Natsuki Hokami

While I was drawing, I remembered something: I really like those jelly drinks that you have to shake. There was a vending machine at the high school I went that sold a mango gelatin in the summer, and I bought a ton of them. I suppose those gelatins are probably gone by now.

Natsuki Hokami's first serialized manga, *Hell Warden Higuma*, was published in *Weekly Shonen Jump* in 2018.

Demon Slayer: Kimetsu Academy

VOLUME 2
SHONEN JUMP EDITION

STORY AND ART BY
NATSUKI HOKAMI

Translation / John Werry
Touch-Up Art & Lettering / E.K. Weaver
Design / Yukiko Whitley
Editor / Andrew Kuhre Bartosh

KIMETSU GAKUEN! © 2021 by Koyoharu Gotouge, Natsuki Hokami
All rights reserved.
First published in Japan in 2021 by SHUEISHA Inc., Tokyo.
English translation rights arranged by SHUEISHA Inc.

The stories, characters, and incidents mentioned in
this publication are entirely fictional.

Printed in the U.S.A.

Published by VIZ Media, LLC
P.O. Box 77010
San Francisco, CA 94107

10 9 8 7 6 5 4 3 2 1
First printing, April 2024

PARENTAL ADVISORY
DEMON SLAYER: KIMETSU ACADEMY is rated
T for Teen and is recommended for ages 13 and
up. This volume contains fantasy violence.

2

The Kimetsu Academy Night Tour

DEMON SLAYER

KIMETSU ACADEMY

Story and Art by
Natsuki Hokami

Based on Koyoharu Gotouge's
Demon Slayer: Kimetsu no Yaiba

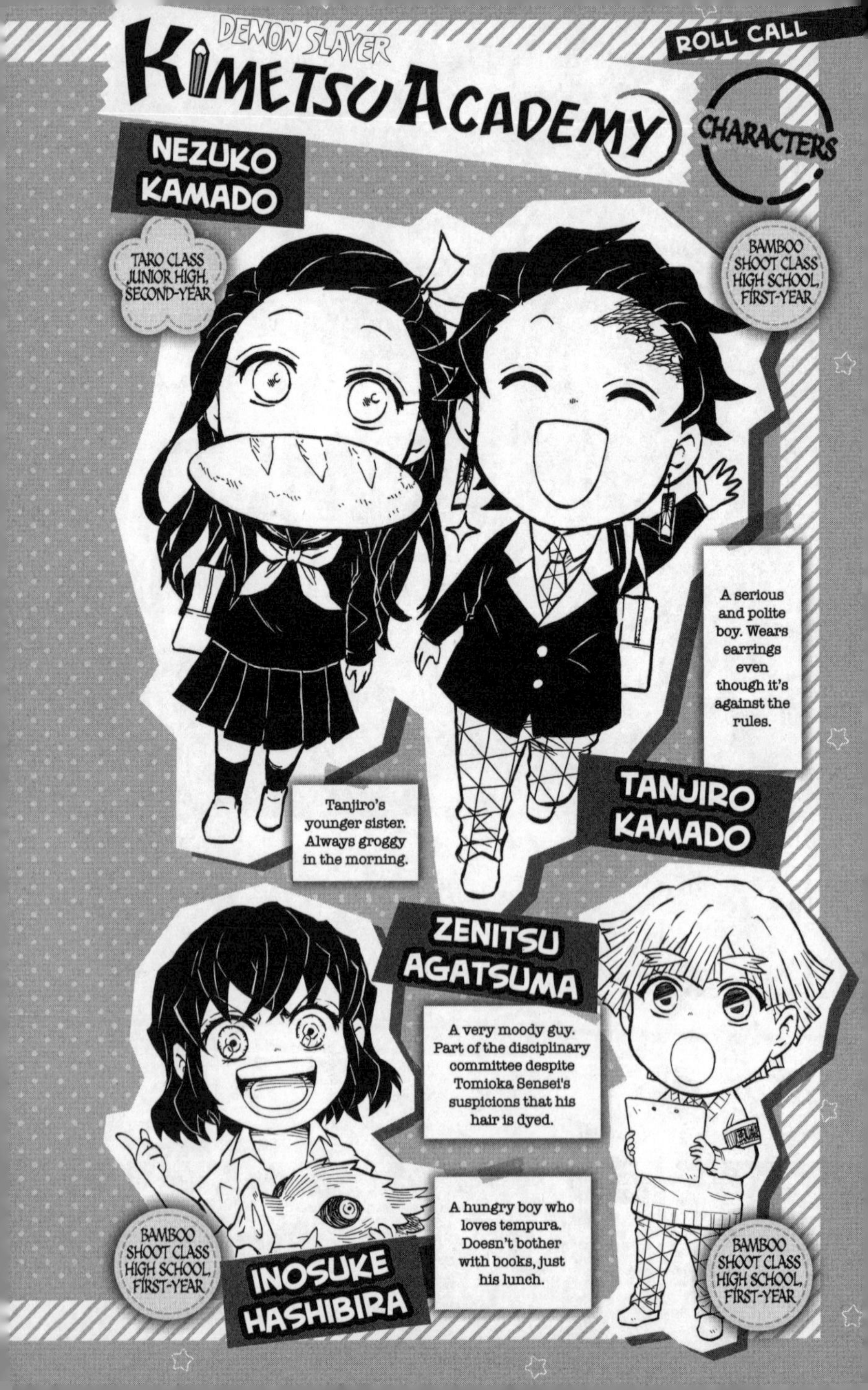
DEMON SLAYER
KIMETSU ACADEMY
ROLL CALL
CHARACTERS
NEZUKO KAMADO
TARO CLASS JUNIOR HIGH, SECOND-YEAR
Tanjiro's younger sister. Always groggy in the morning.
TANJIRO KAMADO
BAMBOO SHOOT CLASS HIGH SCHOOL, FIRST-YEAR
A serious and polite boy. Wears earrings even though it's against the rules.
ZENITSU AGATSUMA
A very moody guy. Part of the disciplinary committee despite Tomioka Sensei's suspicions that his hair is dyed.
BAMBOO SHOOT CLASS HIGH SCHOOL, FIRST-YEAR
INOSUKE HASHIBIRA
BAMBOO SHOOT CLASS HIGH SCHOOL, FIRST-YEAR
A hungry boy who loves tempura. Doesn't bother with books, just his lunch.

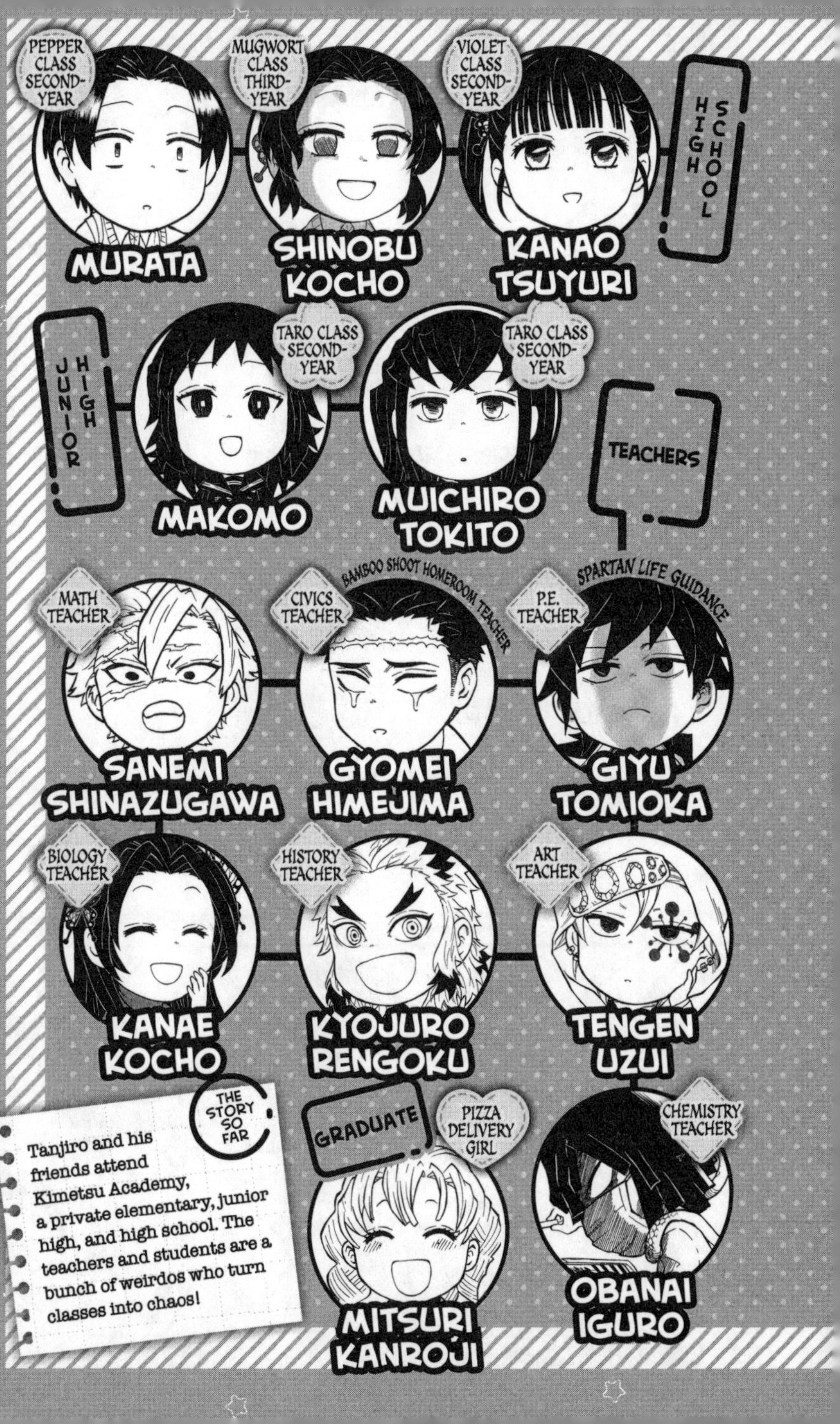
PEPPER CLASS SECOND-YEAR
MURATA
MUGWORT CLASS THIRD-YEAR
SHINOBU KOCHO
VIOLET CLASS SECOND-YEAR
KANAO TSUYURI
HIGH SCHOOL
JUNIOR HIGH
TARO CLASS SECOND-YEAR
MAKOMO
TARO CLASS SECOND-YEAR
MUICHIRO TOKITO
TEACHERS
MATH TEACHER
SANEMI SHINAZUGAWA
BAMBOO SHOOT HOMEROOM TEACHER
CIVICS TEACHER
GYOMEI HIMEJIMA
SPARTAN LIFE GUIDANCE
P.E. TEACHER
GIYU TOMIOKA
BIOLOGY TEACHER
KANAE KOCHO
HISTORY TEACHER
KYOJURO RENGOKU
ART TEACHER
TENGEN UZUI
THE STORY SO FAR
Tanjiro and his friends attend Kimetsu Academy, a private elementary, junior high, and high school. The teachers and students are a bunch of weirdos who turn classes into chaos!
GRADUATE
PIZZA DELIVERY GIRL
MITSURI KANROJI
CHEMISTRY TEACHER
OBANAI IGURO

CONTENTS

2 The Kimetsu Academy Night Tour

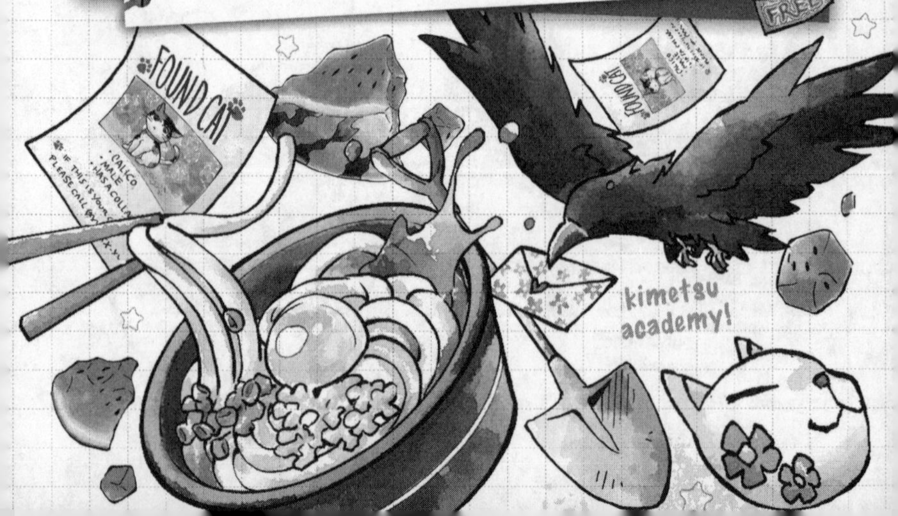

FOUND CAT
kimetsu academy!

CHAPTER 6: CATNIP FOR KITTIES, KITTIES FOR HIMEJIMA

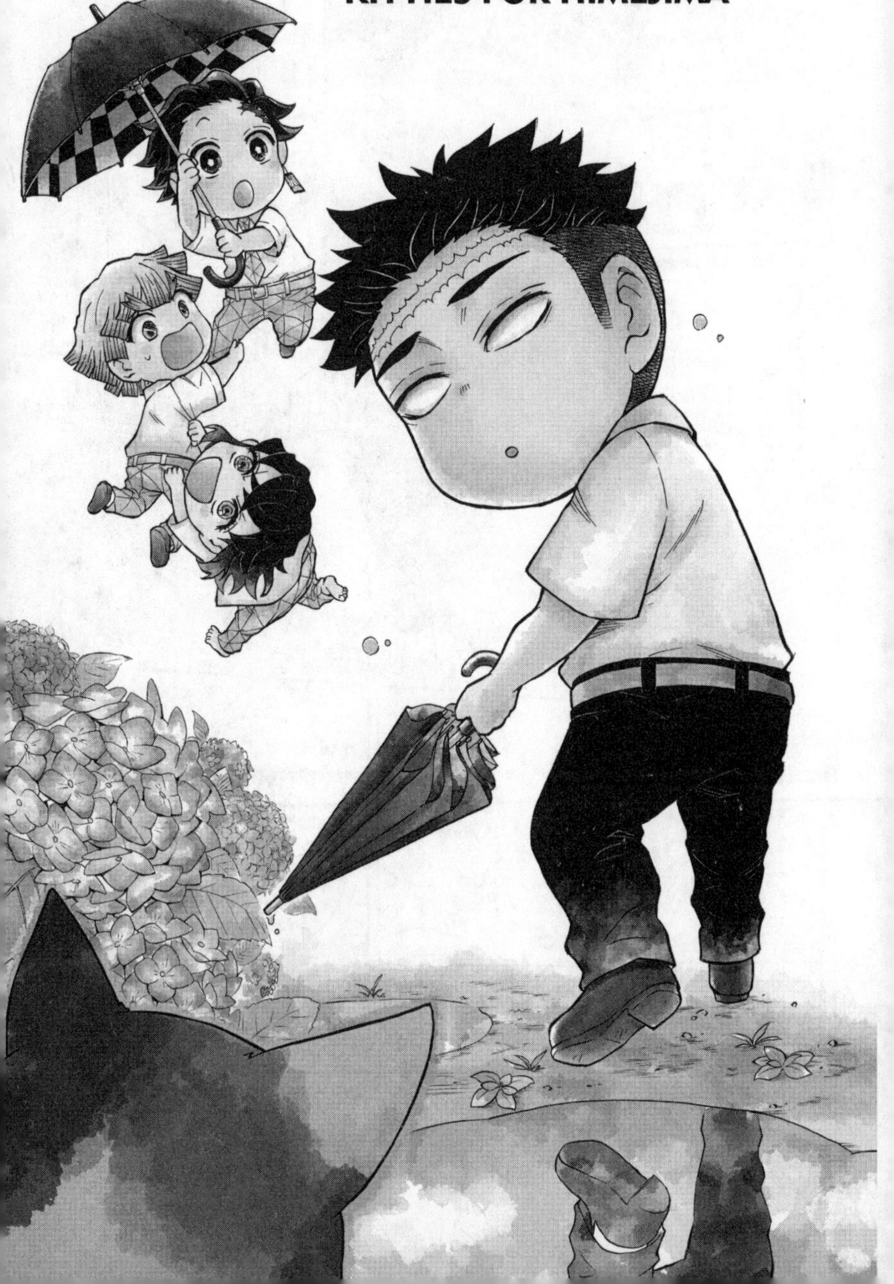

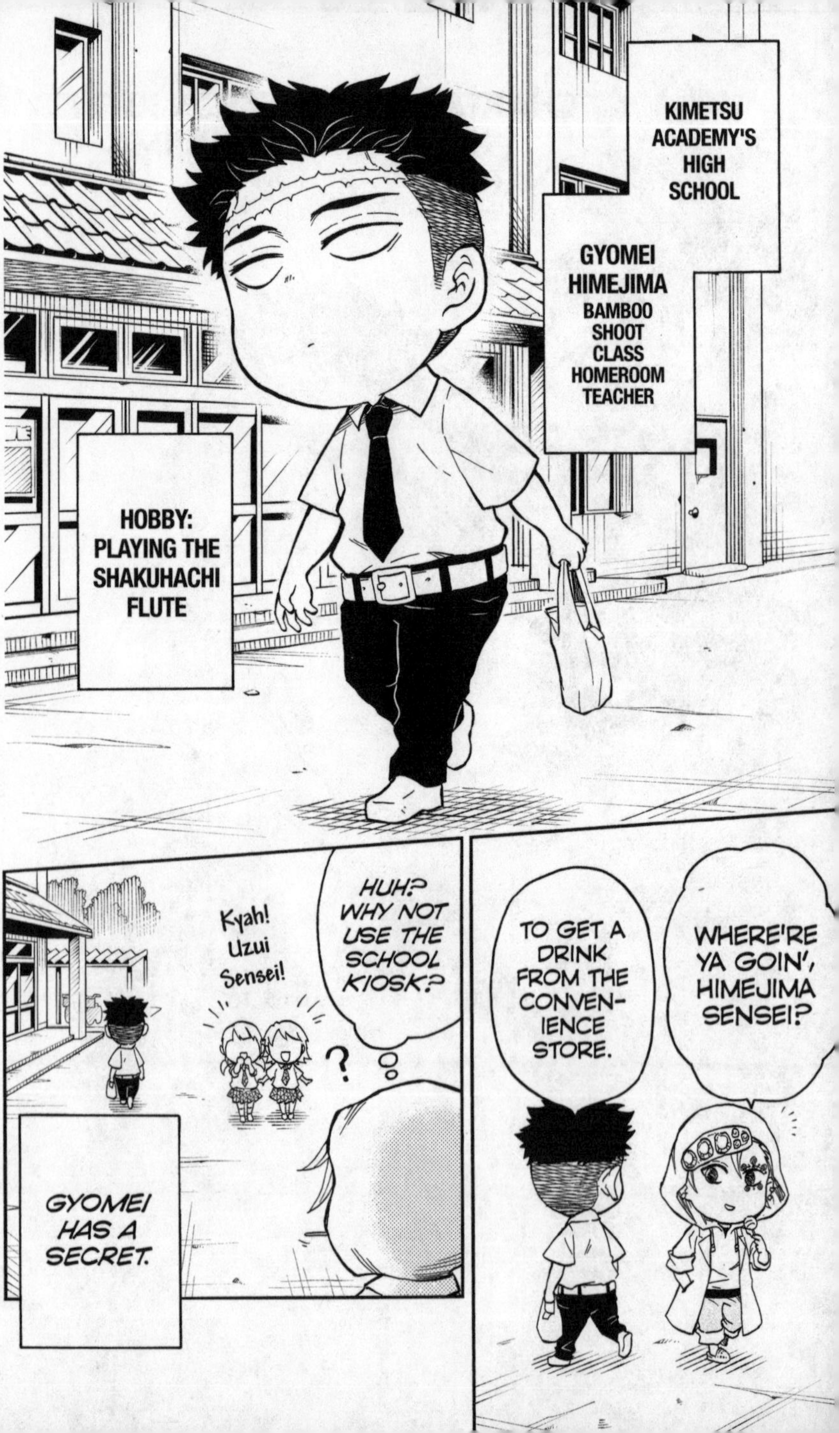
KIMETSU ACADEMY'S HIGH SCHOOL
GYOMEI HIMEJIMA
BAMBOO SHOOT CLASS HOMEROOM TEACHER
HOBBY: PLAYING THE SHAKUHACHI FLUTE
WHERE'RE YA GOIN', HIMEJIMA SENSEI?
TO GET A DRINK FROM THE CONVEN-IENCE STORE.
HUH? WHY NOT USE THE SCHOOL KIOSK?
Kyah! Uzui Sensei!
?
GYOMEI HAS A SECRET.

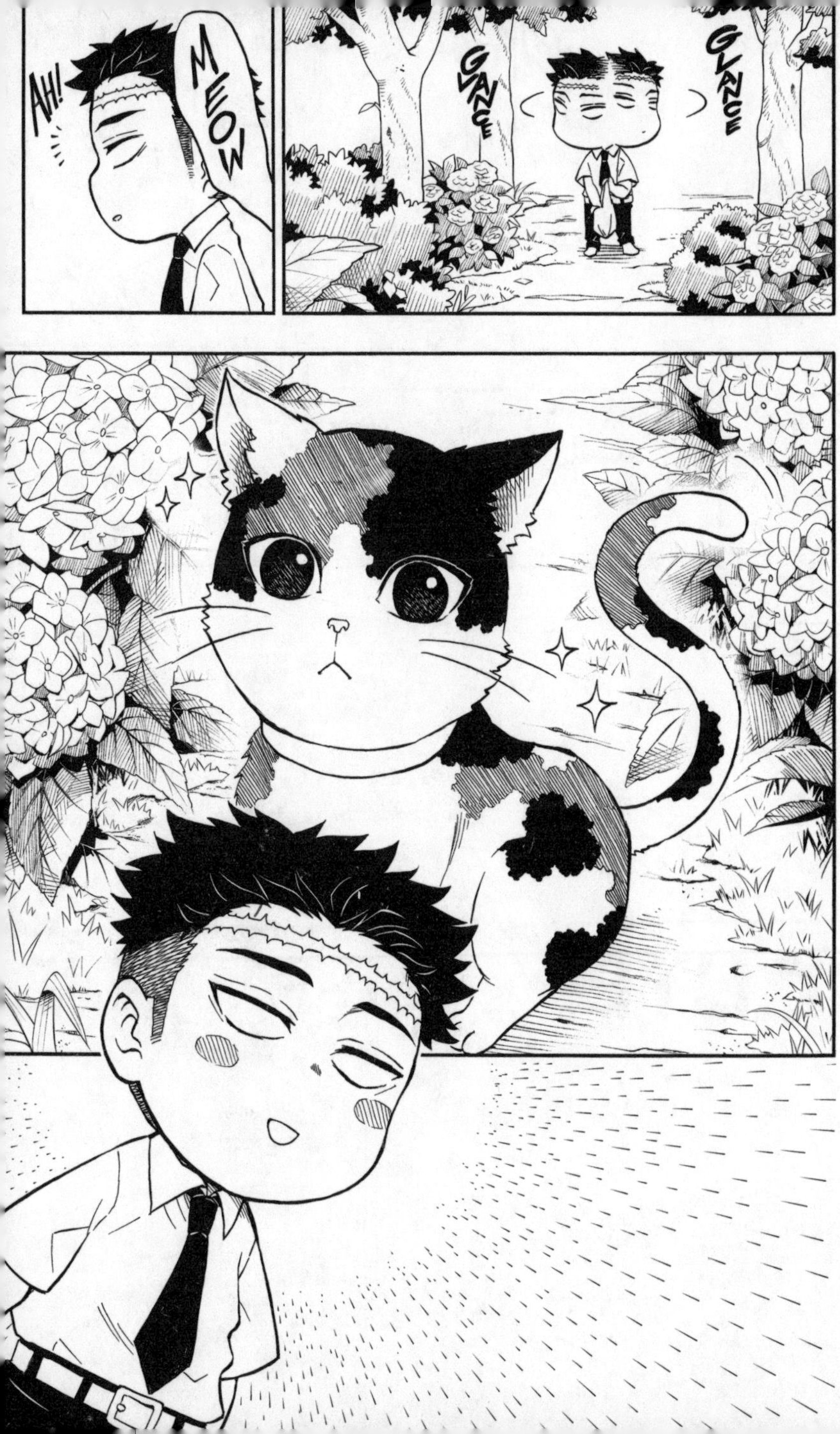
GLANCE
GLANCE
MEOW
AH!

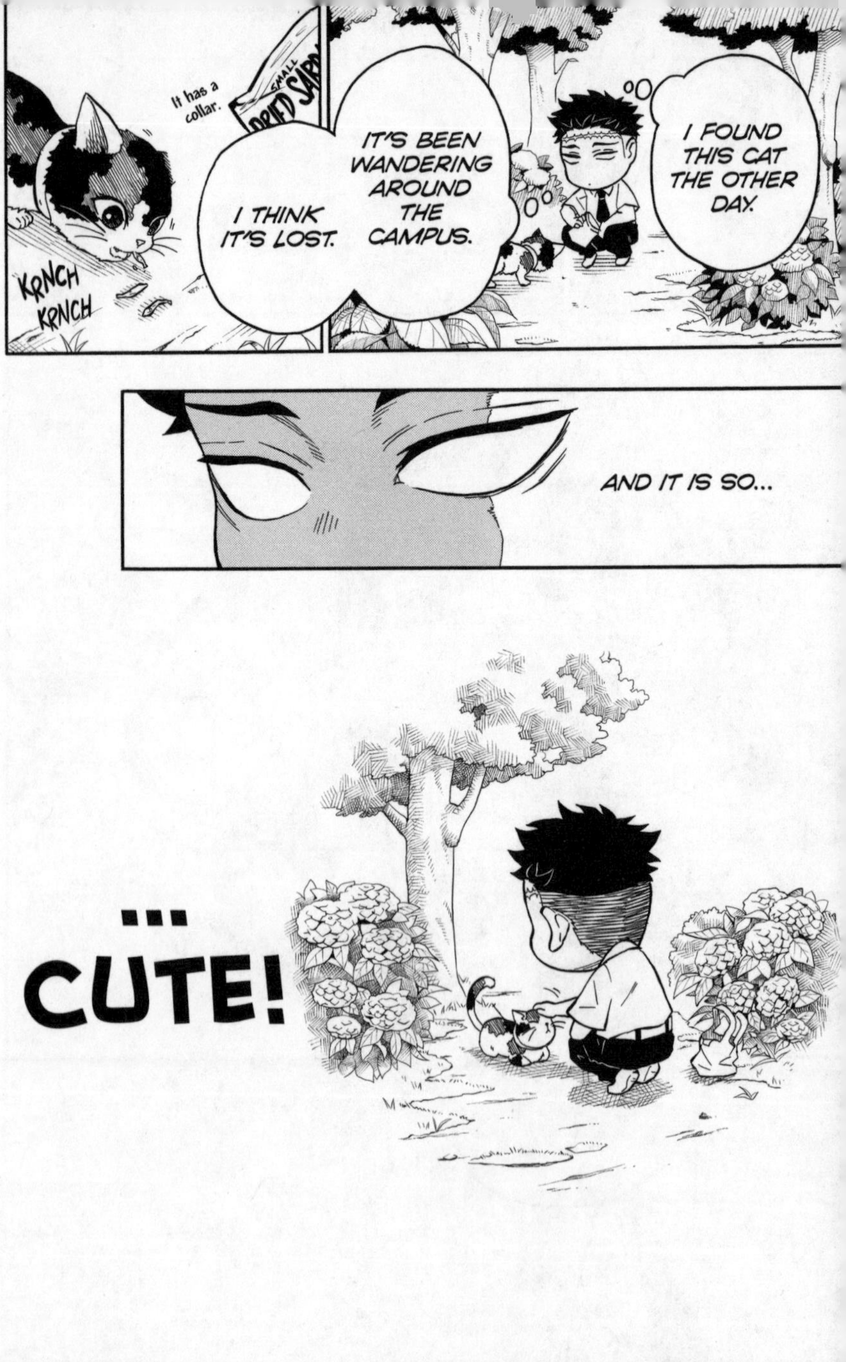
I FOUND THIS CAT THE OTHER DAY.
IT'S BEEN WANDERING AROUND THE CAMPUS.
I THINK IT'S LOST.
It has a collar.
KRNCH
KRNCH
AND IT IS SO...
...CUTE!

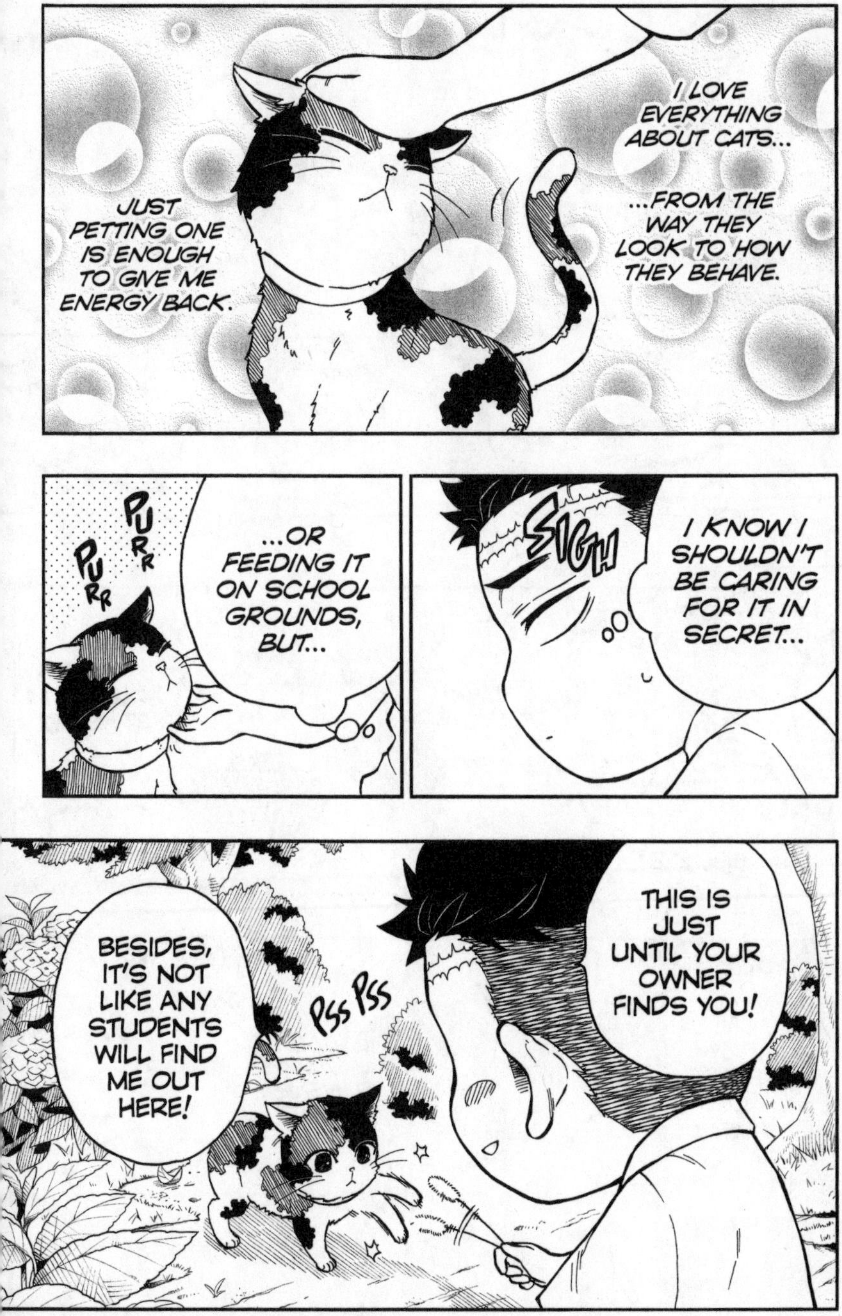
I LOVE EVERYTHING ABOUT CATS...
...FROM THE WAY THEY LOOK TO HOW THEY BEHAVE.
JUST PETTING ONE IS ENOUGH TO GIVE ME ENERGY BACK.
I KNOW I SHOULDN'T BE CARING FOR IT IN SECRET...
SIGH
...OR FEEDING IT ON SCHOOL GROUNDS, BUT...
PURR
PURR
THIS IS JUST UNTIL YOUR OWNER FINDS YOU!
PSS PSS
BESIDES, IT'S NOT LIKE ANY STUDENTS WILL FIND ME OUT HERE!

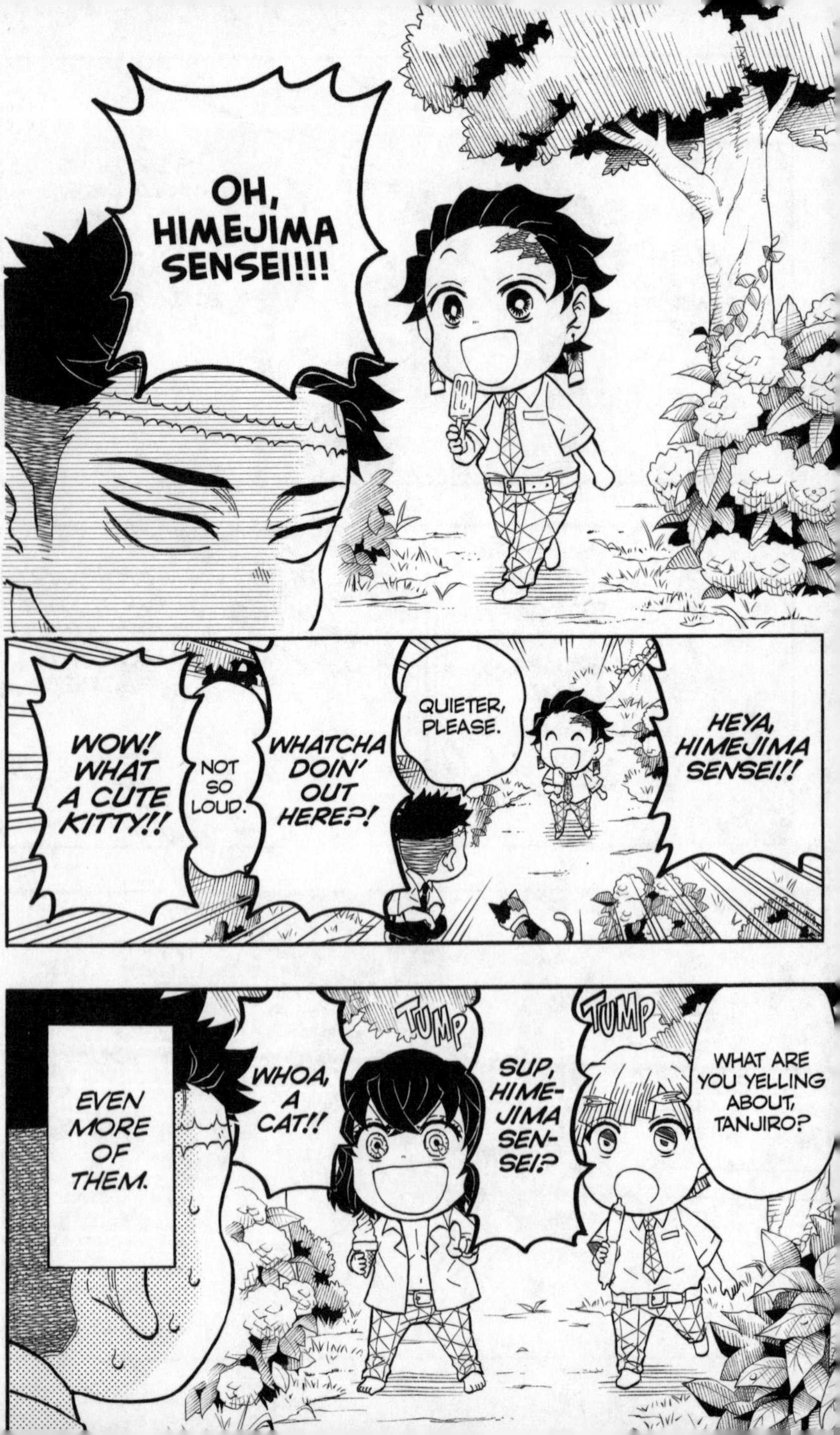
OH, HIMEJIMA SENSEI!!!!
HEYA, HIMEJIMA SENSEI!!
QUIETER, PLEASE.
WHATCHA DOIN' OUT HERE?!
NOT SO LOUD.
WOW! WHAT A CUTE KITTY!!
TUMP
WHAT ARE YOU YELLING ABOUT, TANJIRO?
TUMP
SUP, HIME-JIMA SEN-SEI?
WHOA, A CAT!!
EVEN MORE OF THEM.

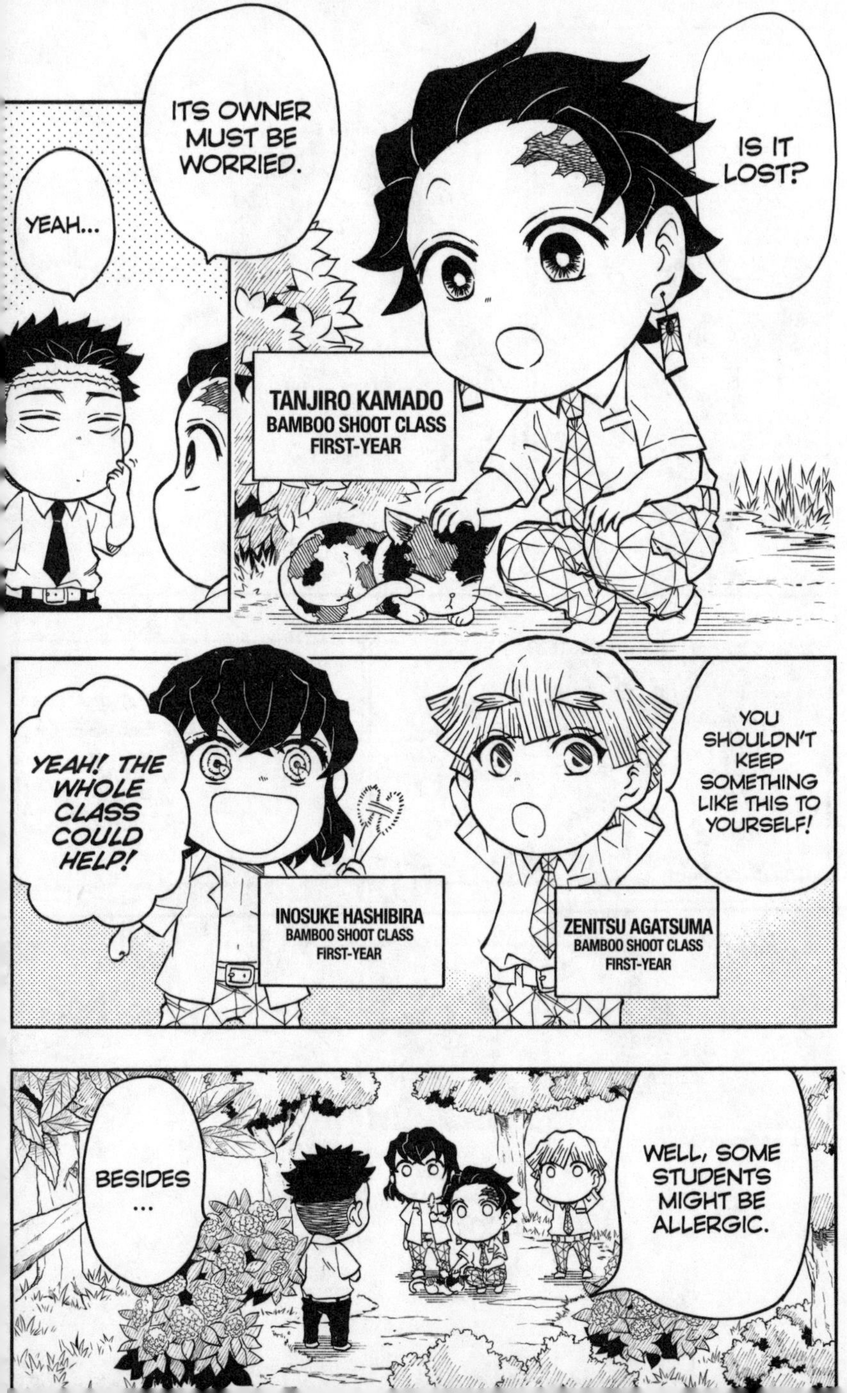
IS IT LOST?
TANJIRO KAMADO BAMBOO SHOOT CLASS FIRST-YEAR
ITS OWNER MUST BE WORRIED.
YEAH...
YOU SHOULDN'T KEEP SOMETHING LIKE THIS TO YOURSELF!
ZENITSU AGATSUMA BAMBOO SHOOT CLASS FIRST-YEAR
INOSUKE HASHIBIRA BAMBOO SHOOT CLASS FIRST-YEAR
YEAH! THE WHOLE CLASS COULD HELP!
WELL, SOME STUDENTS MIGHT BE ALLERGIC.
BESIDES ...

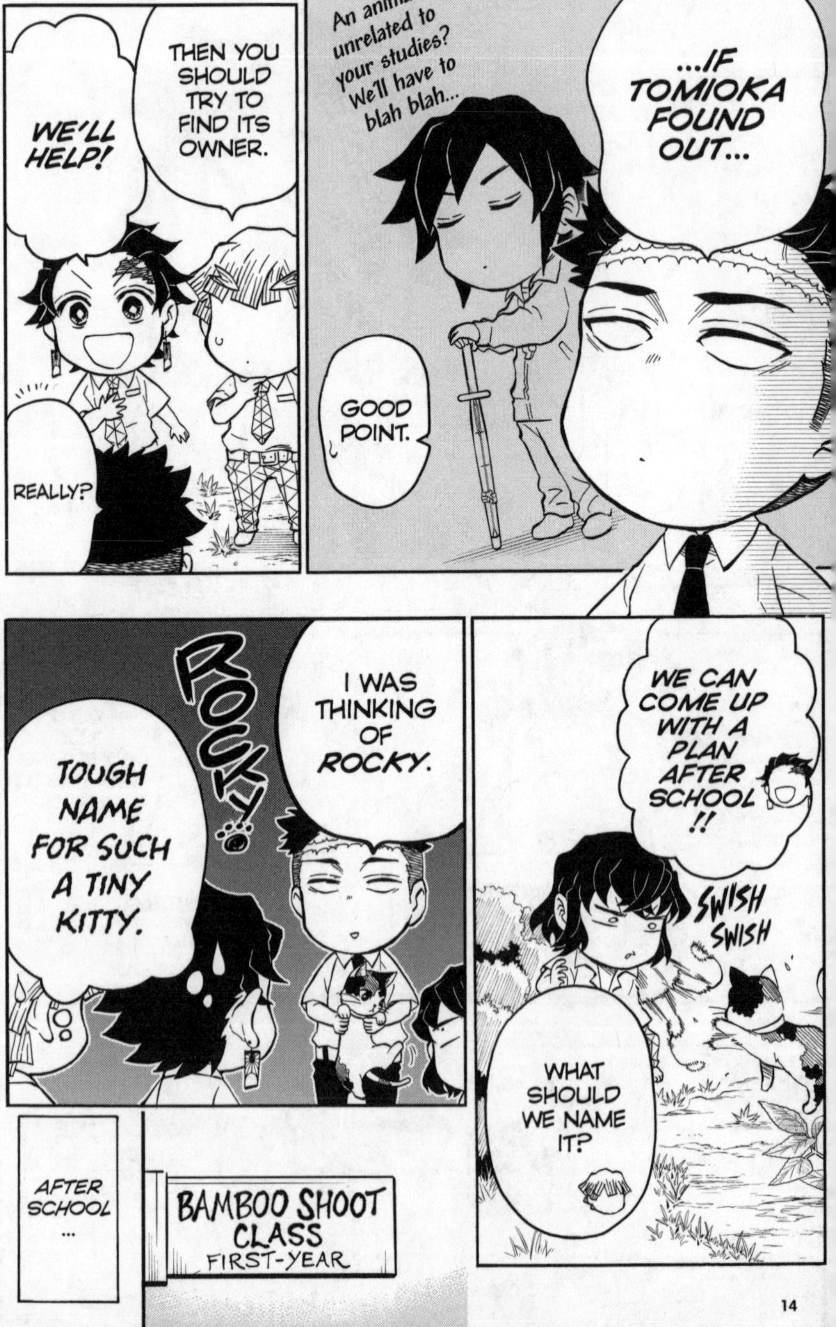
...IF TOMIOKA FOUND OUT...
An animal unrelated to your studies? We'll have to blah blah...
GOOD POINT.
THEN YOU SHOULD TRY TO FIND ITS OWNER.
WE'LL HELP!
REALLY?
WE CAN COME UP WITH A PLAN AFTER SCHOOL!!
SWISH SWISH
WHAT SHOULD WE NAME IT?
I WAS THINKING OF ROCKY.
ROCKY!
TOUGH NAME FOR SUCH A TINY KITTY.
BAMBOO SHOOT CLASS
FIRST-YEAR
AFTER SCHOOL...

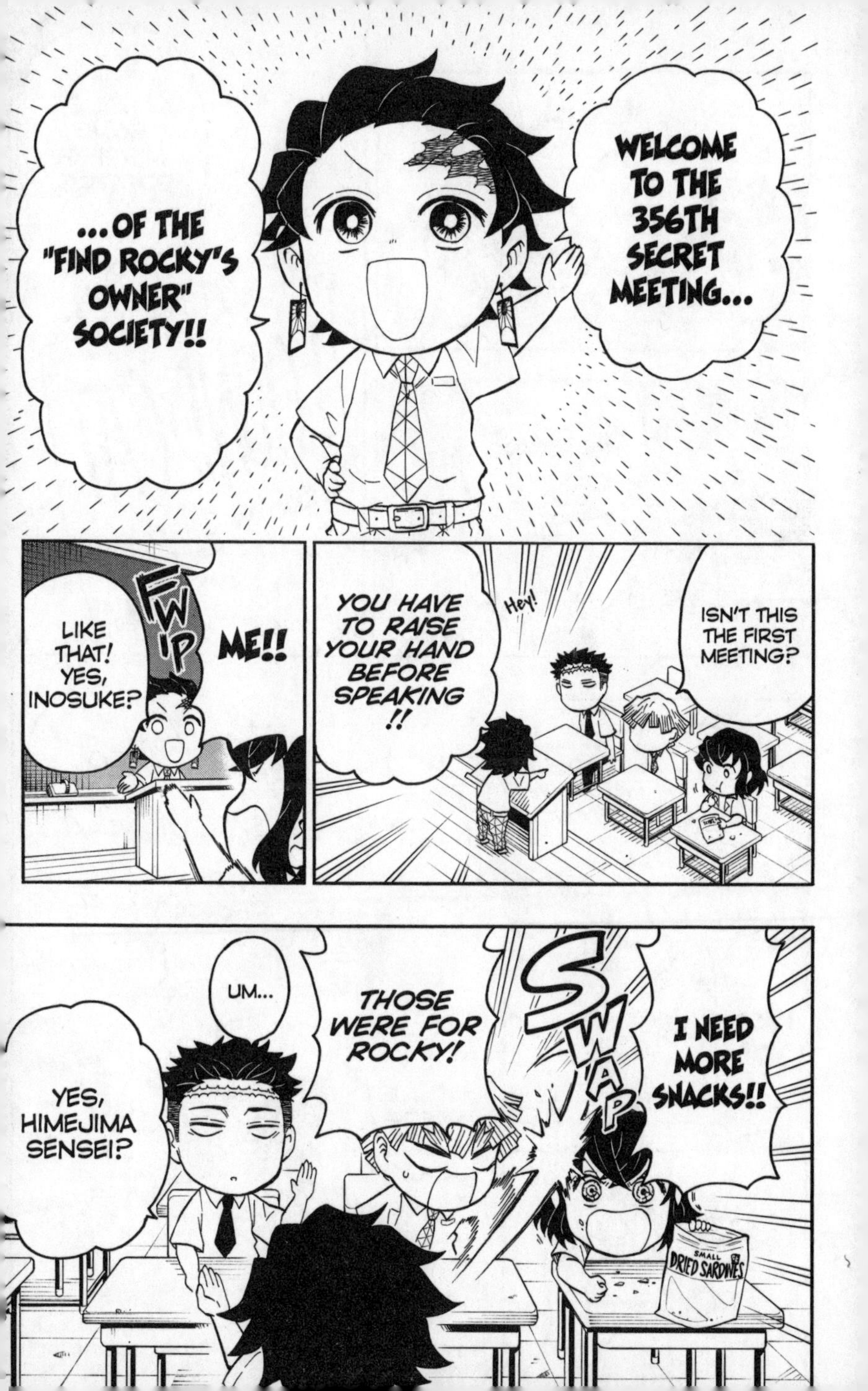
WELCOME TO THE 356TH SECRET MEETING...
...OF THE "FIND ROCKY'S OWNER" SOCIETY!!
ISN'T THIS THE FIRST MEETING?
Hey!
YOU HAVE TO RAISE YOUR HAND BEFORE SPEAKING !!
ME!!
FWIP
LIKE THAT! YES, INOSUKE?
I NEED MORE SNACKS!!
SWAP
SMALL DRIED SARDINES
THOSE WERE FOR ROCKY!
UM...
YES, HIMEJIMA SENSEI?

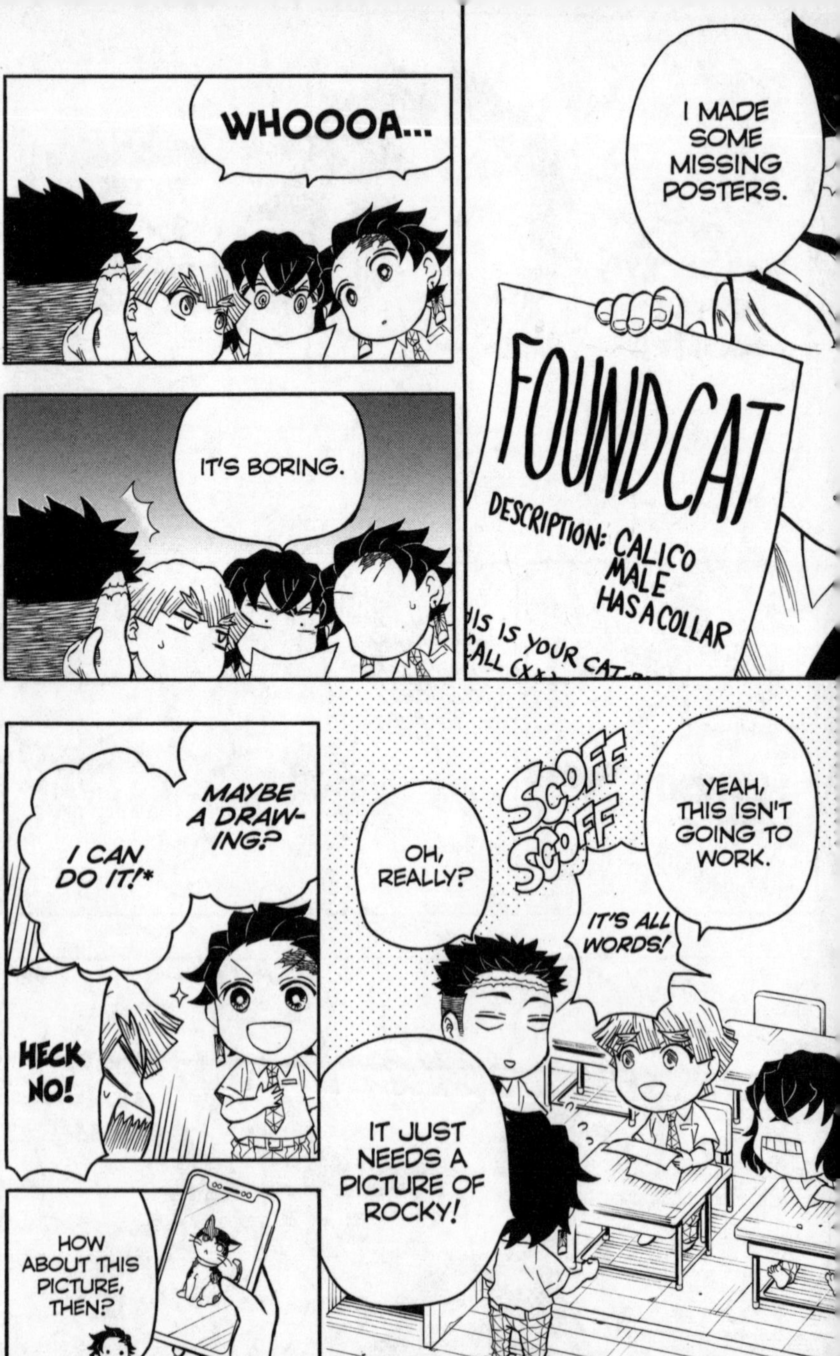
I MADE SOME MISSING POSTERS.
FOUNDCAT
DESCRIPTION: CALICO
MALE
HAS A COLLAR
WHOOOA...
IT'S BORING.
YEAH, THIS ISN'T GOING TO WORK.
IT'S ALL WORDS!
SCOFF SCOFF
OH, REALLY?
IT JUST NEEDS A PICTURE OF ROCKY!
MAYBE A DRAW-ING?
I CAN DO IT!*
HECK NO!
HOW ABOUT THIS PICTURE, THEN?

*CHECK VOLUME 1 TO SEE TANJIRO'S ARTISTIC "SKILLS."

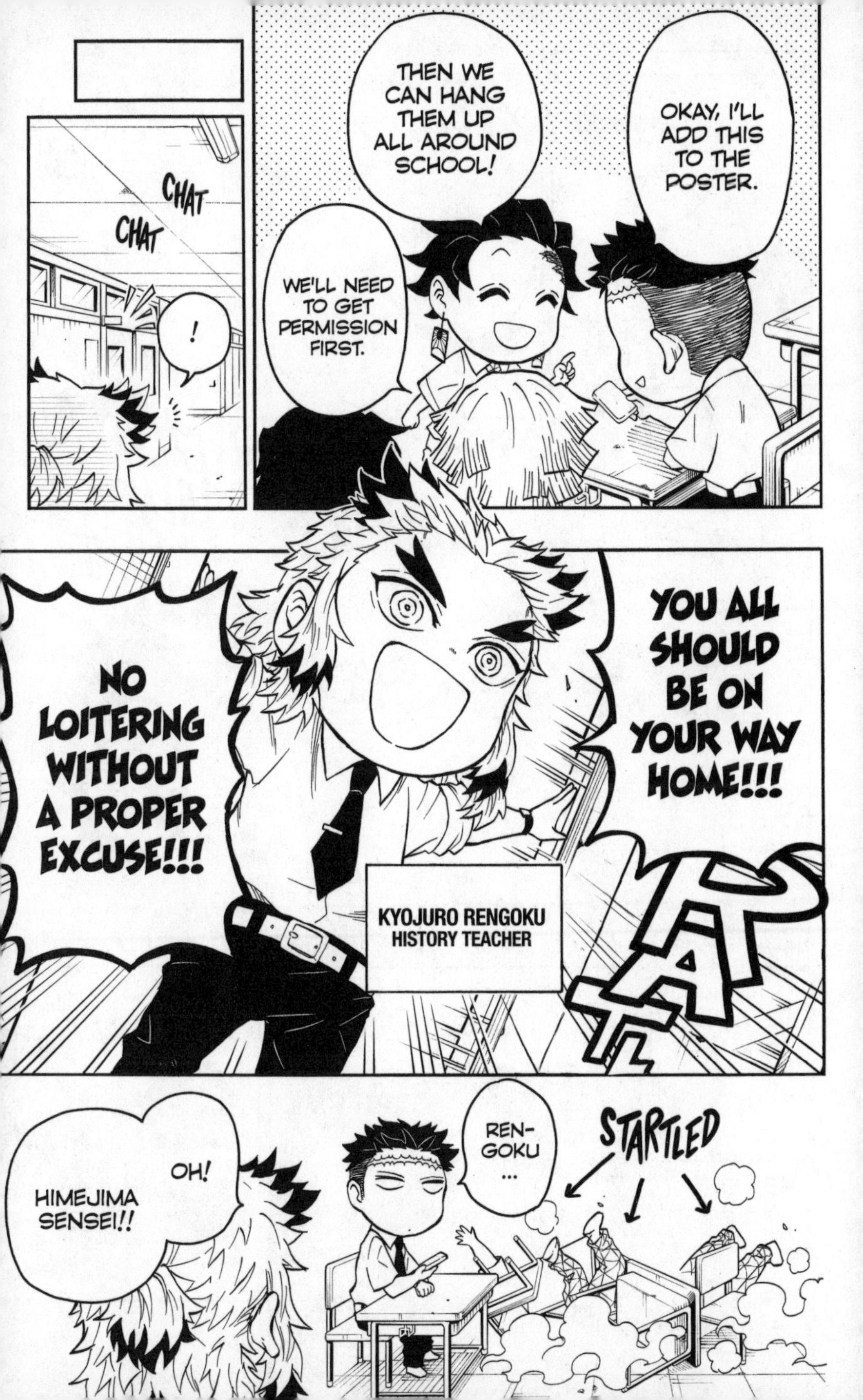
OKAY, I'LL ADD THIS TO THE POSTER.
THEN WE CAN HANG THEM UP ALL AROUND SCHOOL!
WE'LL NEED TO GET PERMISSION FIRST.
CHAT
CHAT
!
YOU ALL SHOULD BE ON YOUR WAY HOME!!!
NO LOITERING WITHOUT A PROPER EXCUSE!!!
KYOJURO RENGOKU
HISTORY TEACHER
TAP
STARTLED
REN-GOKU ...
OH!
HIMEJIMA SENSEI!!

YOU'RE WITH THEM?
SORRY 'BOUT THAT!
UM...
...WE WERE JUST FINISHING UP.
WHAT WERE YOU ALL TALKING ABOUT?
PLUG
A CA—
NOTHING!!!
WE'RE ALL READY TO GO!
GRIN GRIN GRIN
SEE YOU LATER!!
??
OKAY! SEE YA!!

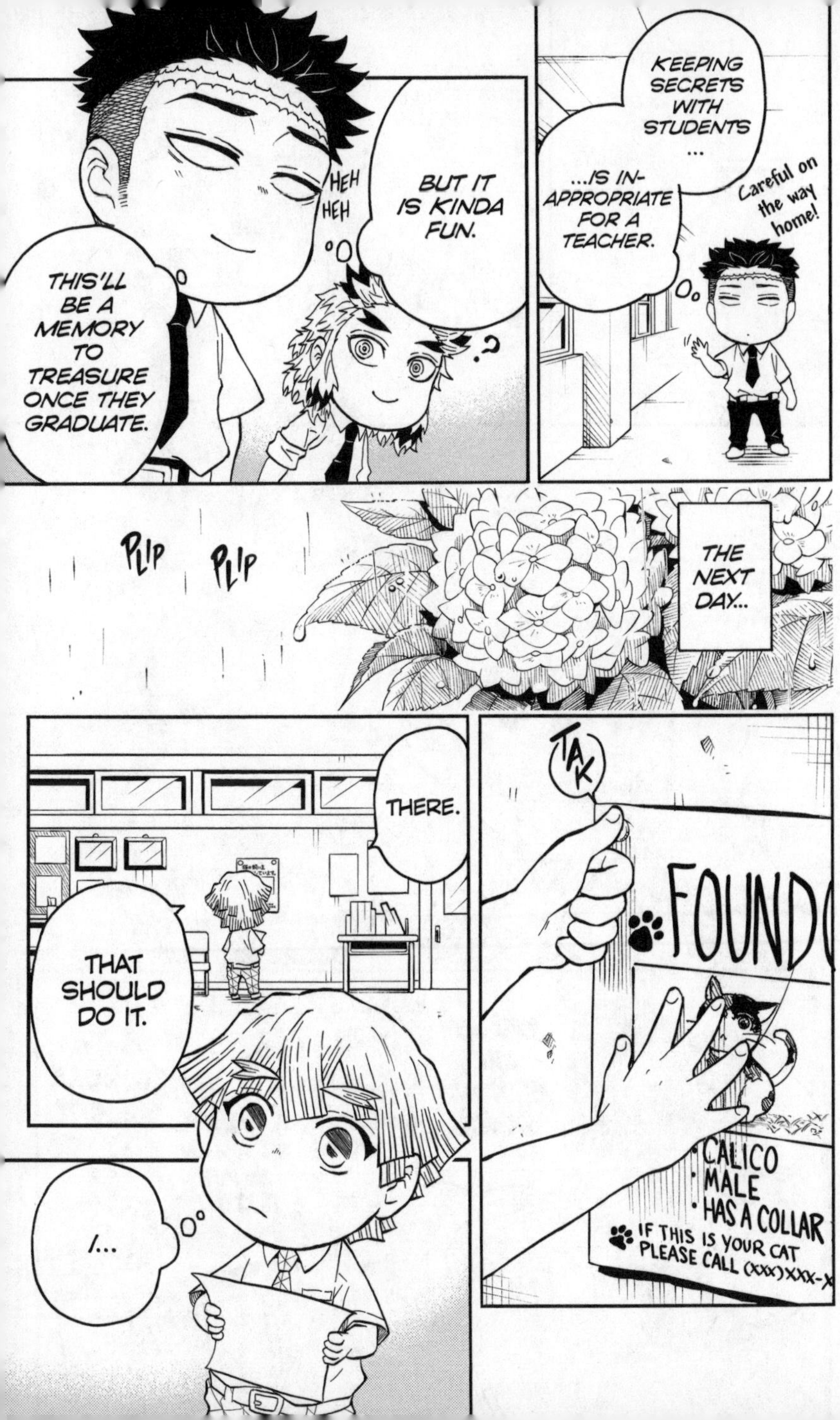
KEEPING SECRETS WITH STUDENTS ...
...IS IN-APPROPRIATE FOR A TEACHER.
Careful on the way home!
THIS'LL BE A MEMORY TO TREASURE ONCE THEY GRADUATE.
HEH HEH
BUT IT IS KINDA FUN.
?
THE NEXT DAY...
PLIP
PLIP
TAK
FOUND
• CALICO
• MALE
• HAS A COLLAR
IF THIS IS YOUR CAT
PLEASE CALL (XXX)XXX-X
THERE.
THAT SHOULD DO IT.
I...

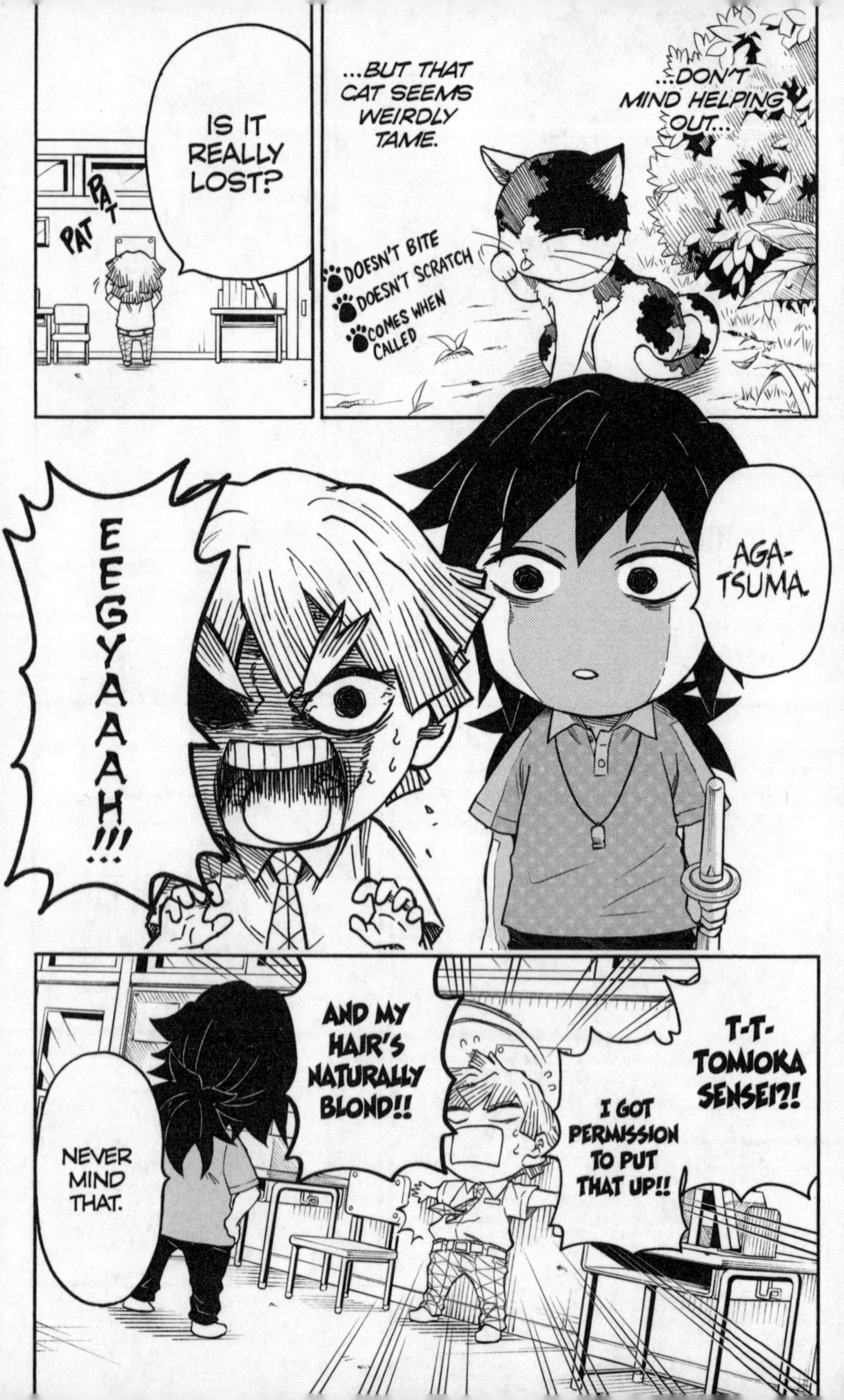
...DON'T MIND HELPING OUT...
...BUT THAT CAT SEEMS WEIRDLY TAME.
DOESN'T BITE
DOESN'T SCRATCH
COMES WHEN CALLED
IS IT REALLY LOST?
PAT PAT
AGA-TSUMA.
EEGYAAAH!!!
T-T-TOMIOKA SENSEI?!
I GOT PERMISSION TO PUT THAT UP!!
AND MY HAIR'S NATURALLY BLOND!!
NEVER MIND THAT.

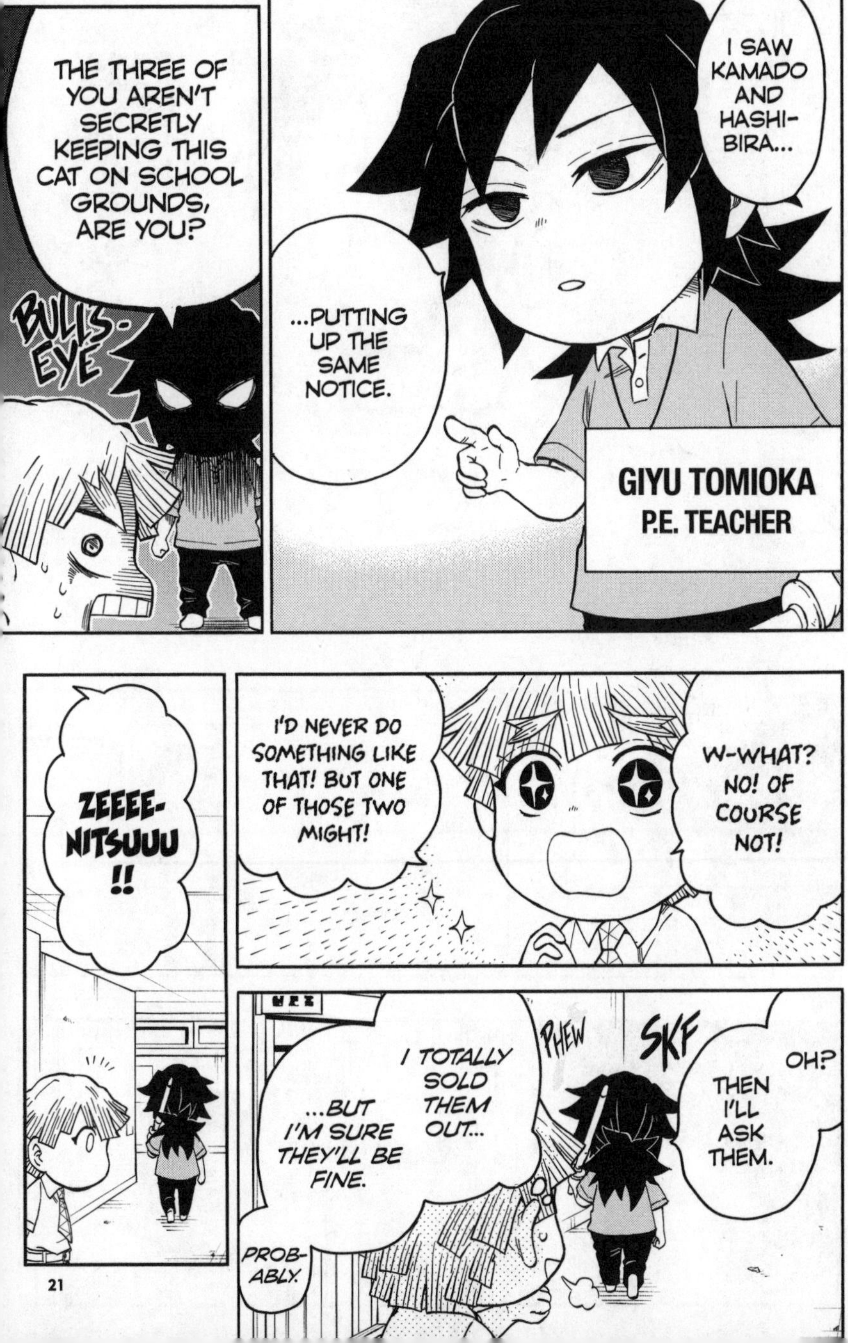

I SAW KAMADO AND HASHIBIRA...
...PUTTING UP THE SAME NOTICE.
GIYU TOMIOKA
P.E. TEACHER
THE THREE OF YOU AREN'T SECRETLY KEEPING THIS CAT ON SCHOOL GROUNDS, ARE YOU?
BULLS-EYE
W-WHAT? NO! OF COURSE NOT!
I'D NEVER DO SOMETHING LIKE THAT! BUT ONE OF THOSE TWO MIGHT!
OH? THEN I'LL ASK THEM.
SKF
PHEW
I TOTALLY SOLD THEM OUT...
...BUT I'M SURE THEY'LL BE FINE.
PROBABLY.
ZEEEE-NITSUUU!!

IT'S WAS RAINING, SO I BROUGHT THE CAT IN!
AH HA HA HA
WHERE SHOULD WE KEEP IT?

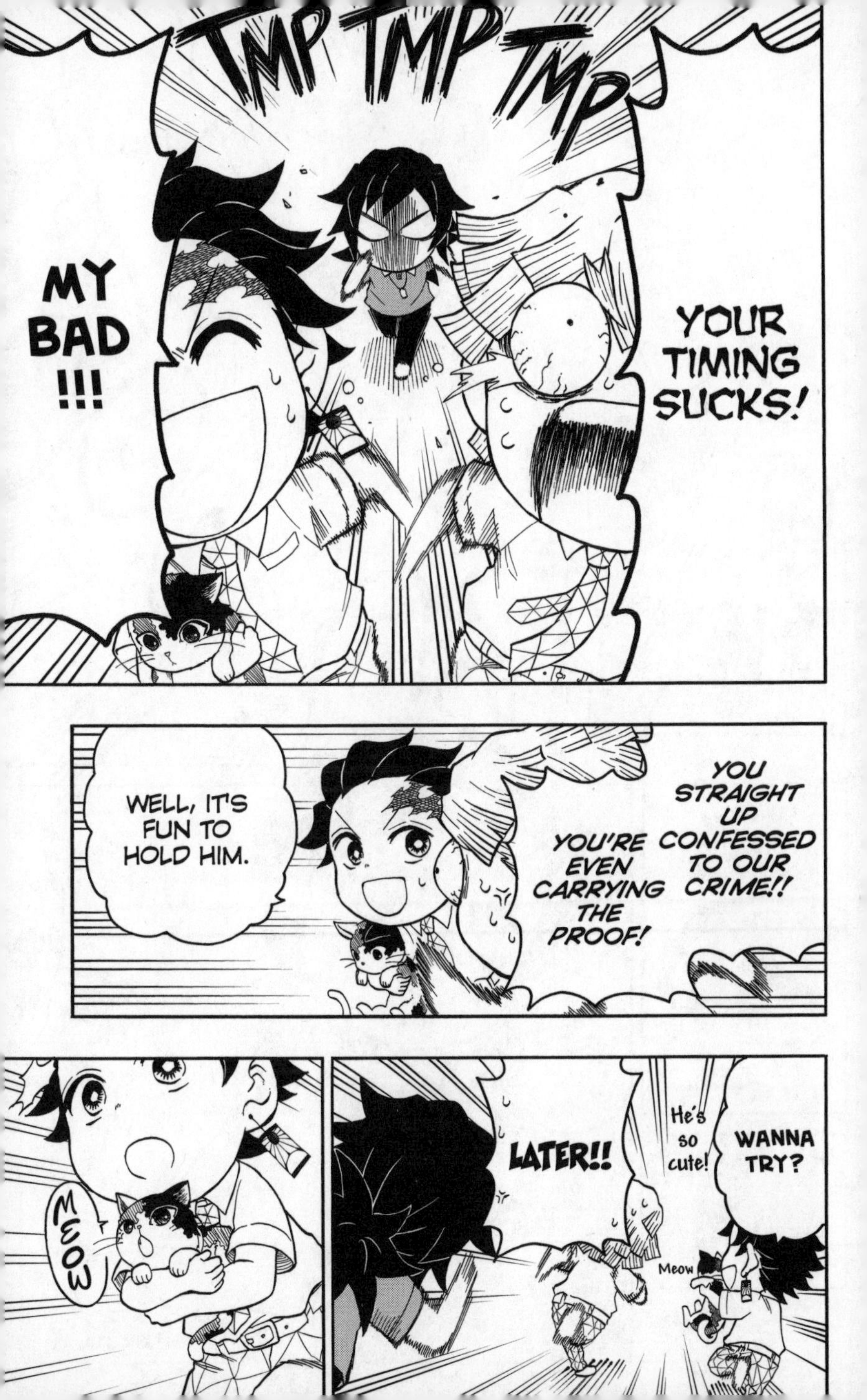
TMP TMP TMP
YOUR TIMING SUCKS!
MY BAD!!!
YOU STRAIGHT UP CONFESSED TO OUR CRIME!!
YOU'RE EVEN CARRYING THE PROOF!
WELL, IT'S FUN TO HOLD HIM.
WANNA TRY?
He's so cute!
LATER!!
Meow
MEOW

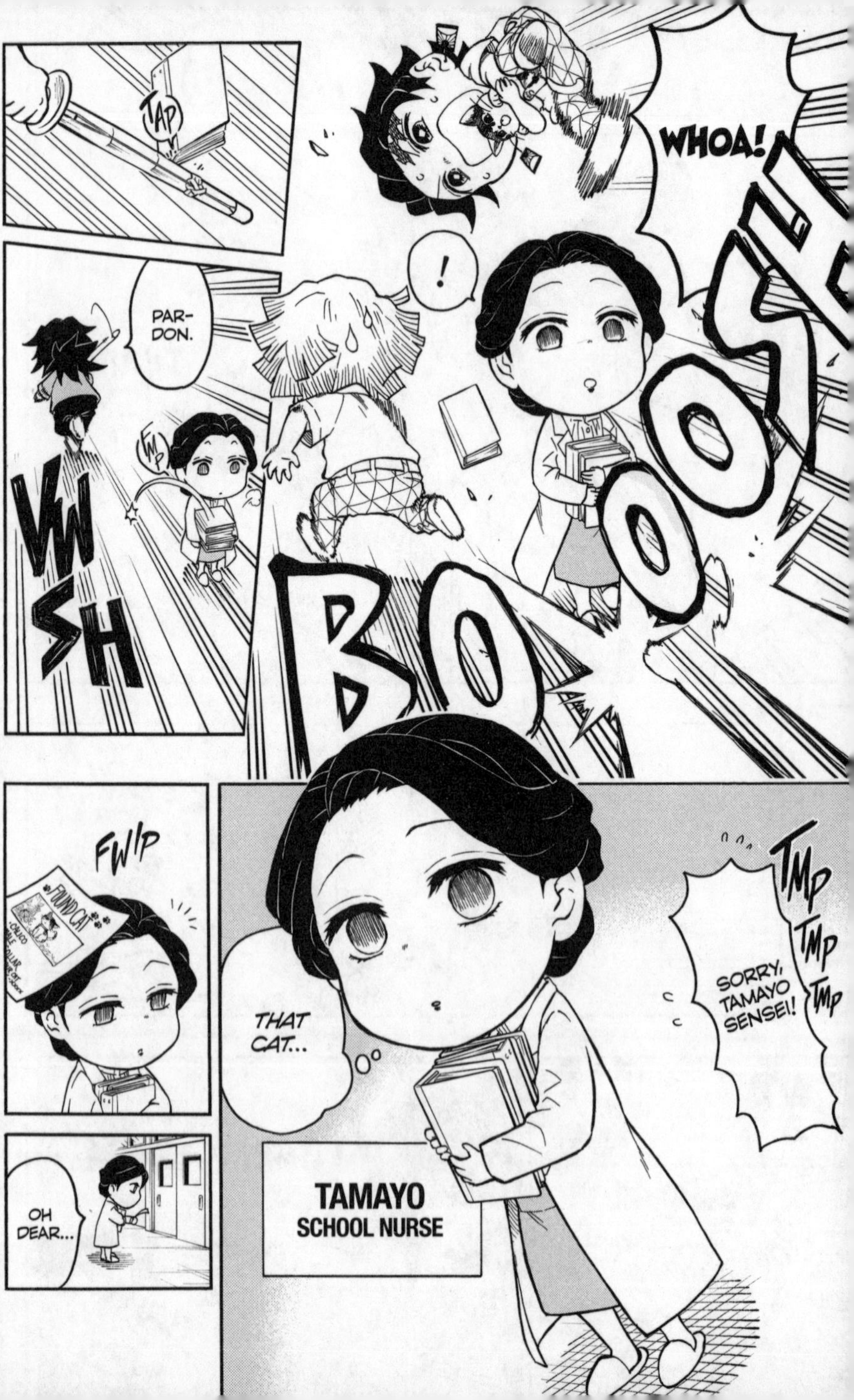
WHOA!
!
BOOOSH
TAP
PAR-DON.
FMP
VWSH
TMP TMP TMP
SORRY, TAMAYO SENSEI!
THAT CAT...
TAMAYO
SCHOOL NURSE
FWIP
FOUND CAT
OH DEAR...

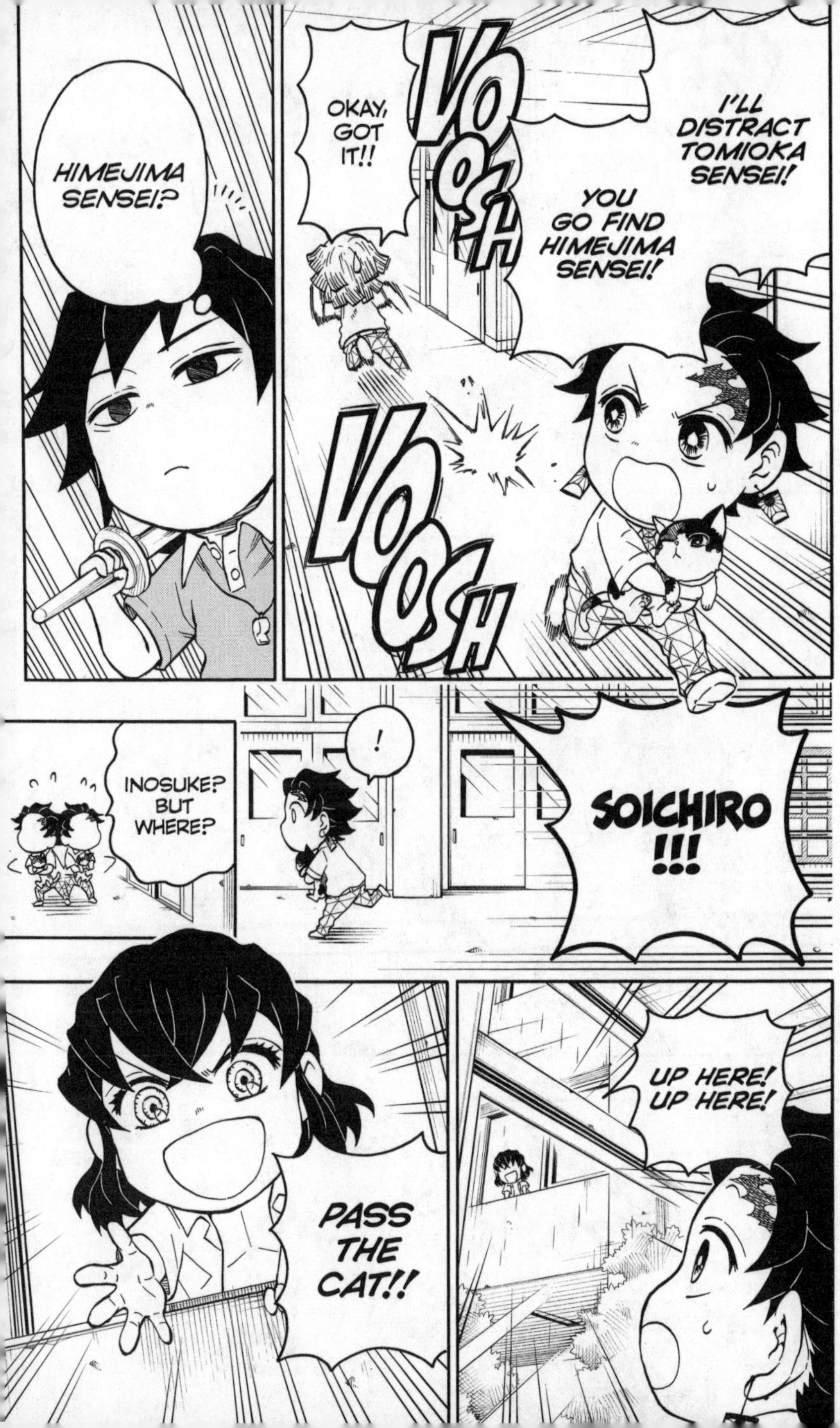
I'LL DISTRACT TOMIOKA SENSEI!
YOU GO FIND HIMEJIMA SENSEI!
OKAY, GOT IT!!
VOOSH
VOOSH
HIMEJIMA SENSEI?
SOICHIRO !!!
!
INOSUKE? BUT WHERE?
UP HERE! UP HERE!
PASS THE CAT!!

TMP TMP TMP TMP
HUH?! HOW?!
HUCK 'IM!!
HOP
NO WAY! THAT'S DAN—
WHA?! ROCKY?!
HOP
HOP
GAH!
FOMP
HE DID IT ALL BY HIMSELF!
WHOA!
YOU'RE SMART, ROCKY!!
INOSUKE!! I'LL SLOW SENSEI DOWN!
TRMBL
TRMBL TRMBL
TRMBL
HIDE ROCKY!
LEAVE IT TO ME!
PWIK
OKAY, KEEP PUSHING!

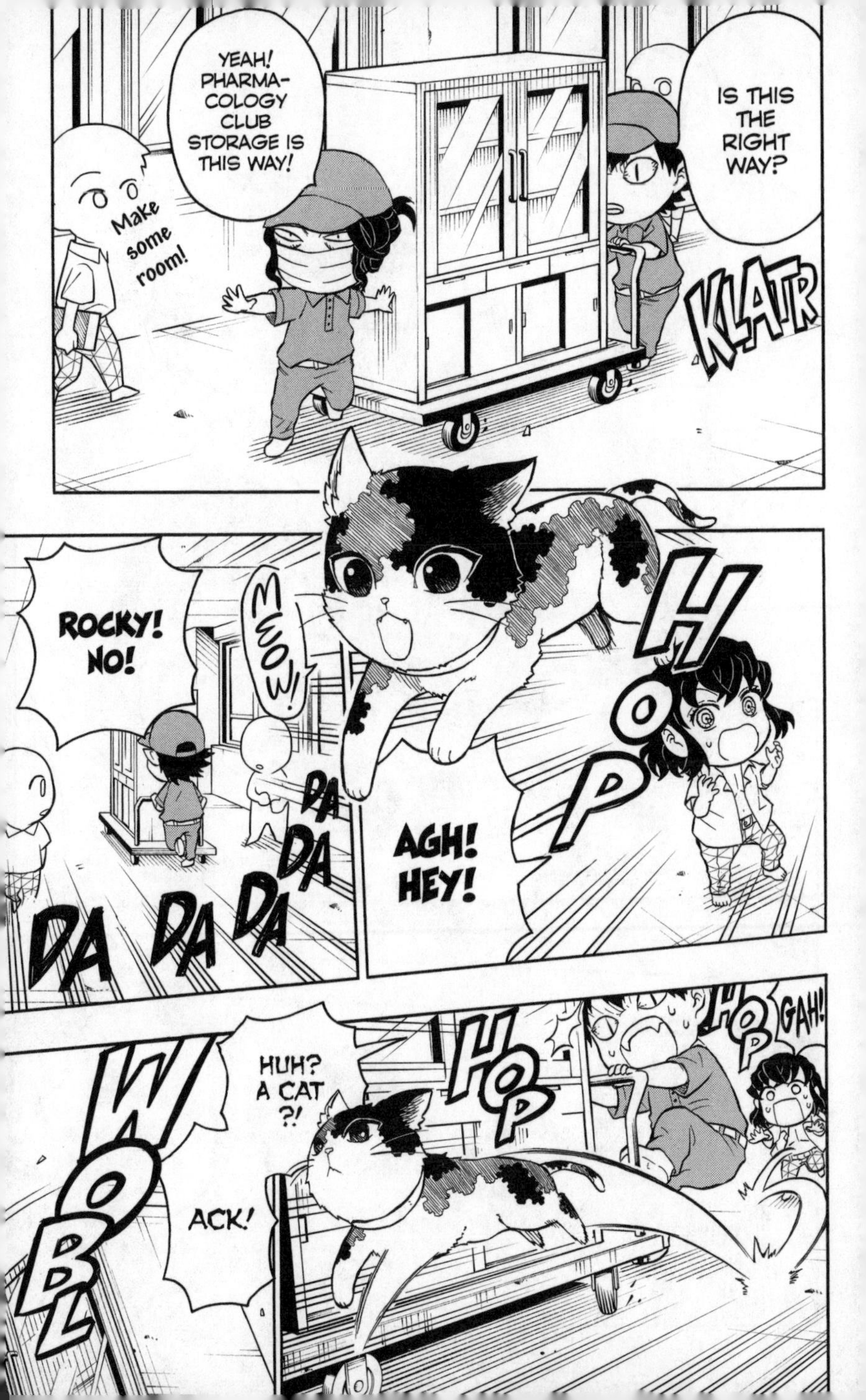
IS THIS THE RIGHT WAY?
YEAH! PHARMA-COLOGY CLUB STORAGE IS THIS WAY!
KLATR
Make some room!
HOP
AGH! HEY!
MEOW!
ROCKY! NO!
DA DA DA DA DA
GAH!
HOP
HOP
HUH? A CAT ?!
WOBL
ACK!

!!
UH-OH!
GASP
INO-SUKE!!

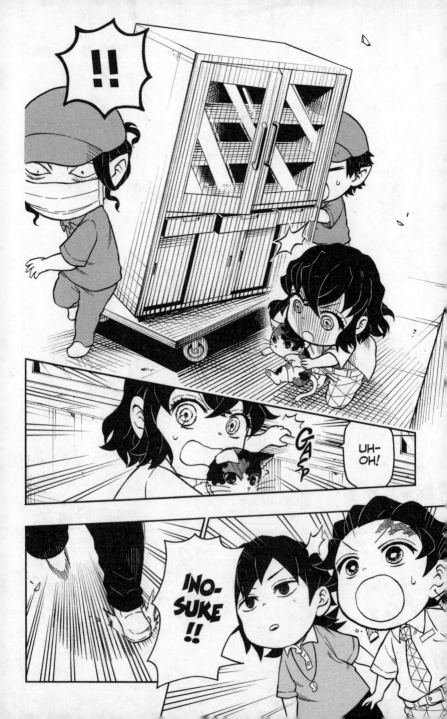

GRAB
HMF !!
SLAM
HIME-JIMA SEN-SEI !!
SLIP
OOPS!
!!

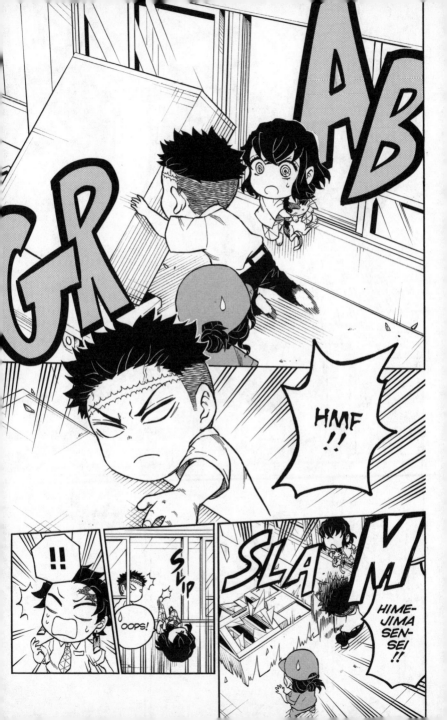

FWSH
TOK
...
DANGL
WHOA ...
...
DOOM
DOOM
SORRY, EVERY-BODY.

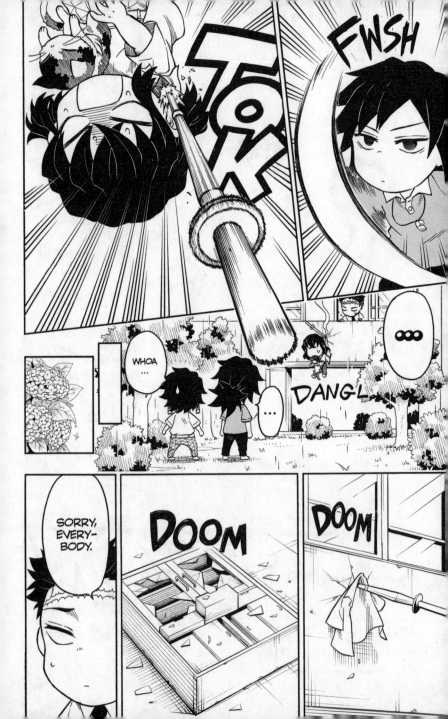

THIS IS ALL MY FAULT.
NO... WELL, YES.
APOLOGETIC
WE SHOULD PROBABLY BE MORE CAREFUL.
THERE YOU ARE, HIMEJIMA SENSEI!!
YOU ALREADY FOUND TANJIRO AND INOSUKE?!
OH, THERE'S ZENITSU.
GRR GRR
TOOK YOU LONG ENOUGH.
ZENITSU DIDN'T BRING YOU?
?
NOPE! I DID SOMETHING MORE IMPORTANT!!
HERE!
I FOUND ROCKY'S OWNERS!!

THANK YOU.

YUSHIRO ?!

TAMAYO SENSEI ... ... AND ...

THEM?

AH!

THE JUNIOR HIGH'S VERY OWN YOKAI...

YEAH, YUSHIRO !!

YOKAI ?!!

...WITH A MONSTER CRUSH ON TAMAYO SENSEI!!

HOP

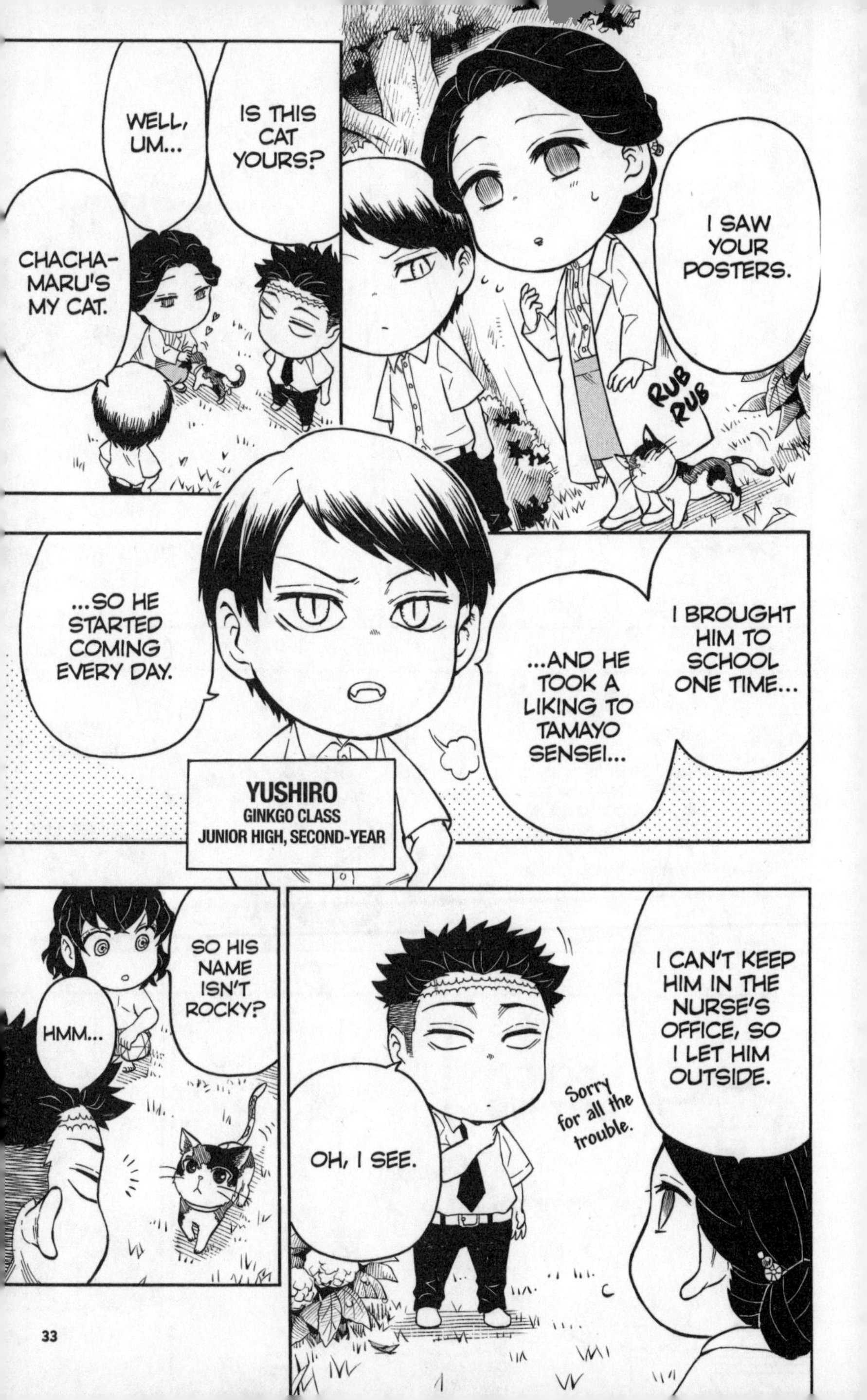
I SAW YOUR POSTERS.
RUB RUB
IS THIS CAT YOURS?
WELL, UM...
CHACHA-MARU'S MY CAT.
I BROUGHT HIM TO SCHOOL ONE TIME...
...AND HE TOOK A LIKING TO TAMAYO SENSEI...
...SO HE STARTED COMING EVERY DAY.
YUSHIRO
GINKGO CLASS
JUNIOR HIGH, SECOND-YEAR
I CAN'T KEEP HIM IN THE NURSE'S OFFICE, SO I LET HIM OUTSIDE.
Sorry for all the trouble.
OH, I SEE.
SO HIS NAME ISN'T ROCKY?
HMM...

WELL...
...I'M GLAD WE FOUND YOUR OWNER.
POOR SENSEI...
CHACHA-MARU'S A NICE NAME.
THANK YOU FOR MAKING MY DAYS BETTER.
RUB RUB
PURR PURR
...
YOU CAN TAKE HIM HOME NOW.
Here.
DON'T BOTHER.
?!

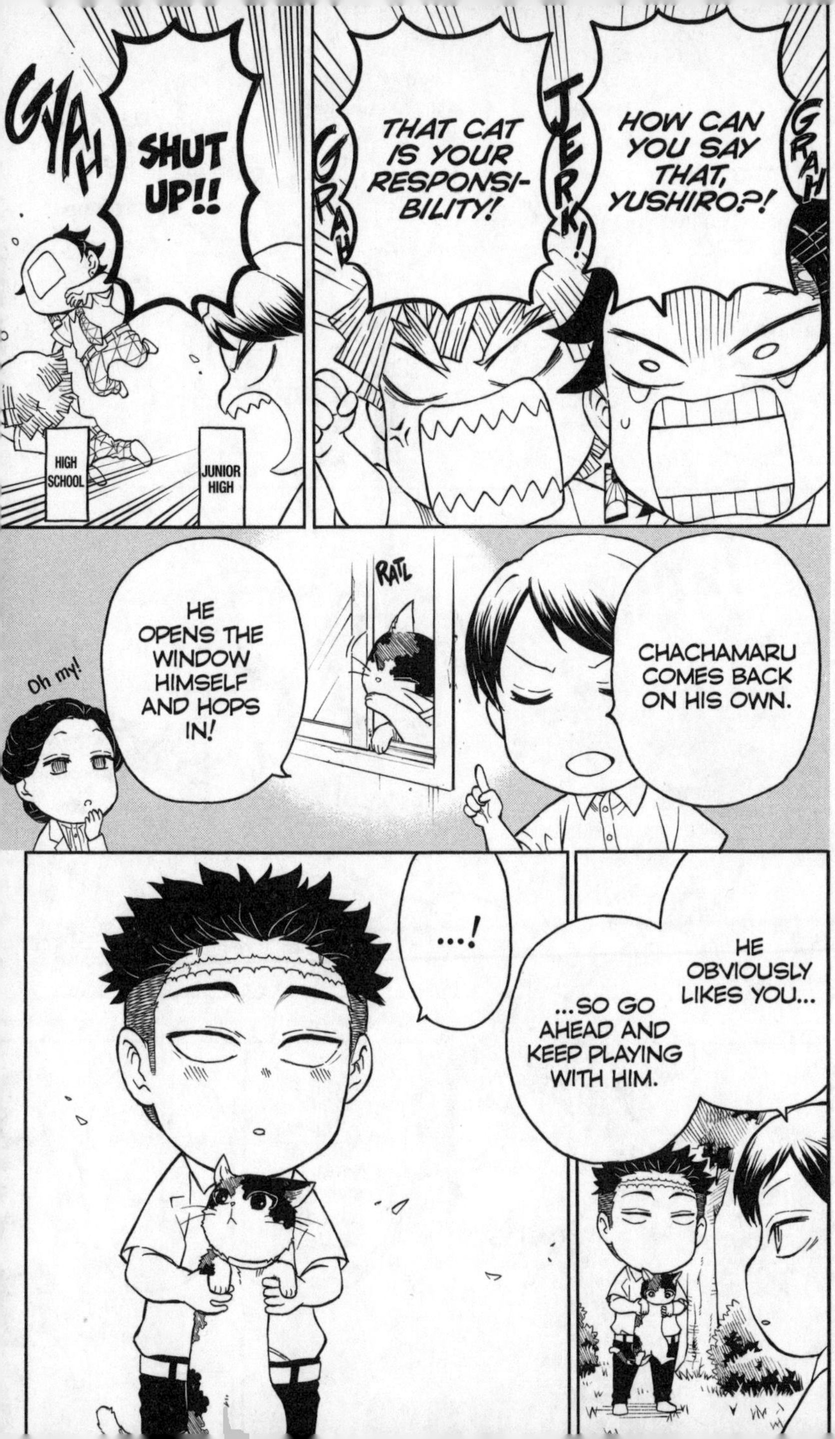
GRAH
HOW CAN YOU SAY THAT, YUSHIRO?!
JERK!
GRAH
THAT CAT IS YOUR RESPONSIBILITY!
GYAH
SHUT UP!!
JUNIOR HIGH
HIGH SCHOOL
CHACHAMARU COMES BACK ON HIS OWN.
RATL
HE OPENS THE WINDOW HIMSELF AND HOPS IN!
Oh my!
HE OBVIOUSLY LIKES YOU...
...SO GO AHEAD AND KEEP PLAYING WITH HIM.
...!

LUCKY YOU, HIMEJIMA SENSEI!!
YEAH! FOR A MINUTE THERE...
...I THOUGHT YOU WERE GONNA CRY!!
YAAAY!!
O-OKAY ...
BUT, UM...
...CAN YOU?
GACK
THE SCHOOL'S RULES MIGHT POSE A BIT OF A PROBLEM...
THERE ISN'T ACTUALLY A RULE AGAINST THE CAT BEING HERE...
...SO IT'S NOT LIKE I CAN ACTUALLY FORBID IT.

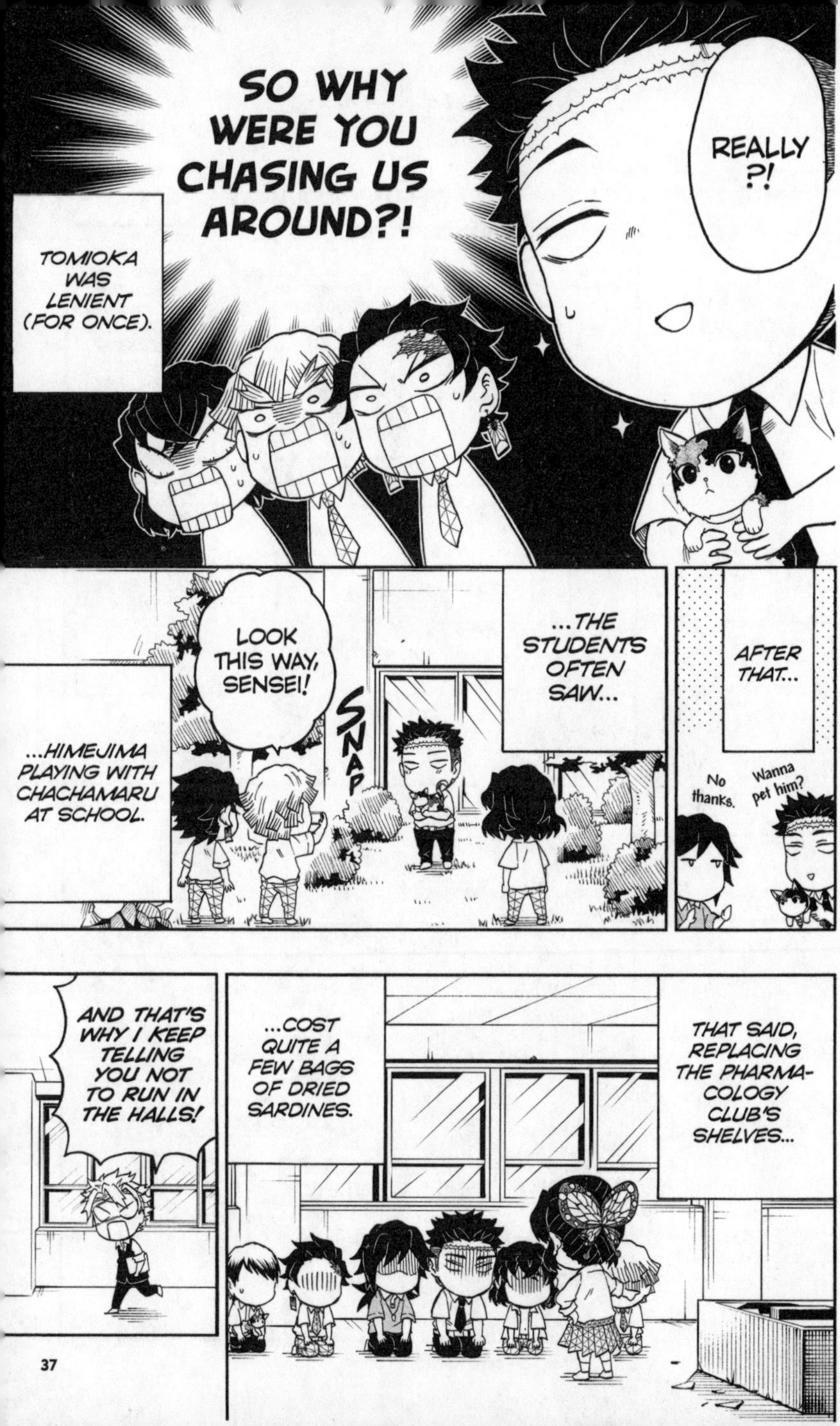
REALLY?!
SO WHY WERE YOU CHASING US AROUND?!
TOMIOKA WAS LENIENT (FOR ONCE).
AFTER THAT...
Wanna pet him?
No thanks.
...THE STUDENTS OFTEN SAW...
LOOK THIS WAY, SENSEI!
SNAP
...HIMEJIMA PLAYING WITH CHACHAMARU AT SCHOOL.
THAT SAID, REPLACING THE PHARMACOLOGY CLUB'S SHELVES...
...COST QUITE A FEW BAGS OF DRIED SARDINES.
AND THAT'S WHY I KEEP TELLING YOU NOT TO RUN IN THE HALLS!

AWESOME ACADEMY

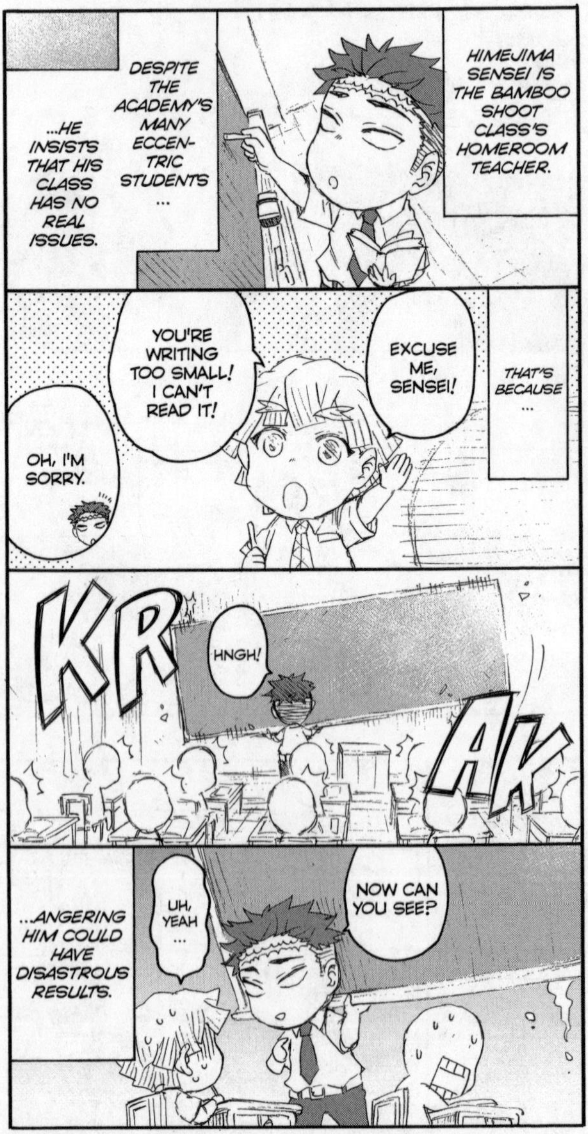
HIMEJIMA SENSEI IS THE BAMBOO SHOOT CLASS'S HOMEROOM TEACHER.
DESPITE THE ACADEMY'S MANY ECCENTRIC STUDENTS...
...HE INSISTS THAT HIS CLASS HAS NO REAL ISSUES.
THAT'S BECAUSE...
EXCUSE ME, SENSEI!
YOU'RE WRITING TOO SMALL! I CAN'T READ IT!
OH, I'M SORRY.
HNGH!
KR
AK
NOW CAN YOU SEE?
UH, YEAH...
...ANGERING HIM COULD HAVE DISASTROUS RESULTS.

But no one has ever seen him angry.

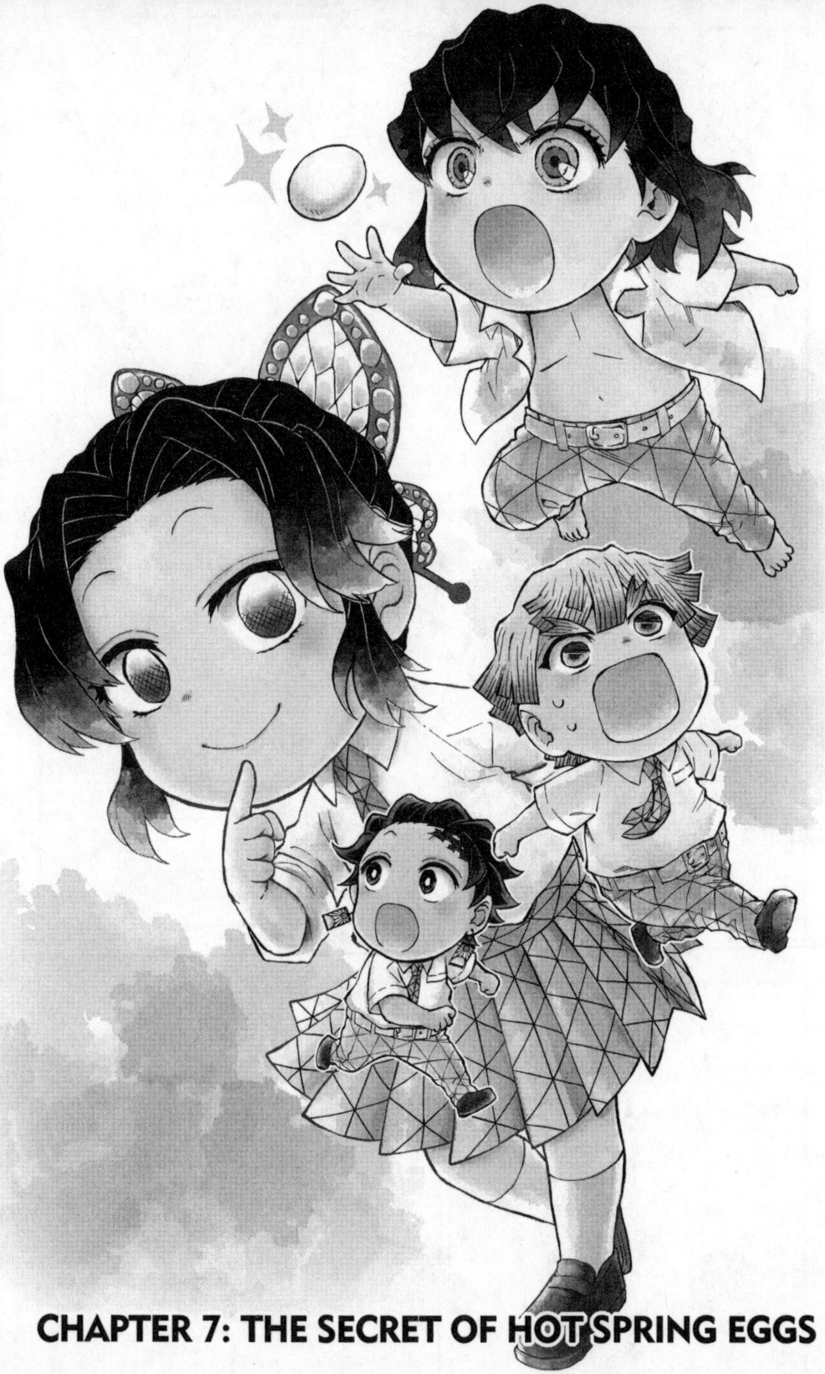

CHAPTER 7: THE SECRET OF HOT SPRING EGGS

I MADE PLENTY OF CURRY...
...AND PUT IT IN THE FRIDGE ...
...SO YOU CAN GET IT OUT AND WARM SOME UP EVERY DAY.
PAT
YOU ALREADY TOLD ME THAT!
WHY WOULD YOU WANNA...
...TAKE A TRIP TO SOME HOT SPRING RIGHT NOW ANYWAY?!
It's too hot!
INOSUKE HASHIBIRA
BAMBOO SHOOT CLASS
FIRST-YEAR
HOT SPRINGS IN THE SUMMER HAVE THEIR OWN CHARM.
SMILE
HISA
INOSUKE'S FOSTER PARENT
THERE'S ALSO CHILLED WATER-MELON ...
...SO SHARE IT WITH YOUR FRIENDS.
I KNOW !!
JUNK

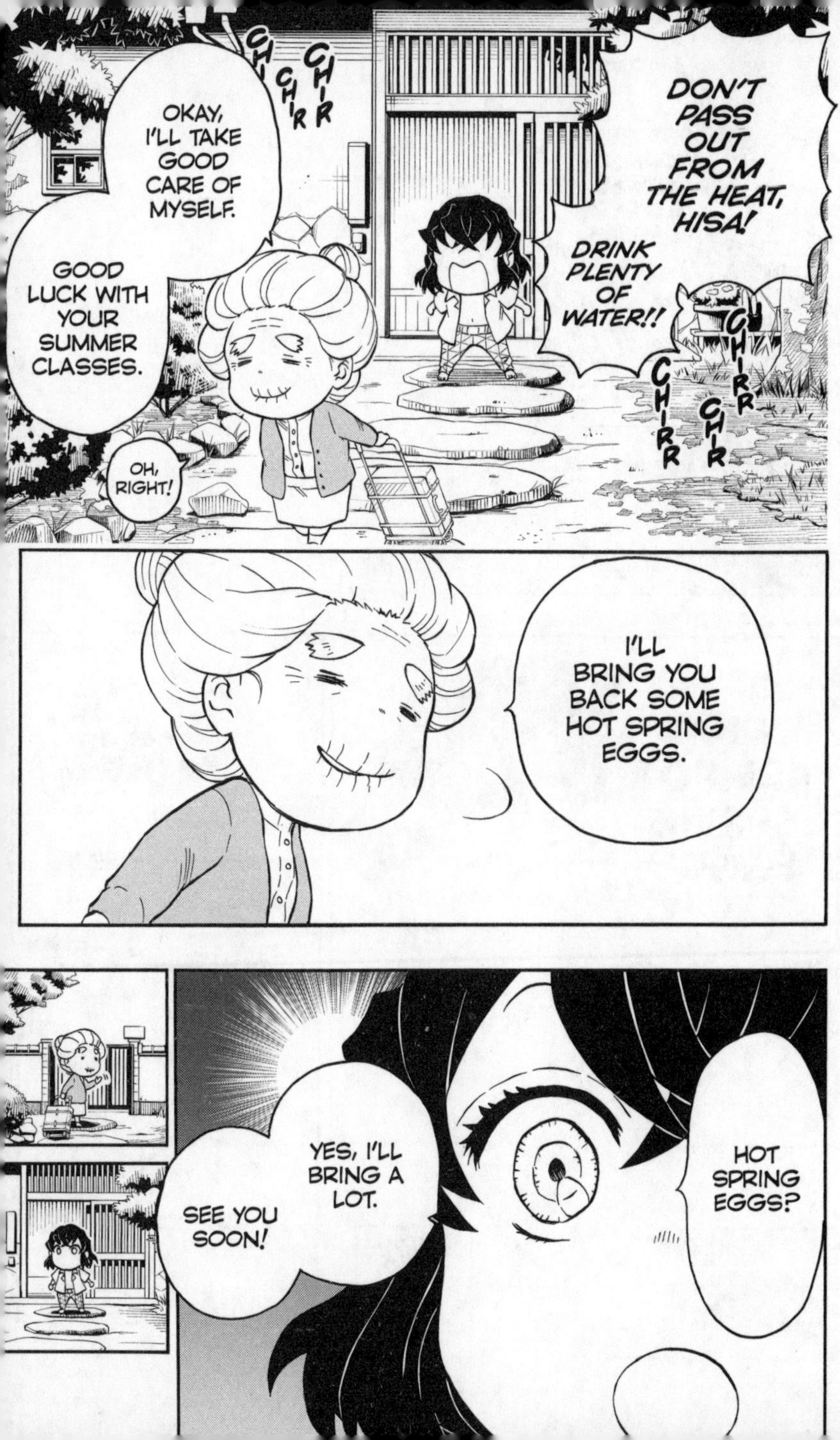
DON'T PASS OUT FROM THE HEAT, HISA!
DRINK PLENTY OF WATER!!
CHIRR
CHIRR
CHIR
CHIRR
CHIR
CHIR
OKAY, I'LL TAKE GOOD CARE OF MYSELF.
GOOD LUCK WITH YOUR SUMMER CLASSES.
OH, RIGHT!
I'LL BRING YOU BACK SOME HOT SPRING EGGS.
HOT SPRING EGGS?
YES, I'LL BRING A LOT.
SEE YOU SOON!

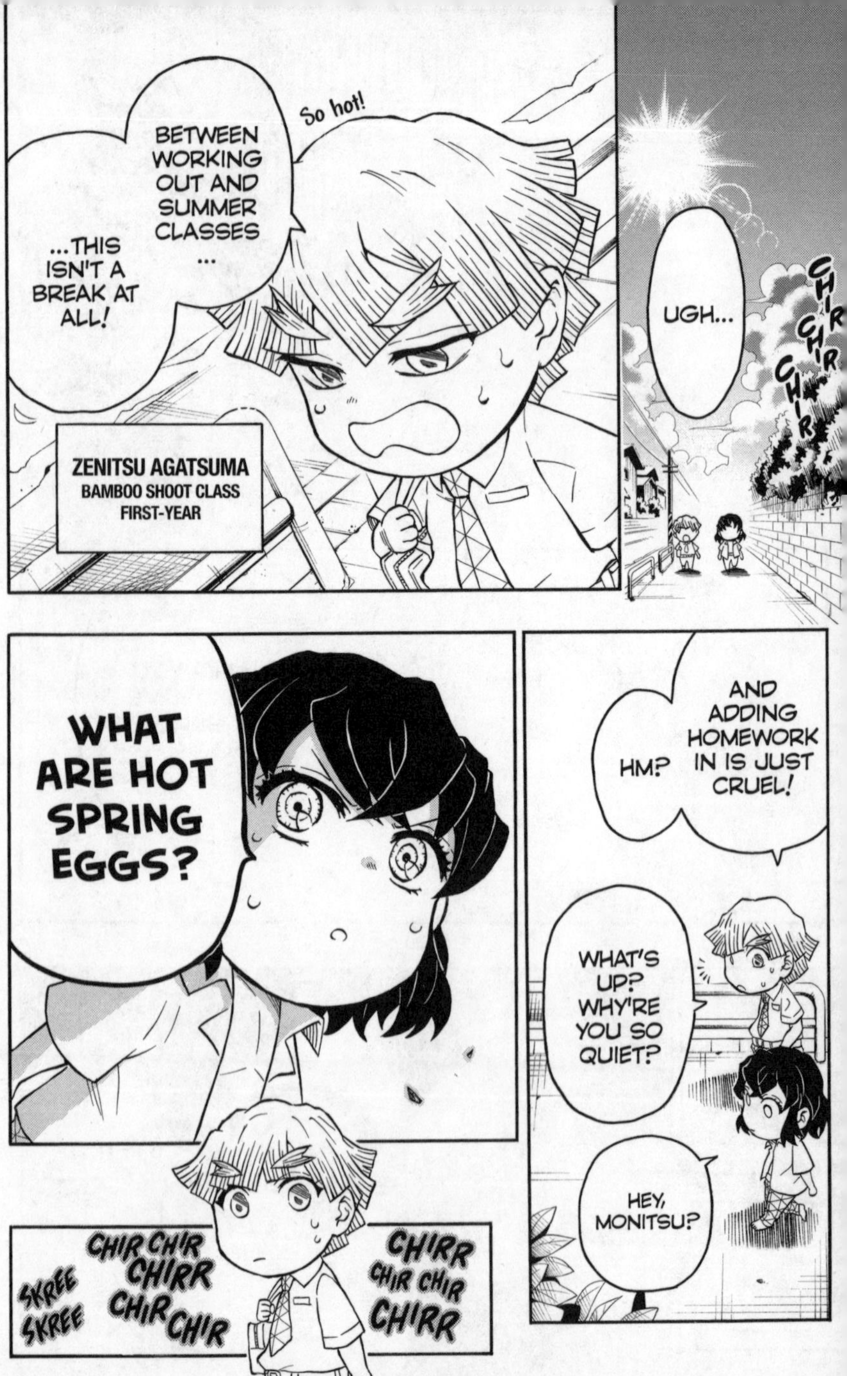
UGH...
CHIR CHIR CHIR
So hot!
BETWEEN WORKING OUT AND SUMMER CLASSES ...
...THIS ISN'T A BREAK AT ALL!
ZENITSU AGATSUMA
BAMBOO SHOOT CLASS
FIRST-YEAR
AND ADDING HOMEWORK IN IS JUST CRUEL!
HM?
WHAT'S UP? WHY'RE YOU SO QUIET?
HEY, MONITSU?
WHAT ARE HOT SPRING EGGS?
CHIRR CHIR CHIR CHIRR
CHIR CHIR CHIRR CHIR CHIR
SKREE SKREE

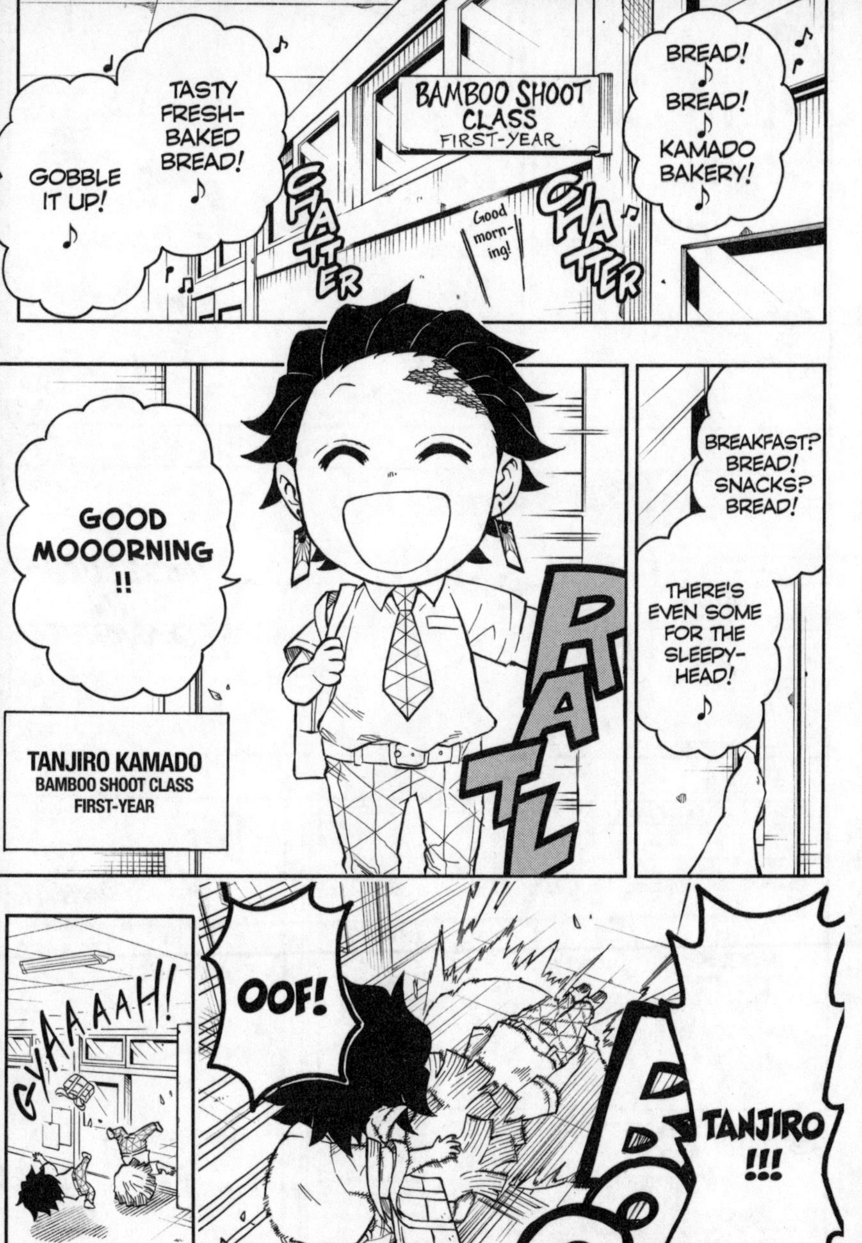

BREAD! ♪ BREAD! ♪ KAMADO BAKERY! ♪
BAMBOO SHOOT CLASS FIRST-YEAR
CHATTER
Good morn-ing!
CHATTER
TASTY FRESH-BAKED BREAD! ♪
GOBBLE IT UP! ♪
BREAKFAST? BREAD! SNACKS? BREAD!
THERE'S EVEN SOME FOR THE SLEEPY-HEAD! ♪
RATTL
GOOD MOOORNING!!
TANJIRO KAMADO
BAMBOO SHOOT CLASS
FIRST-YEAR
TANJIRO!!!
OOF!
GYAAAAH!

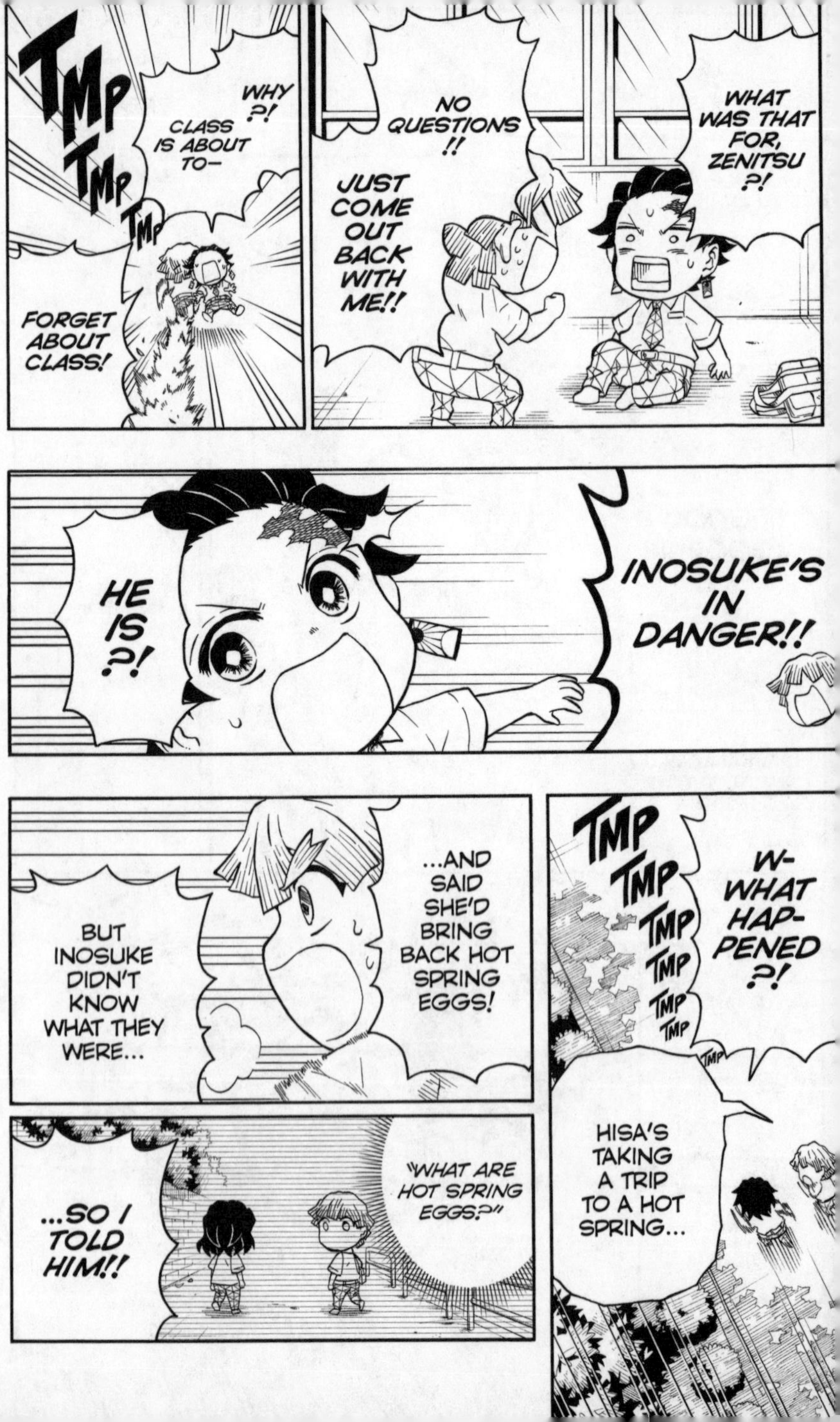
WHAT WAS THAT FOR, ZENITSU?!
NO QUESTIONS!!
JUST COME OUT BACK WITH ME!!
WHY?!
CLASS IS ABOUT TO—
TMP TMP TMP
FORGET ABOUT CLASS!
INOSUKE'S IN DANGER!!
HE IS?!
TMP TMP TMP TMP TMP TMP TMP
W-WHAT HAPPENED?!
HISA'S TAKING A TRIP TO A HOT SPRING...
...AND SAID SHE'D BRING BACK HOT SPRING EGGS!
BUT INOSUKE DIDN'T KNOW WHAT THEY WERE...
"WHAT ARE HOT SPRING EGGS?"
...SO I TOLD HIM!!

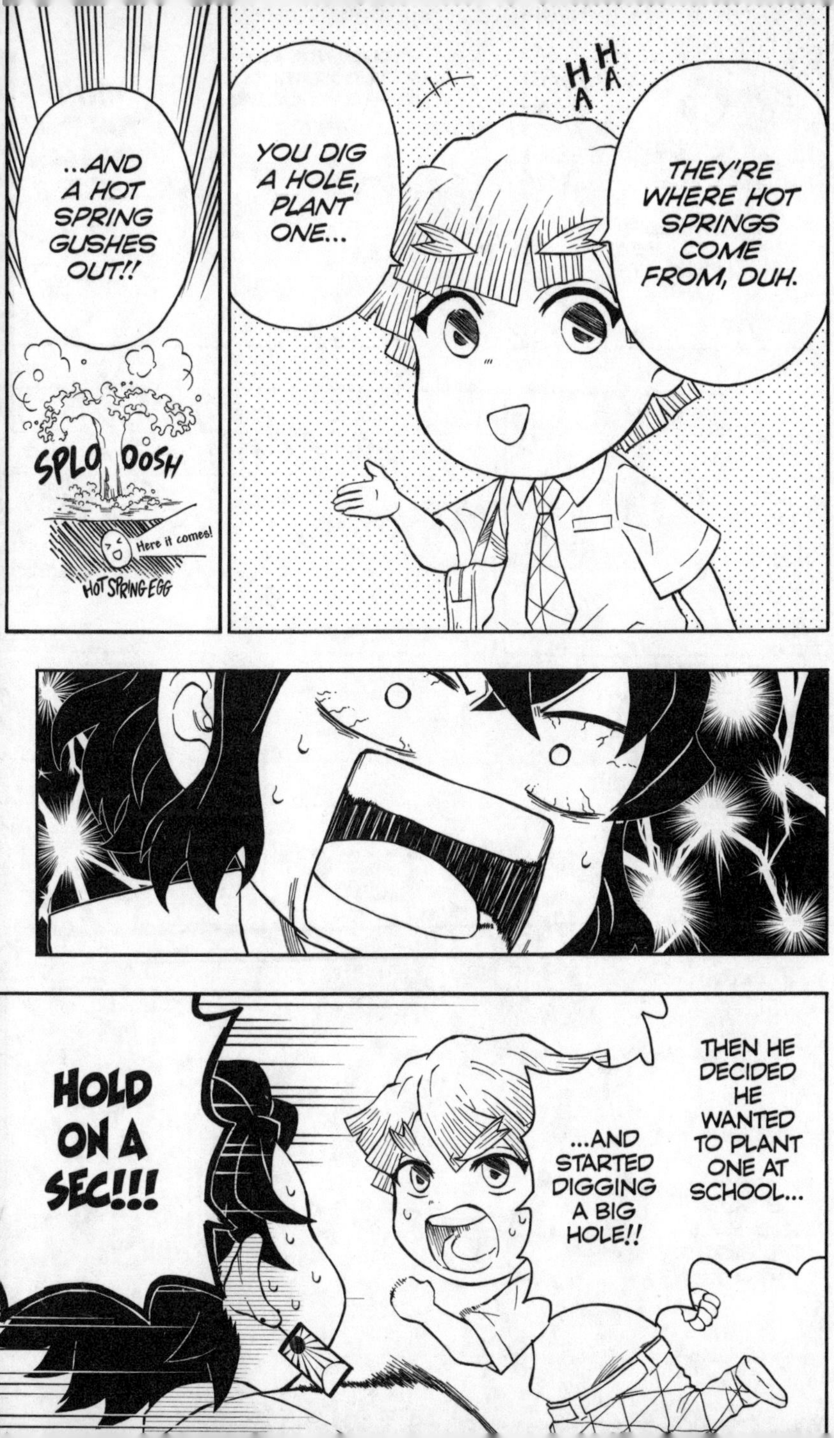
HA HA
THEY'RE WHERE HOT SPRINGS COME FROM, DUH.
YOU DIG A HOLE, PLANT ONE...
...AND A HOT SPRING GUSHES OUT!!
SPLODOSH
Here it comes!
HOT SPRING EGG
THEN HE DECIDED HE WANTED TO PLANT ONE AT SCHOOL...
...AND STARTED DIGGING A BIG HOLE!!
HOLD ON A SEC!!!

WHY'D YOU TELL HIM SUCH A STUPID LIE?!
—HOT SPRING EGGS (REAL)— EGGS THAT HAVE BEEN BOILED SLOWLY AT LOW HEAT. YUM!
I DIDN'T THINK HE'D BELIEVE ME!
I THOUGHT IT'D BE MORE LIKE THIS!
Oh you!!!!
AH HA HA!
CHAT CHAT
!
WHOOOSH
GRAAAAAH!
?
GRAAAH!
CHIRR CHIRR CHIRR
KIMETSU ACADEMY WESTERN GROUNDS
MOUNTAIN OUT BACK (FOOTHILLS)
CHIRR
CHIR CHIR CHIR
CHIRRR
CHIRR
SHINK
SHINK
SHINK
WHEW!
THE BIGGER THE HOLE, THE BETTER, RIGHT?!

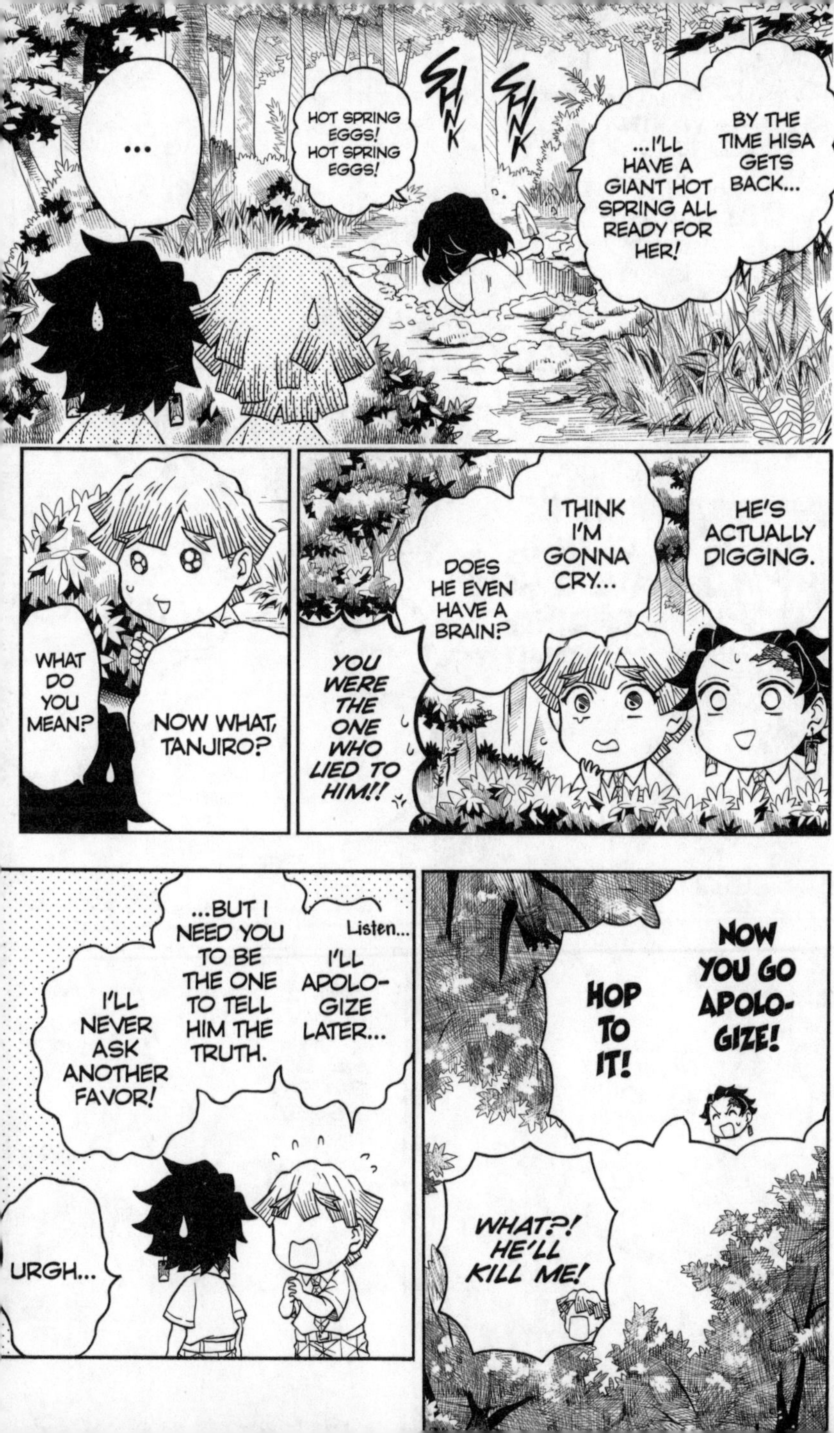
BY THE TIME HISA GETS BACK...
...I'LL HAVE A GIANT HOT SPRING ALL READY FOR HER!
SHNK
SHNK
HOT SPRING EGGS! HOT SPRING EGGS!
...
HE'S ACTUALLY DIGGING.
I THINK I'M GONNA CRY...
DOES HE EVEN HAVE A BRAIN?
YOU WERE THE ONE WHO LIED TO HIM!!
NOW WHAT, TANJIRO?
WHAT DO YOU MEAN?
NOW YOU GO APOLO-GIZE!
HOP TO IT!
WHAT?! HE'LL KILL ME!
Listen...
I'LL APOLO-GIZE LATER...
...BUT I NEED YOU TO BE THE ONE TO TELL HIM THE TRUTH.
I'LL NEVER ASK ANOTHER FAVOR!
URGH...

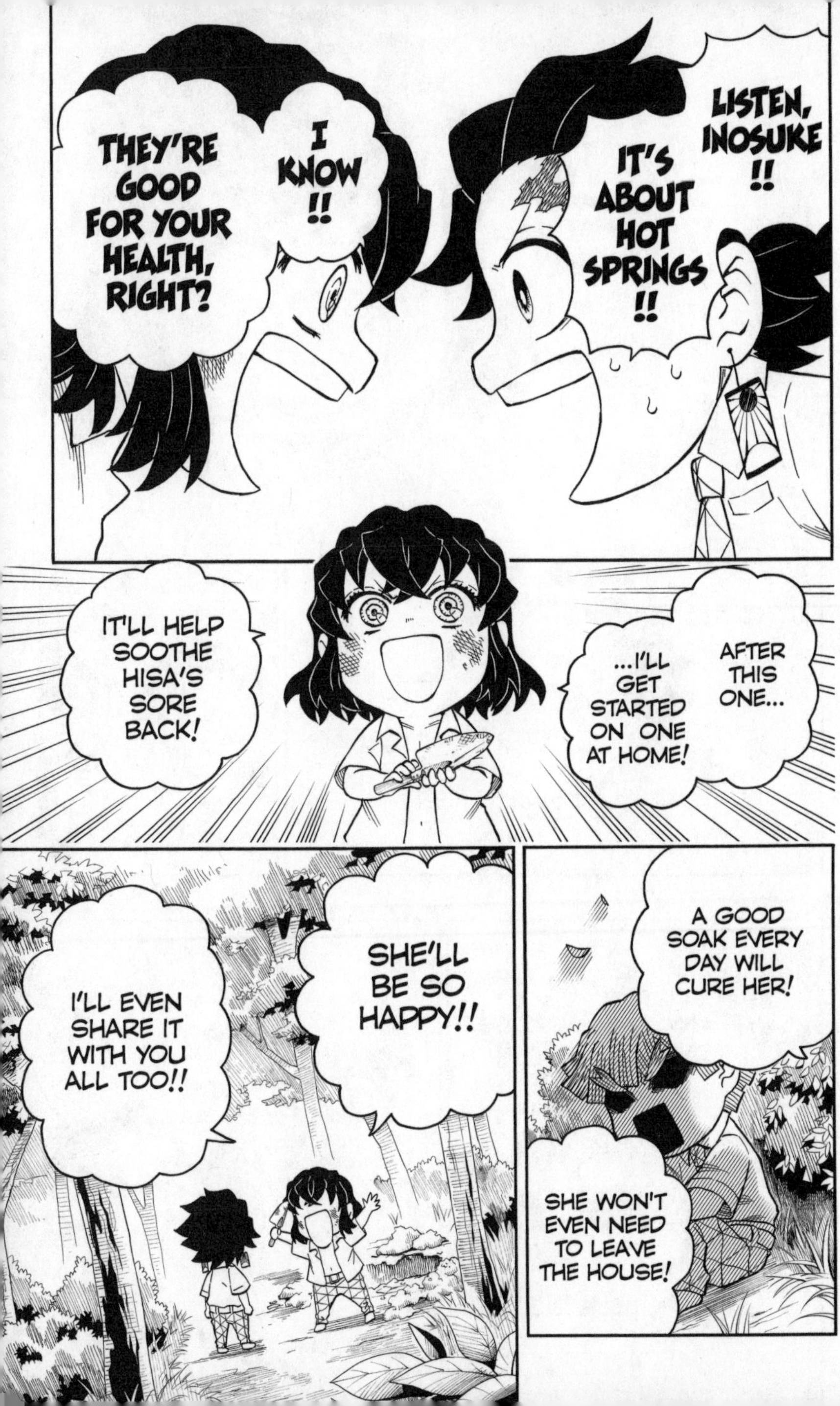
LISTEN, INOSUKE!!
IT'S ABOUT HOT SPRINGS!!
I KNOW!!
THEY'RE GOOD FOR YOUR HEALTH, RIGHT?
AFTER THIS ONE...
...I'LL GET STARTED ON ONE AT HOME!
IT'LL HELP SOOTHE HISA'S SORE BACK!
A GOOD SOAK EVERY DAY WILL CURE HER!
SHE WON'T EVEN NEED TO LEAVE THE HOUSE!
SHE'LL BE SO HAPPY!!
I'LL EVEN SHARE IT WITH YOU ALL TOO!!

AIN'T THAT GREAT?
I COULDN'T TELL HIM.
WHAT ?!!
I THOUGHT YOU WERE THE HONEST TYPE!!
DON'T EVEN START WITH ME!
BESIDES, I RE-MEMBERED SOME-THING.

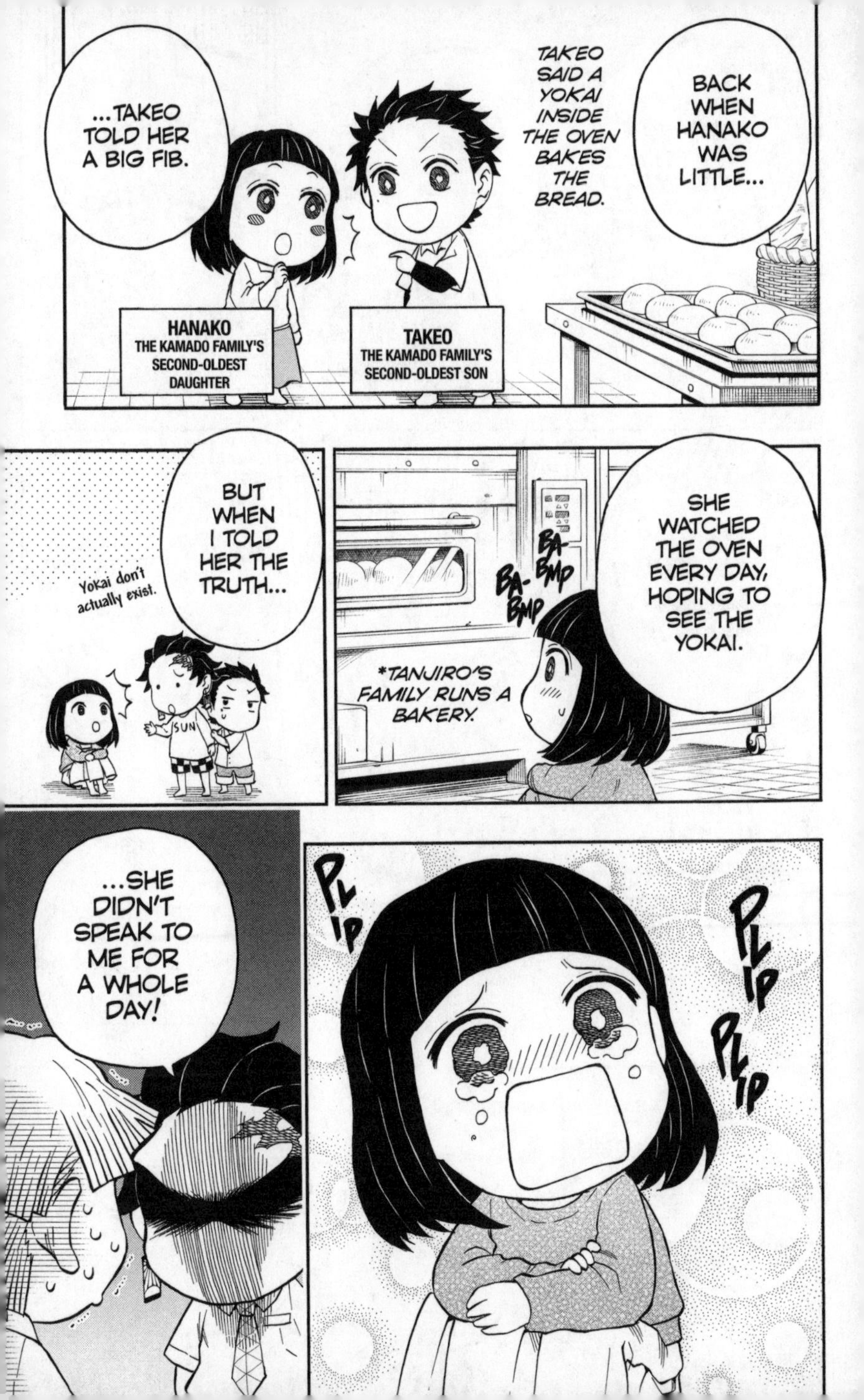
BACK WHEN HANAKO WAS LITTLE...
TAKEO SAID A YOKAI INSIDE THE OVEN BAKES THE BREAD.
TAKEO
THE KAMADO FAMILY'S SECOND-OLDEST SON
HANAKO
THE KAMADO FAMILY'S SECOND-OLDEST DAUGHTER
...TAKEO TOLD HER A BIG FIB.
SHE WATCHED THE OVEN EVERY DAY, HOPING TO SEE THE YOKAI.
BA-BMP
BA-BMP
*TANJIRO'S FAMILY RUNS A BAKERY.
BUT WHEN I TOLD HER THE TRUTH...
Yokai don't actually exist.
SUN
PLIP
PLIP
PLIP
PLIP
...SHE DIDN'T SPEAK TO ME FOR A WHOLE DAY!

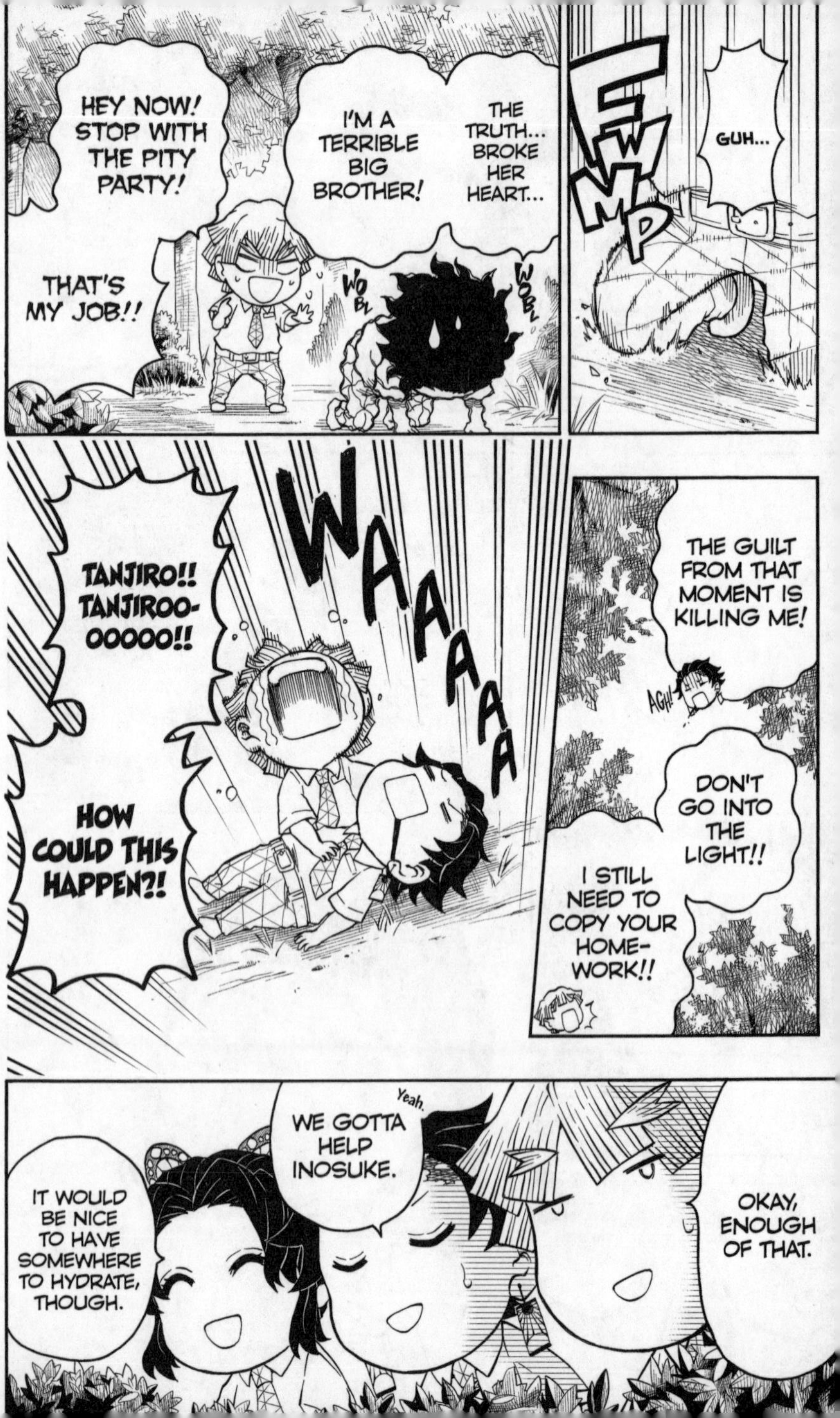
FWMP
GUH...
THE TRUTH... BROKE HER HEART...
I'M A TERRIBLE BIG BROTHER!
WOBL
WOBL
HEY NOW! STOP WITH THE PITY PARTY!
THAT'S MY JOB!!
THE GUILT FROM THAT MOMENT IS KILLING ME!
AGH!
DON'T GO INTO THE LIGHT!!
I STILL NEED TO COPY YOUR HOME-WORK!!
WAAAAAA
TANJIRO!! TANJIROO-OOOOO!!
HOW COULD THIS HAPPEN?!
OKAY, ENOUGH OF THAT.
Yeah.
WE GOTTA HELP INOSUKE.
IT WOULD BE NICE TO HAVE SOMEWHERE TO HYDRATE, THOUGH.

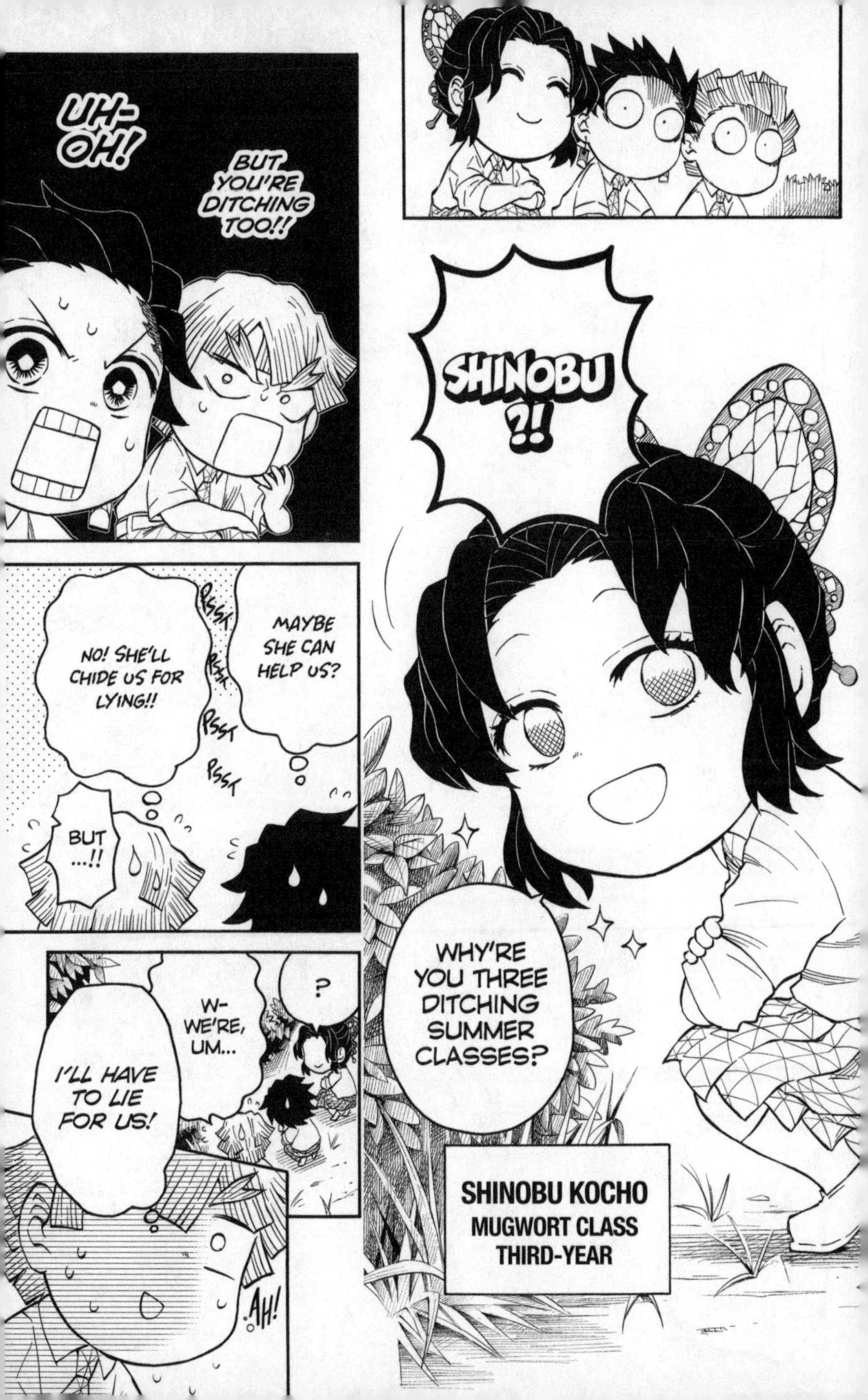
SHINOBU ?!!
WHY'RE YOU THREE DITCHING SUMMER CLASSES?
SHINOBU KOCHO
MUGWORT CLASS
THIRD-YEAR
UH-OH!
BUT YOU'RE DITCHING TOO!!
MAYBE SHE CAN HELP US?
PSSST
NO! SHE'LL CHIDE US FOR LYING!!
BUT ...!!
?
W-WE'RE, UM...
I'LL HAVE TO LIE FOR US!
AH!

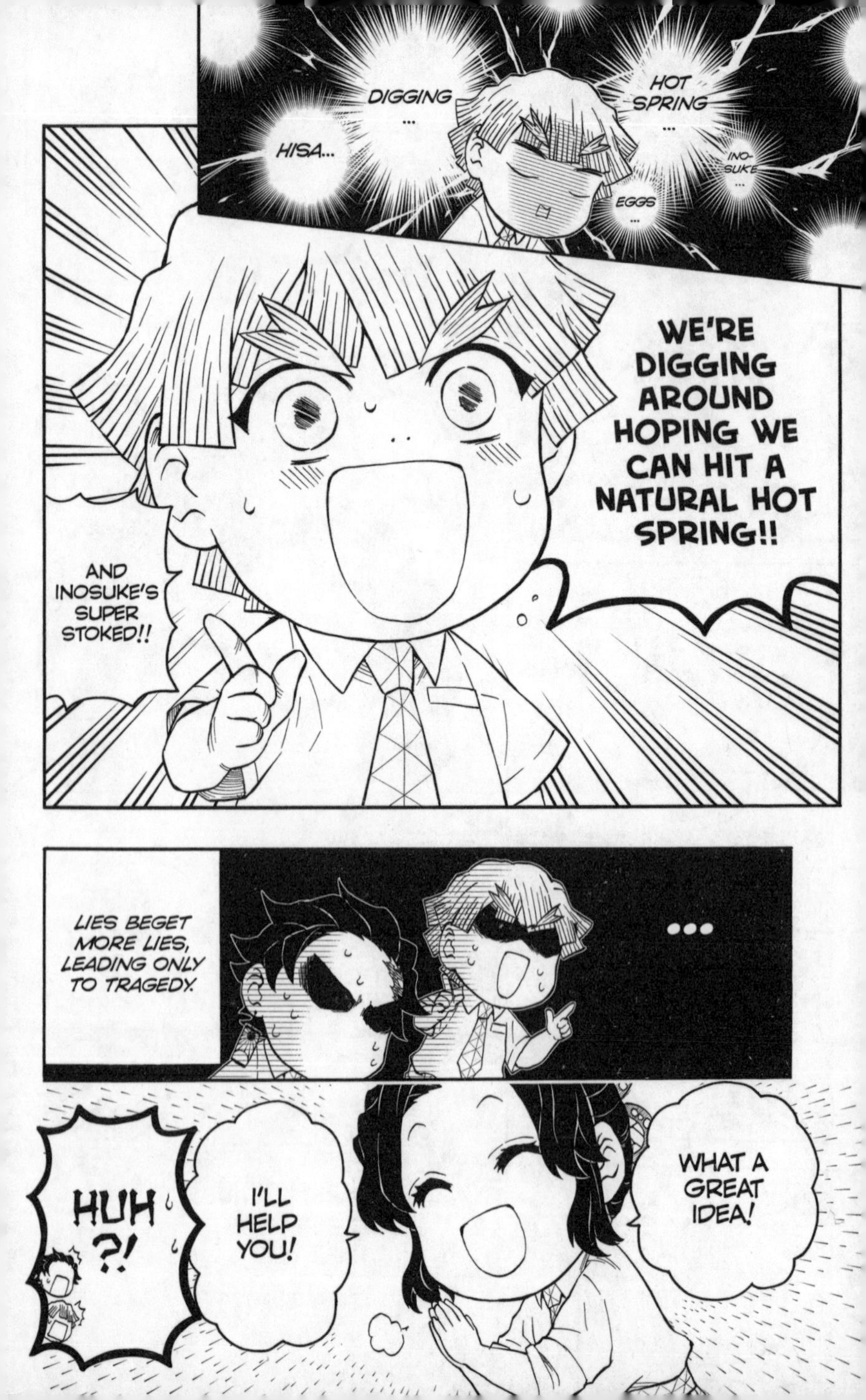
HOT SPRING ...
INO-SUKE ...
EGGS ...
DIGGING ...
HISA...
WE'RE DIGGING AROUND HOPING WE CAN HIT A NATURAL HOT SPRING!!
AND INOSUKE'S SUPER STOKED!!
...
LIES BEGET MORE LIES, LEADING ONLY TO TRAGEDY.
WHAT A GREAT IDEA!
I'LL HELP YOU!
HUH ?!

MAYBE WE'LL GET LUCKY AND ACTUALLY FIND ONE!
HUH? NO, UM...
I DOUBT THAT!
WANNA KNOW SOMETHING NEAT?
BEFORE THEY BUILT THE SCHOOL ...
...THIS AREA WAS KNOWN FOR ITS HOT SPRINGS.
IT'S ENTIRELY POSSIBLE THERE COULD STILL BE SOME HIDING UNDER-GROUND.
?!
WAIT, REALLY?!
YOU'VE NEVER HEARD OF...
...KIMETSU HOT SPRING?
KIMETSU HOT SPRING?!
WE COULD ACTUALLY SUCCEED?!
AND VISIT A HOT SPRING AT SCHOOL?!
THAT MEANS...

WHAT?! HOT SPRING EGGS ARE JUST A KIND OF FOOD?!
YOU DON'T HATCH HOT SPRINGS FROM THEM?!
SORRY!
HMPH!
FINE. I FORGIVE YOU...
WHO COULD COMPLAIN WHILE THEY'RE IN A HOT SPRING?
...SINCE WE ACTUALLY DUG ONE UP!!
AHHH!
THIS FEELS GREAT!
NEXT TIME, I'LL BRING HISA!!
YES!!

BAM!!
GUYS! SHINOBU!!
YOU'RE ALL HERE TO HELP ME DIG TOO?!
YES. IT LOOKS LIKE YOU COULD USE A HAND.
GWOOOOO
SHNK

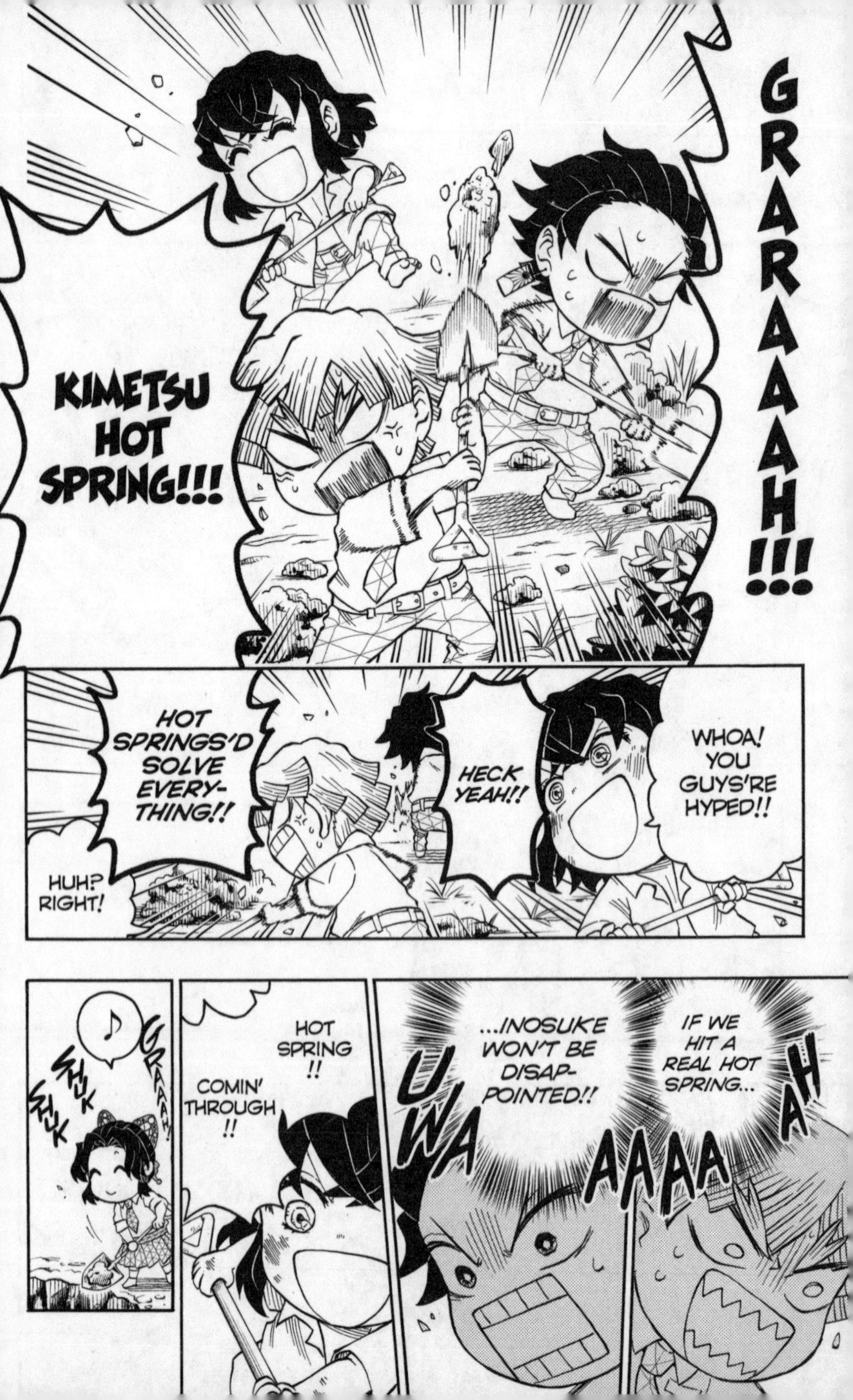
GRARAAAH!!!
KIMETSU HOT SPRING!!!
WHOA! YOU GUYS'RE HYPED!!
HECK YEAH!!
HOT SPRINGS'D SOLVE EVERY-THING!!
HUH? RIGHT!
IF WE HIT A REAL HOT SPRING...
...INOSUKE WON'T BE DISAP-POINTED!!
UWAAAAAAH
HOT SPRING !!
COMIN' THROUGH !!
GRAAAH!
♪
SHUK SHUK

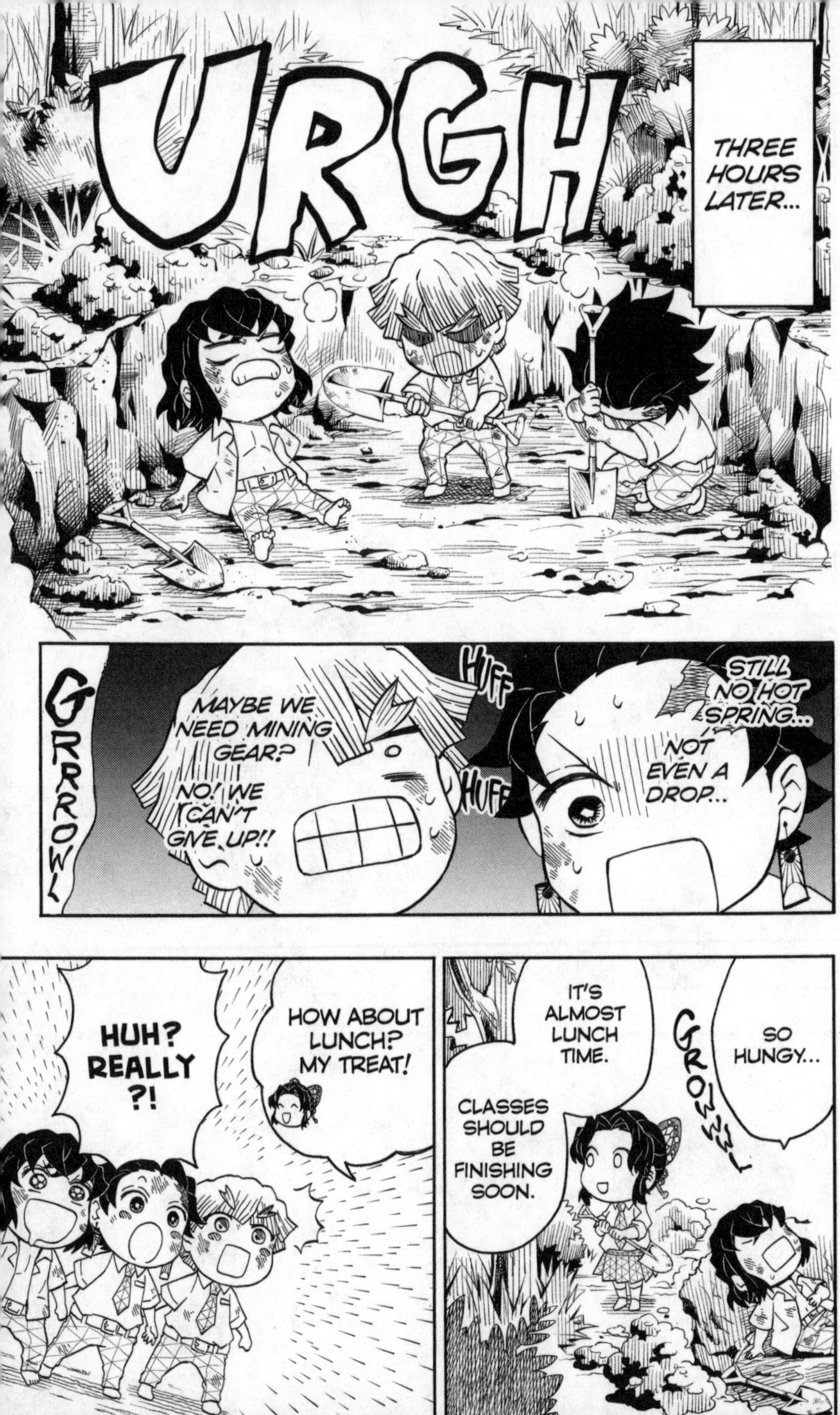
THREE HOURS LATER...
URGH
STILL NO HOT SPRING...
NOT EVEN A DROP...
HUFF
HUFF
MAYBE WE NEED MINING GEAR?
NO! WE CAN'T GIVE UP!!
GRRROWL
SO HUNGY...
GROWWL
IT'S ALMOST LUNCH TIME.
CLASSES SHOULD BE FINISHING SOON.
HOW ABOUT LUNCH? MY TREAT!
HUH? REALLY?!

SHINOBU IS AN ANGEL!!
I ACTUALLY FEEL BAD ABOUT LYING TO HER!!
I ORDERED FOOD FROM THE DINER.
DELIVERY FOR KOCHO!
HINATSURU SENT FOOD!
GOTO
ENGLISH TEACHER
YOU DOIN' OKAY OUT HERE?
RUSTL
RUSTL
THANK YOU, GOTO SENSEI!
NO PROBLEM. BUT WHY'D YOU NEED FOUR—
OH.

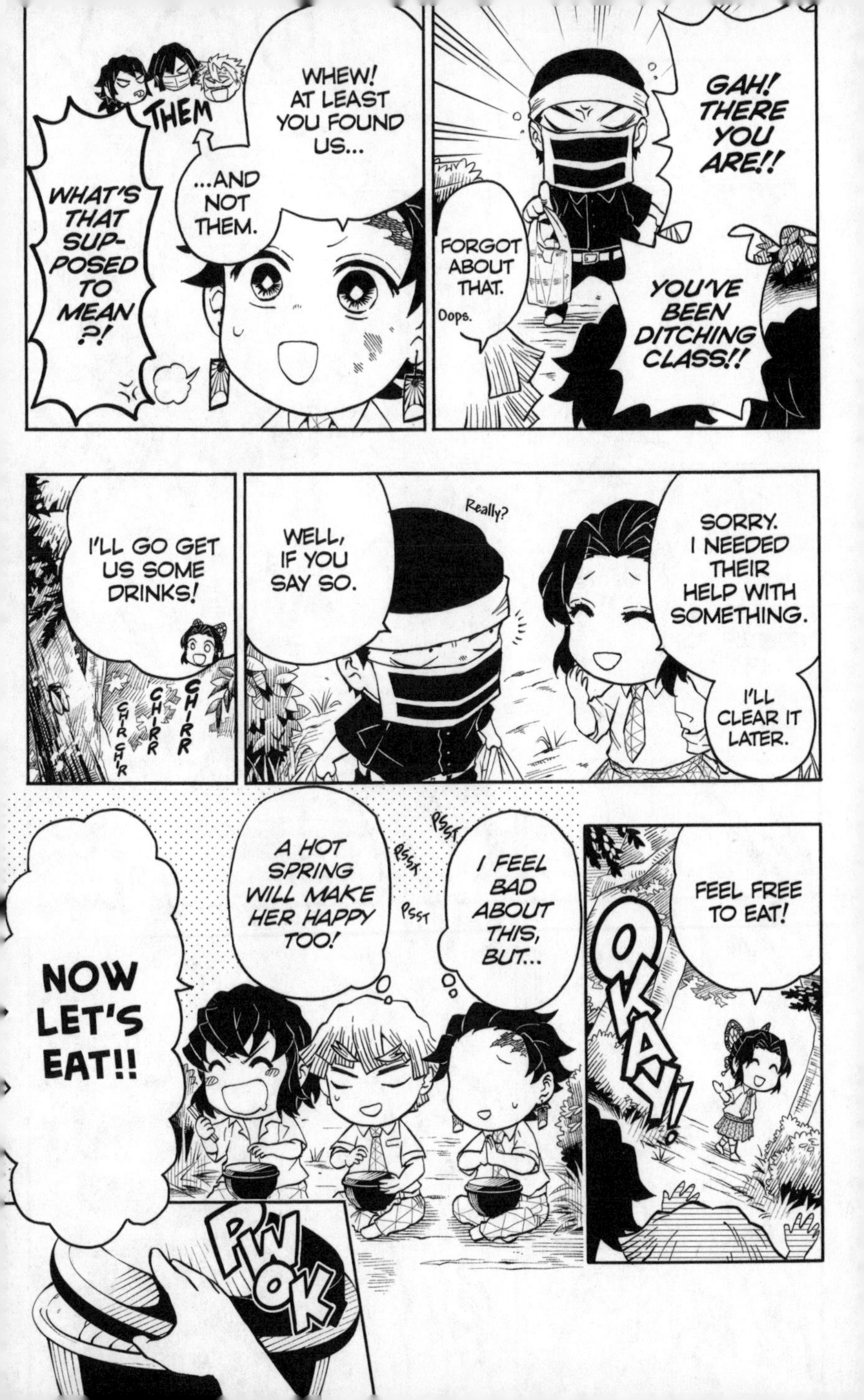
GAH! THERE YOU ARE!!
YOU'VE BEEN DITCHING CLASS!!
FORGOT ABOUT THAT.
Oops.
WHEW! AT LEAST YOU FOUND US...
...AND NOT THEM.
THEM
WHAT'S THAT SUP-POSED TO MEAN?!
SORRY. I NEEDED THEIR HELP WITH SOMETHING.
I'LL CLEAR IT LATER.
Really?
WELL, IF YOU SAY SO.
I'LL GO GET US SOME DRINKS!
CHIRR CHIRR CHIR CHIR
FEEL FREE TO EAT!
OKAY!
PSST
I FEEL BAD ABOUT THIS, BUT...
PSSST
PSST
A HOT SPRING WILL MAKE HER HAPPY TOO!
NOW LET'S EAT!!
PWOK

UDON
GLEAM
THIS...
...LOOKS....
YUMMY !!
IT'S THE DINER'S TOP ITEM!
PERFECT FOR SUMMER!
COLD UDON WITH HOT SPRING EGG!!
UWAAAAAH!!
HOT SPRING EGG?
GYAAAAAH!

WHY ARE YOU SHOUT-ING?!
SHAKE NO SHAKE NO SHAKE NO
DID YOU SAY HOT SPRING EGG?!
HM?
YEAH! HOT SPRING EGG!
I LOVE 'EM. IN FACT, I SHOULD MAKE SOME LATER.
ALL IT TAKES ARE SOME NORMAL EGGS.
HM?
STOP RUNNING!!!
TMP TMP TMP TMP
YIIIKES!

WE'RE SORRY, INOSUKE! WE CAN EXPLAIN!!
DON'T BOTHER!
GOTO JUST SAID THEY'RE NORMAL EGGS!!
NO WAY!
THEY'RE MORE THAN JUST NORMAL EGGS!!
?!
FWP
THEY'RE ...
...EXTRA-TASTY EGGS!
CRAZY CUTTING !!
YIKES!
ZEN-ITSU !!
THAT'S STILL JUST A FOOD!!
AH! THERE'S SHINOBU!

SENPAI! HELP US!
WSH
ARE YOU FIGHTING?
WSH
WE'LL TELL YOU EVERY-THING!
BLAH
BLAH
BLAH
OH, IS THAT WHAT HAPPENED?
AND THAT'S WHY YOU WERE RUNNING?
POUT
WHAT A SILLY LIE THAT WAS, ZENITSU!
YEAH... SORRY.
SORRY, INOSUKE.
Er...
DON'T BE MAD, OKAY?

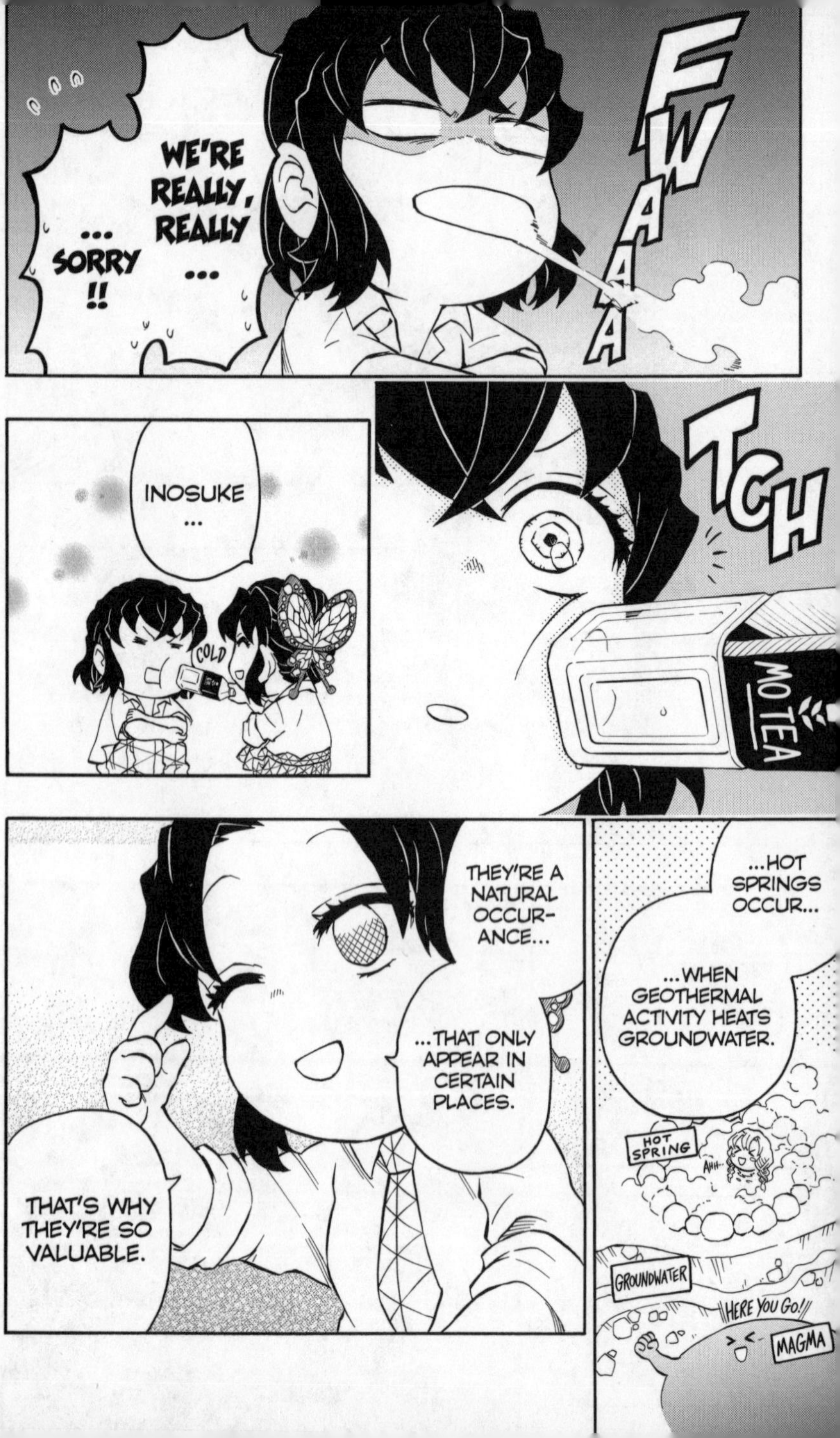
FWAAAA
WE'RE REALLY, REALLY ... ... SORRY!!
TCH
MO TEA
INOSUKE ...
COLD
...HOT SPRINGS OCCUR...
...WHEN GEOTHERMAL ACTIVITY HEATS GROUNDWATER.
HOT SPRING
AHH...
GROUNDWATER
HERE YOU GO!!
MAGMA
THEY'RE A NATURAL OCCUR-ANCE...
...THAT ONLY APPEAR IN CERTAIN PLACES.
THAT'S WHY THEY'RE SO VALUABLE.

THEY COULDN'T TELL YOU THE TRUTH ...
... BECAUSE THEY DIDN'T WANT TO DISAP-POINT YOU.
SO HOW ABOUT FORGIVING THEM?
...
HMPH!
THANKS TO SHINOBU, I FORGIVE YOU.
INO-SUKE!!
YOU'RE SO KIND!
WA HA HA
THE BEST!
WA HA HA
THANKS, SHINOBU!
HEY, SHINOBU!
YOU WANT MY HOT SPRING EGG?
YOU DON'T MIND?
Nah!
HISA'S BRINGING SOME HOME FOR ME!

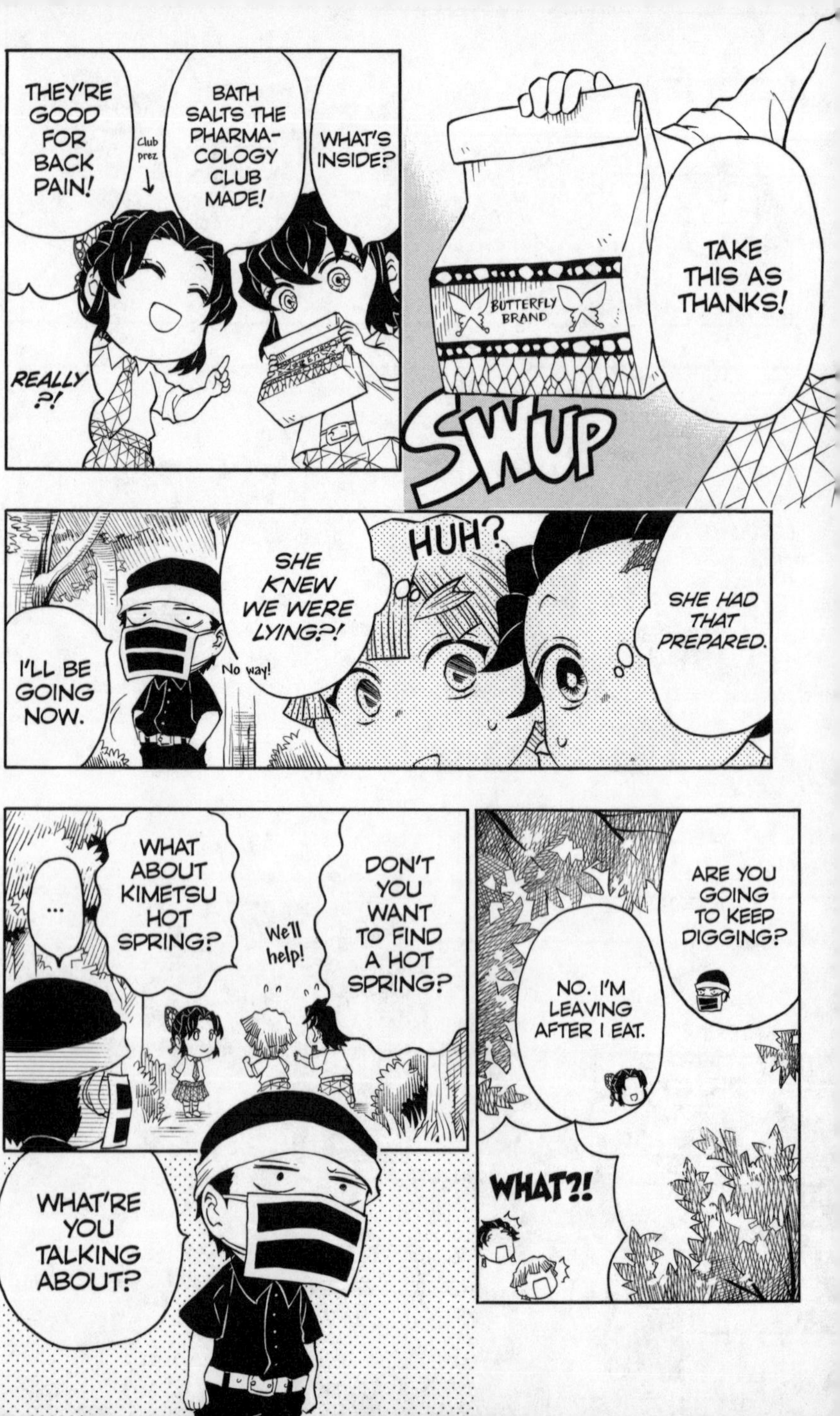
TAKE THIS AS THANKS!
BUTTERFLY BRAND
SWUP
WHAT'S INSIDE?
BATH SALTS THE PHARMA-COLOGY CLUB MADE!
Club prez
THEY'RE GOOD FOR BACK PAIN!
REALLY ?!
SHE HAD THAT PREPARED.
HUH?
SHE KNEW WE WERE LYING?!
No way!
I'LL BE GOING NOW.
ARE YOU GOING TO KEEP DIGGING?
NO. I'M LEAVING AFTER I EAT.
WHAT?!
DON'T YOU WANT TO FIND A HOT SPRING?
We'll help!
WHAT ABOUT KIMETSU HOT SPRING?
...
WHAT'RE YOU TALKING ABOUT?

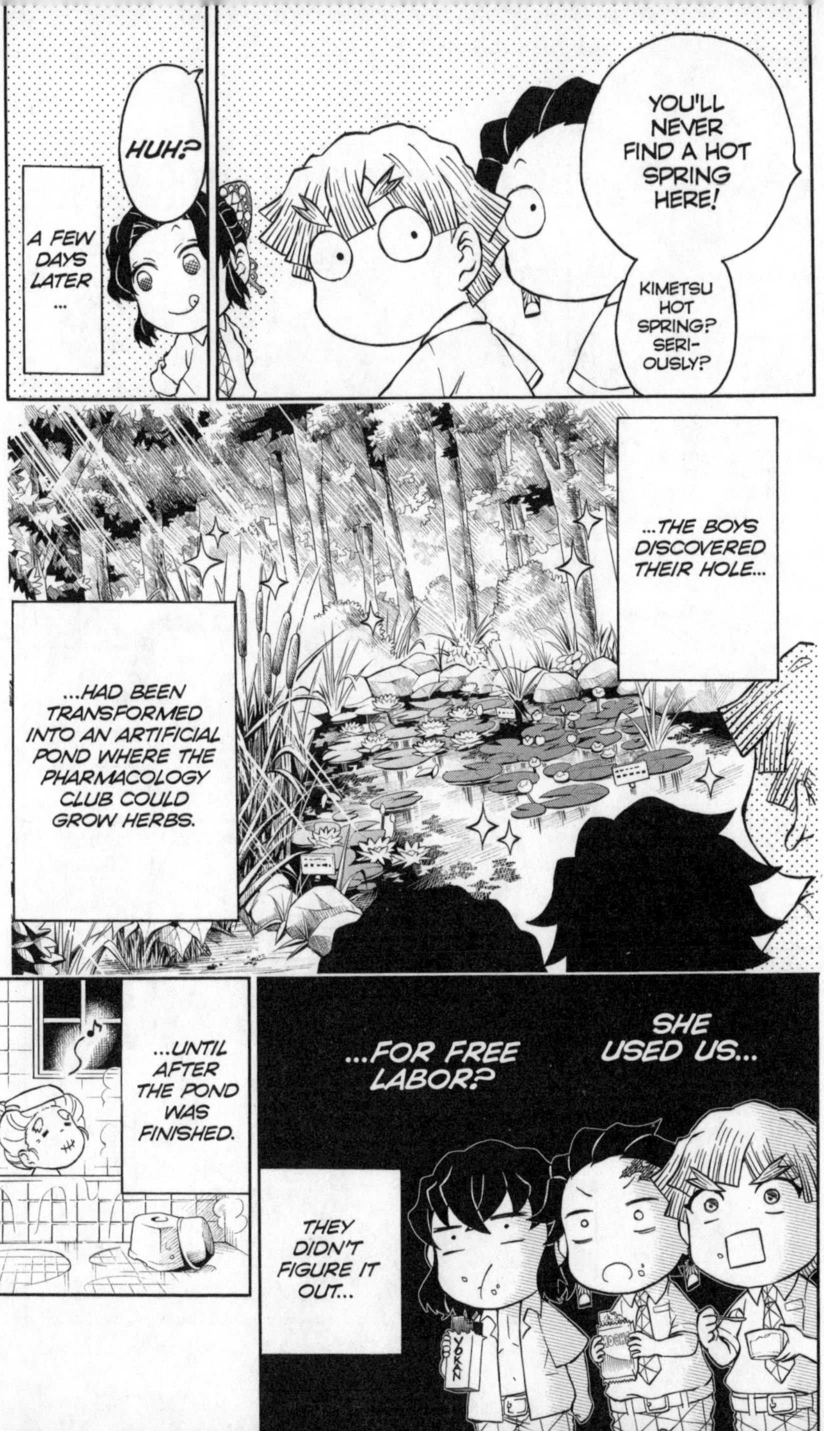
YOU'LL NEVER FIND A HOT SPRING HERE!
KIMETSU HOT SPRING? SERI- OUSLY?
HUH?
A FEW DAYS LATER ...
...THE BOYS DISCOVERED THEIR HOLE...
...HAD BEEN TRANSFORMED INTO AN ARTIFICIAL POND WHERE THE PHARMACOLOGY CLUB COULD GROW HERBS.
SHE USED US...
...FOR FREE LABOR?
THEY DIDN'T FIGURE IT OUT...
YOKAN
...UNTIL AFTER THE POND WAS FINISHED.

DON'T LEAVE IT TO HER

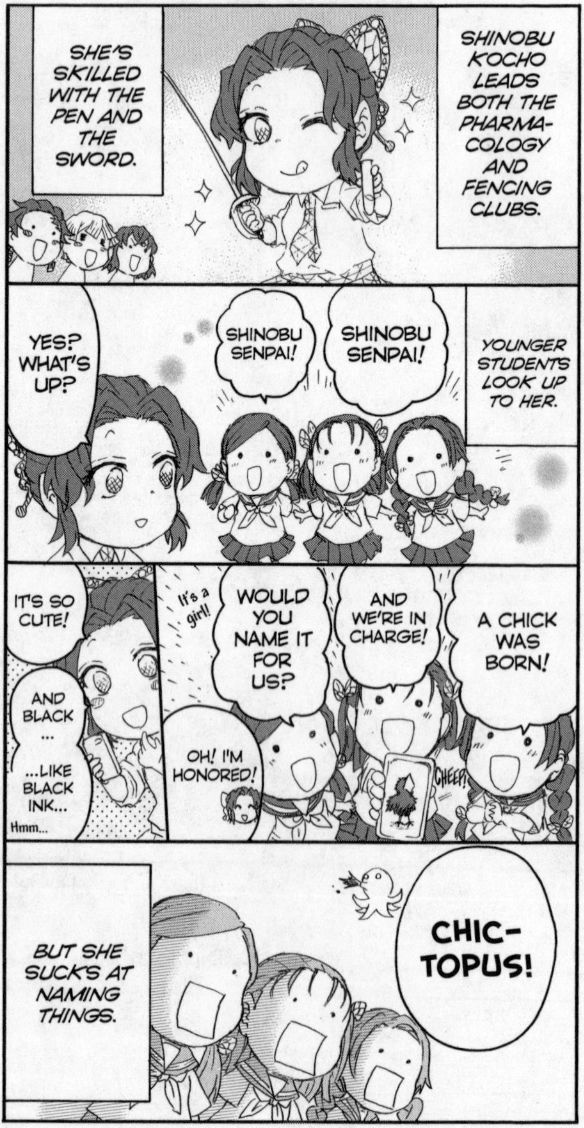

SHINOBU KOCHO LEADS BOTH THE PHARMACOLOGY AND FENCING CLUBS.
SHE'S SKILLED WITH THE PEN AND THE SWORD.
YOUNGER STUDENTS LOOK UP TO HER.
SHINOBU SENPAI!
SHINOBU SENPAI!
YES? WHAT'S UP?
A CHICK WAS BORN!
CHEEP!
AND WE'RE IN CHARGE!
WOULD YOU NAME IT FOR US?
It's a girl!
OH! I'M HONORED!
IT'S SO CUTE!
AND BLACK...
...LIKE BLACK INK...
Hmm...
CHIC-TOPUS!
BUT SHE SUCKS AT NAMING THINGS.

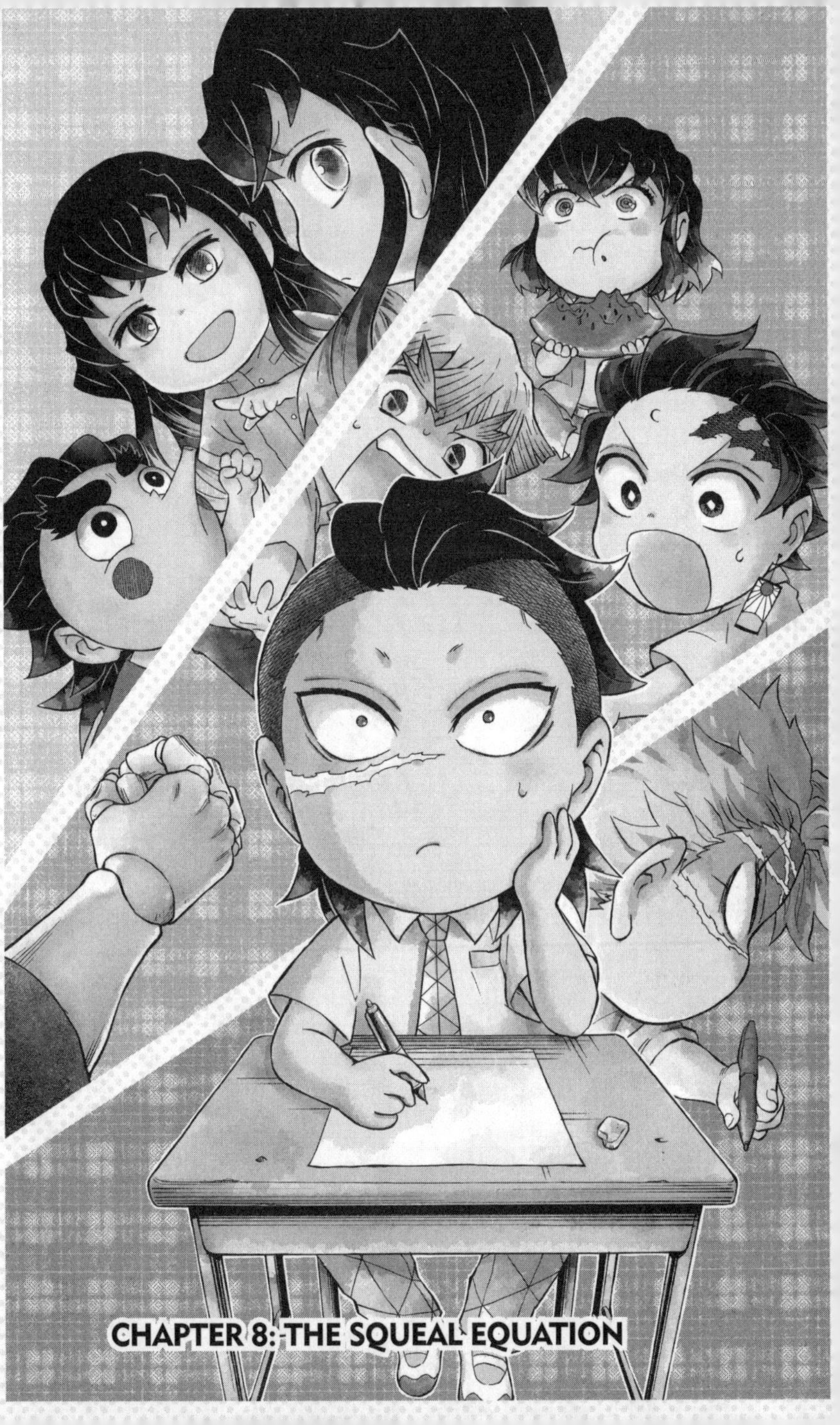

CHAPTER 8: THE SQUEAL EQUATION

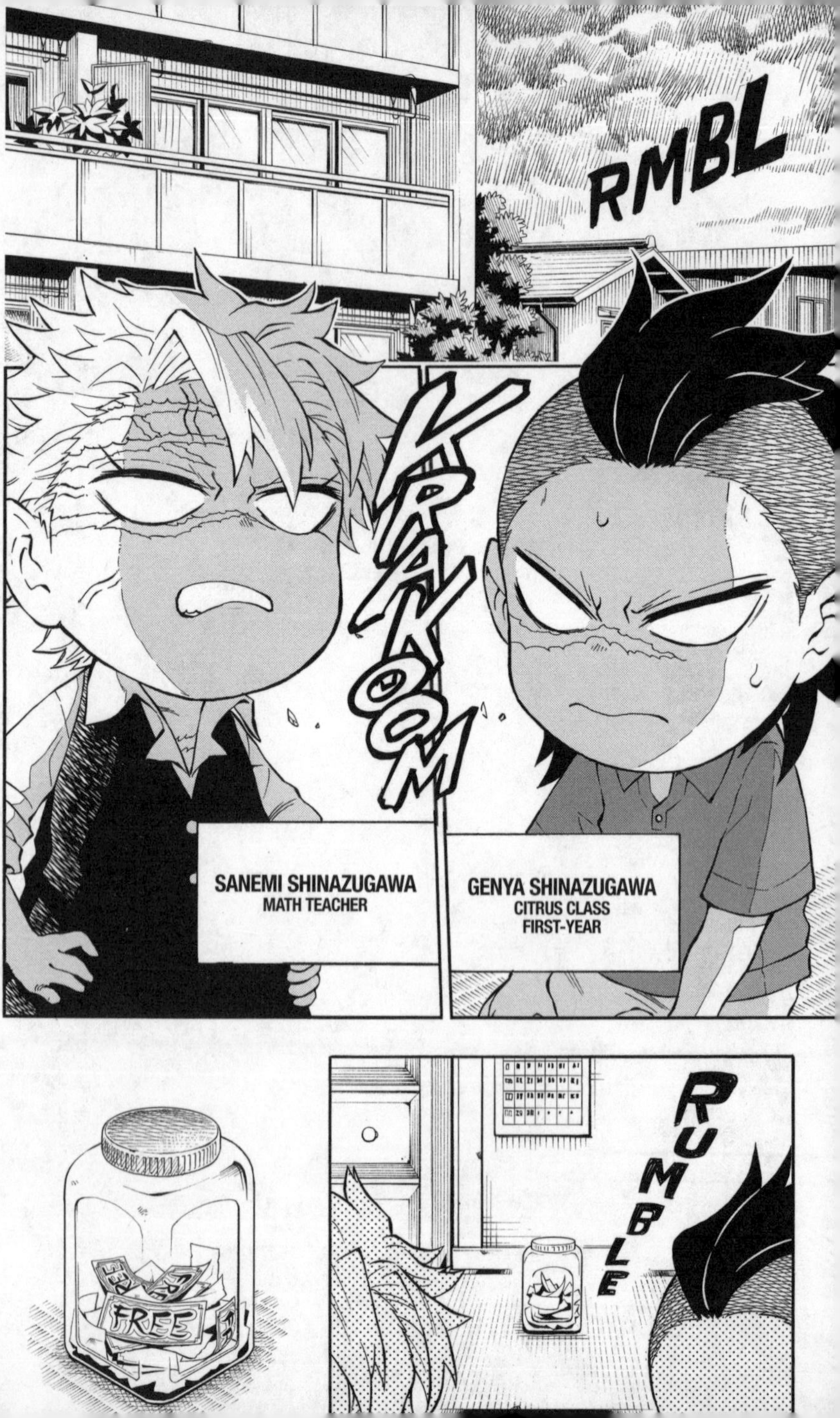
RMBL
VRAKOOM
GENYA SHINAZUGAWA
CITRUS CLASS
FIRST-YEAR
SANEMI SHINAZUGAWA
MATH TEACHER
RUMBLE
FREE

THE NEXT DAY...
...AT KIMETSU ACADEMY'S SUMMER SESSION...
TAP TAP
THAT'S ALL FOR TODAY.
SUMMER SESSION IS ALMOST OVER, SO GET READY FOR EXAMS.
WHEW! IT'S ALMOST OVER!
BUT WE STILL HAVE EXAMS!
CHATTER
CHATTER
I'M STAR-VING!
LET'S GRAB LUNCH AT AOZORA DINER!
CHATTER
SWP
TANJIRO KAMADO!
SLAAM

WE HAD A FIGHT ABOUT MY GRADES!!

I CAN'T ASK HIM!

BAM

MY FINAL EXAM SCORES SUCKED!

WHAT HAPPENED?

YOU CAN FIGHT HIM? RESPECT!

GOT THAT, GENYA?

IF YOU SCORE THIS BADLY AGAIN...

RMMMM

FLASH-BACK

NEVER SCORE THIS LOW AGAIN!

...REDEMP-
TION
VOUCHERS
BACK!!

KRAKOOM

YOU'RE
NOT
GETTING
...

...YOUR
SUMMER
FESTIVAL
...

URGH

...

YEAH...

FOR FREE
GAMES
AND
STUFF?

VOUCH-
ERS?

Oh!

THAT'S
THIS
MONTH!

I HEAR
YOU!

JUST
CALM
DOWN
AND
EAT!

I'VE BEEN
COLLECTING
THOSE LIKE
MAD!!

NO WAY!
I REFUSE
!!

WHAT
WERE YOU
PLANNING
TO DO
WITH 'EM?

WELL,
BETTER
KISS 'EM
GOODBYE.

BUT I
DON'T
WANNA!!

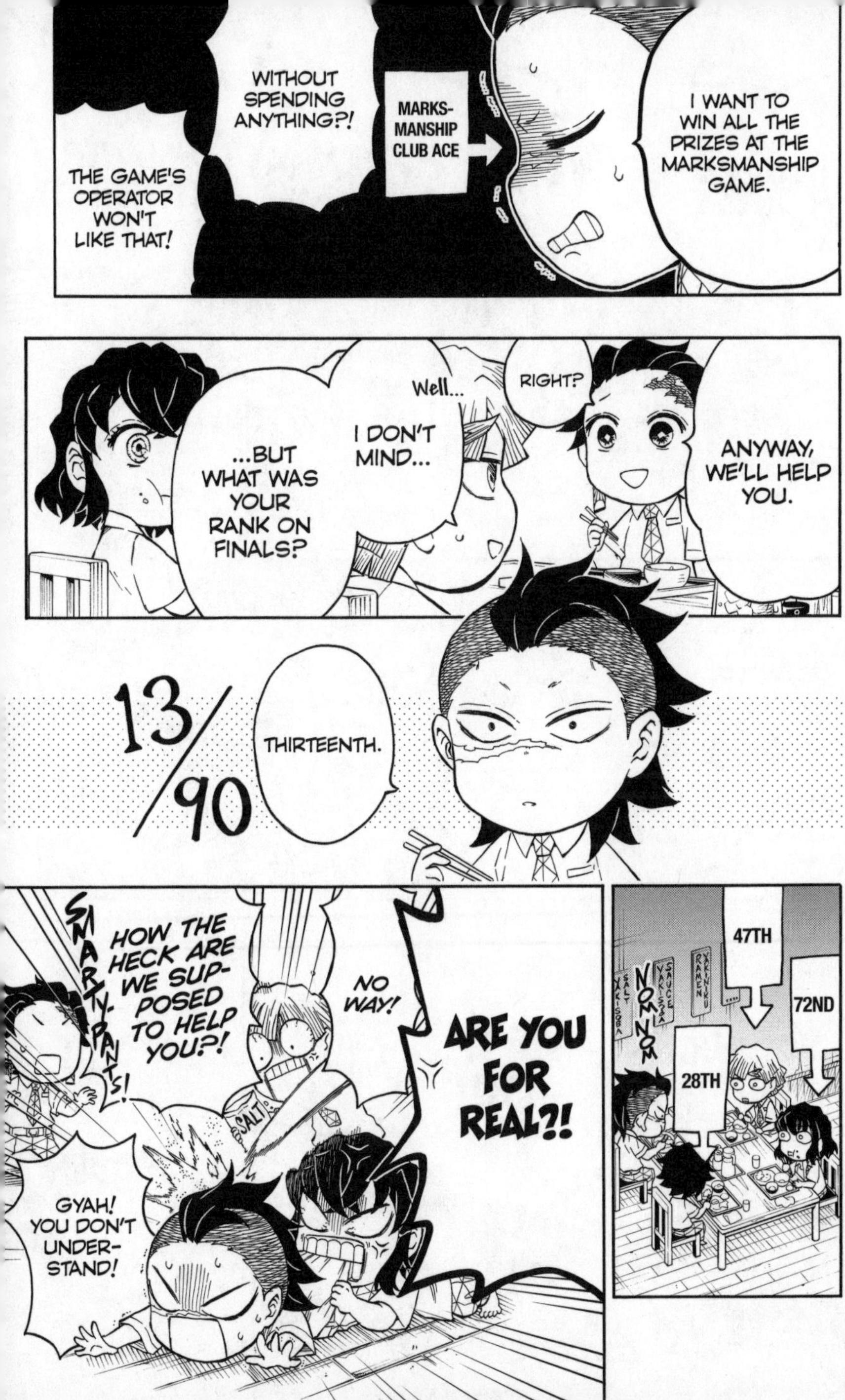
I WANT TO WIN ALL THE PRIZES AT THE MARKSMANSHIP GAME.
MARKS-MANSHIP CLUB ACE
WITHOUT SPENDING ANYTHING?!
THE GAME'S OPERATOR WON'T LIKE THAT!
ANYWAY, WE'LL HELP YOU.
RIGHT?
Well...
I DON'T MIND...
...BUT WHAT WAS YOUR RANK ON FINALS?
THIRTEENTH.
13/90
47TH
72ND
28TH
NOM NOM
SALT YAKISOBA
SAUCE YAKISOBA
RAMEN
YAKINIKU
ARE YOU FOR REAL?!
NO WAY!
HOW THE HECK ARE WE SUP-POSED TO HELP YOU?!
SMARTYPANTS!
SALT
GYAH! YOU DON'T UNDER-STAND!

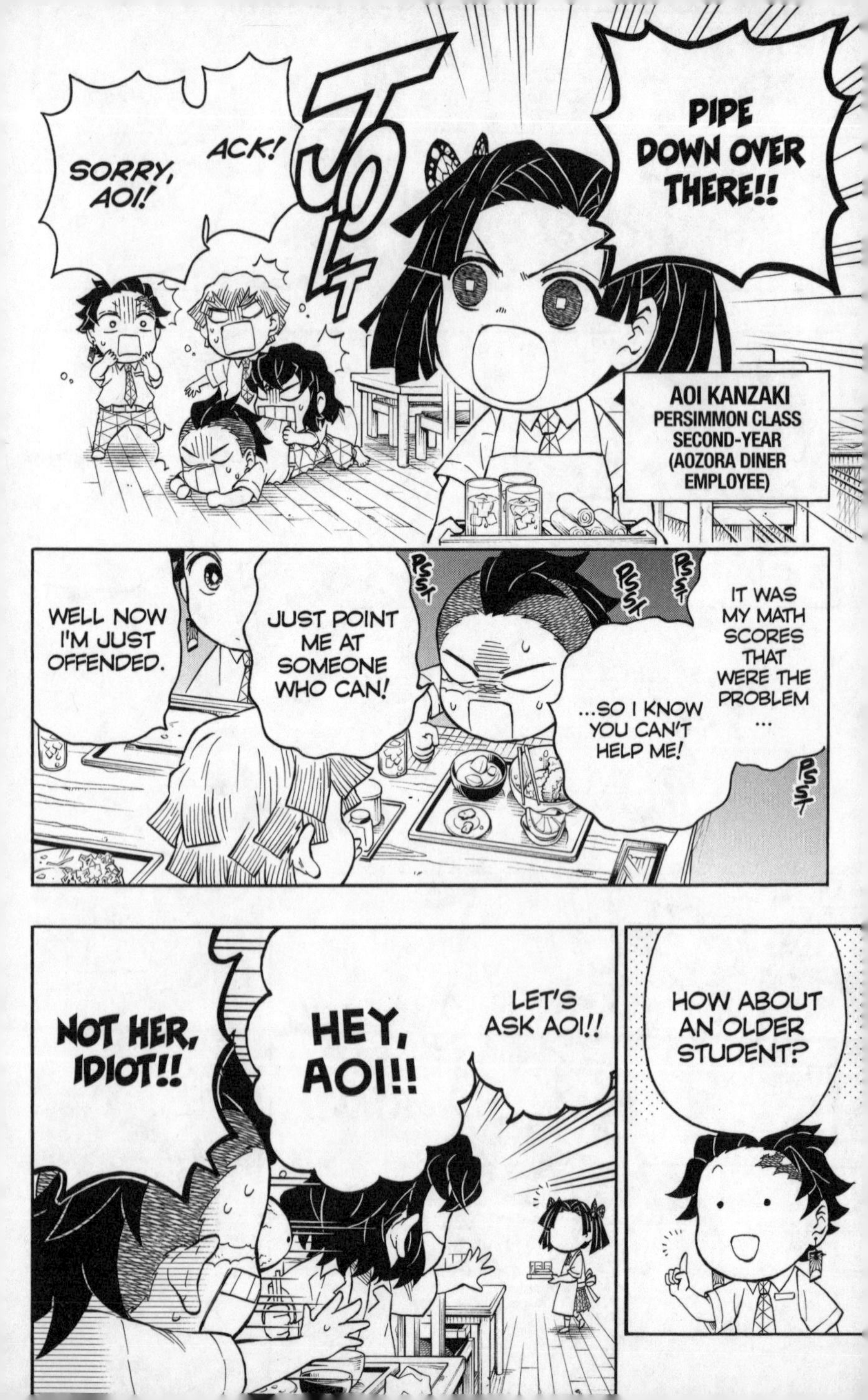
PIPE DOWN OVER THERE!!
AOI KANZAKI
PERSIMMON CLASS SECOND-YEAR (AOZORA DINER EMPLOYEE)
JOLT
ACK!
SORRY, AOI!
PSST
PSST
PSST
IT WAS MY MATH SCORES THAT WERE THE PROBLEM ...
...SO I KNOW YOU CAN'T HELP ME!
PSST
JUST POINT ME AT SOMEONE WHO CAN!
WELL NOW I'M JUST OFFENDED.
HOW ABOUT AN OLDER STUDENT?
LET'S ASK AOI!!
HEY, AOI!!
NOT HER, IDIOT!!

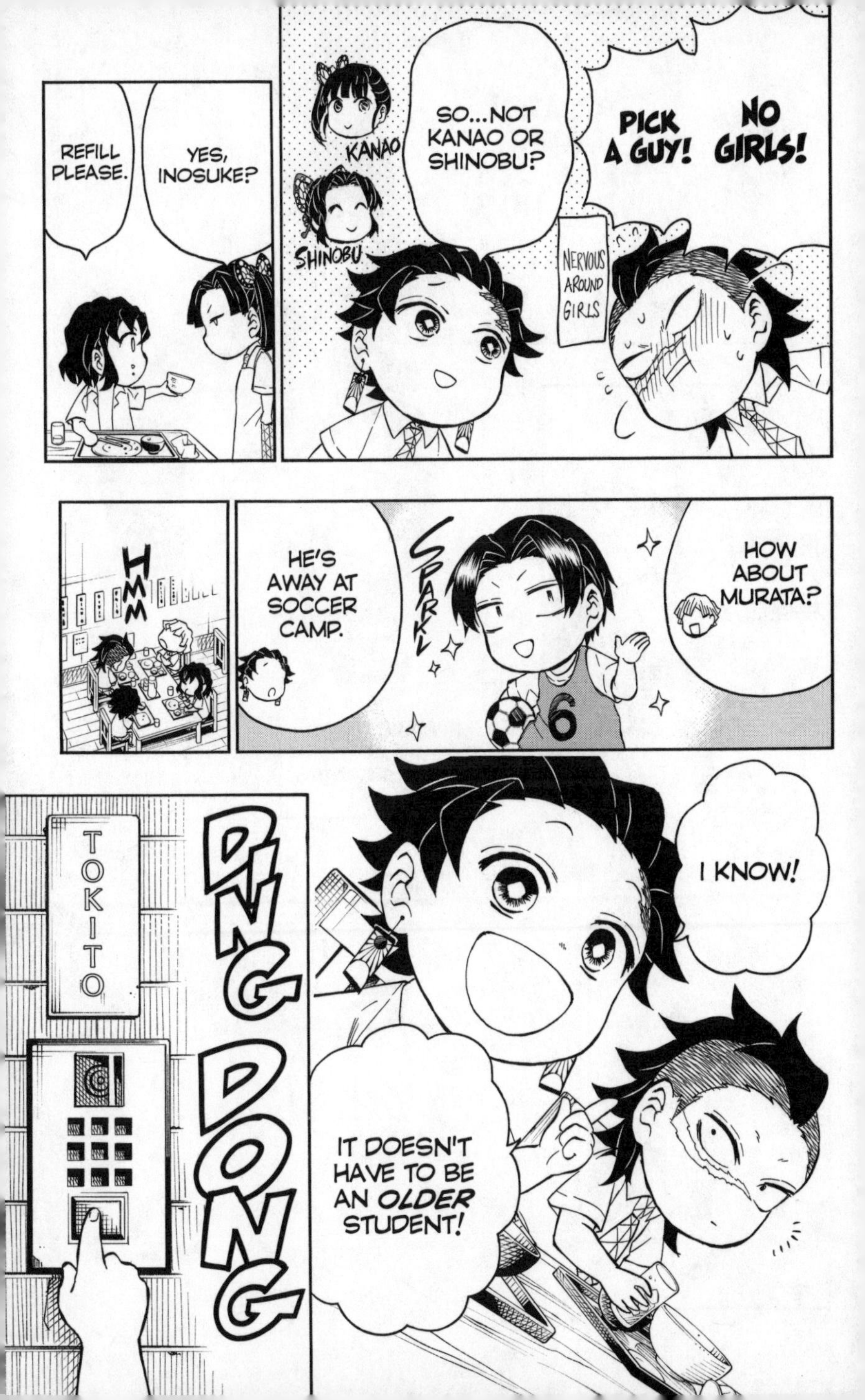
NO GIRLS!
PICK A GUY!
SO...NOT KANAO OR SHINOBU?
KANAO
SHINOBU
NERVOUS AROUND GIRLS
YES, INOSUKE?
REFILL PLEASE.
HOW ABOUT MURATA?
SPARKL
HE'S AWAY AT SOCCER CAMP.
HMM
I KNOW!
IT DOESN'T HAVE TO BE AN *OLDER* STUDENT!
TOKITO
DING DONG

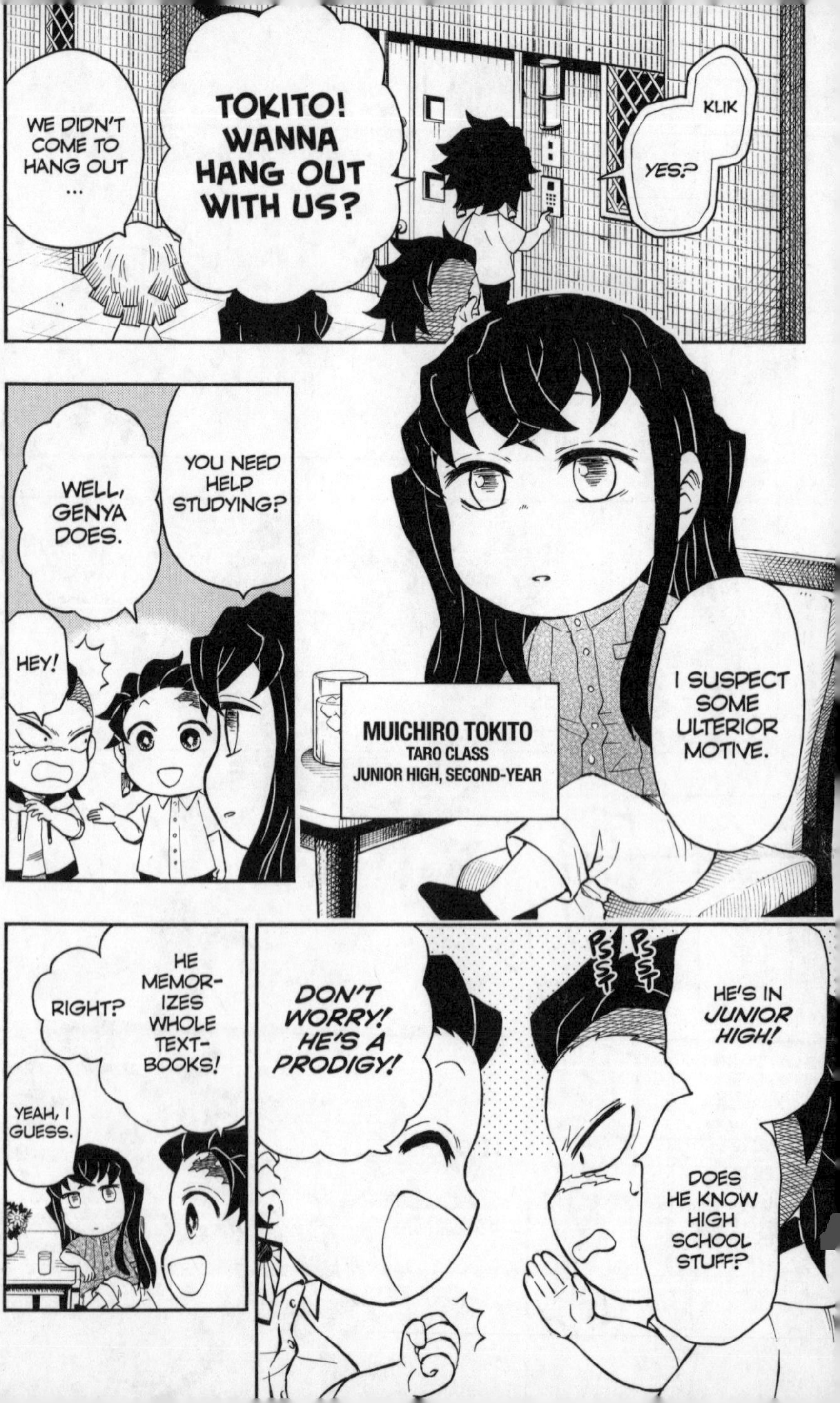
KLIK
YES?
TOKITO! WANNA HANG OUT WITH US?
WE DIDN'T COME TO HANG OUT ...
MUICHIRO TOKITO TARO CLASS JUNIOR HIGH, SECOND-YEAR
I SUSPECT SOME ULTERIOR MOTIVE.
YOU NEED HELP STUDYING?
WELL, GENYA DOES.
HEY!
PSST PSST
HE'S IN JUNIOR HIGH!
DOES HE KNOW HIGH SCHOOL STUFF?
DON'T WORRY! HE'S A PRODIGY!
HE MEMORIZES WHOLE TEXTBOOKS!
RIGHT?
YEAH, I GUESS.

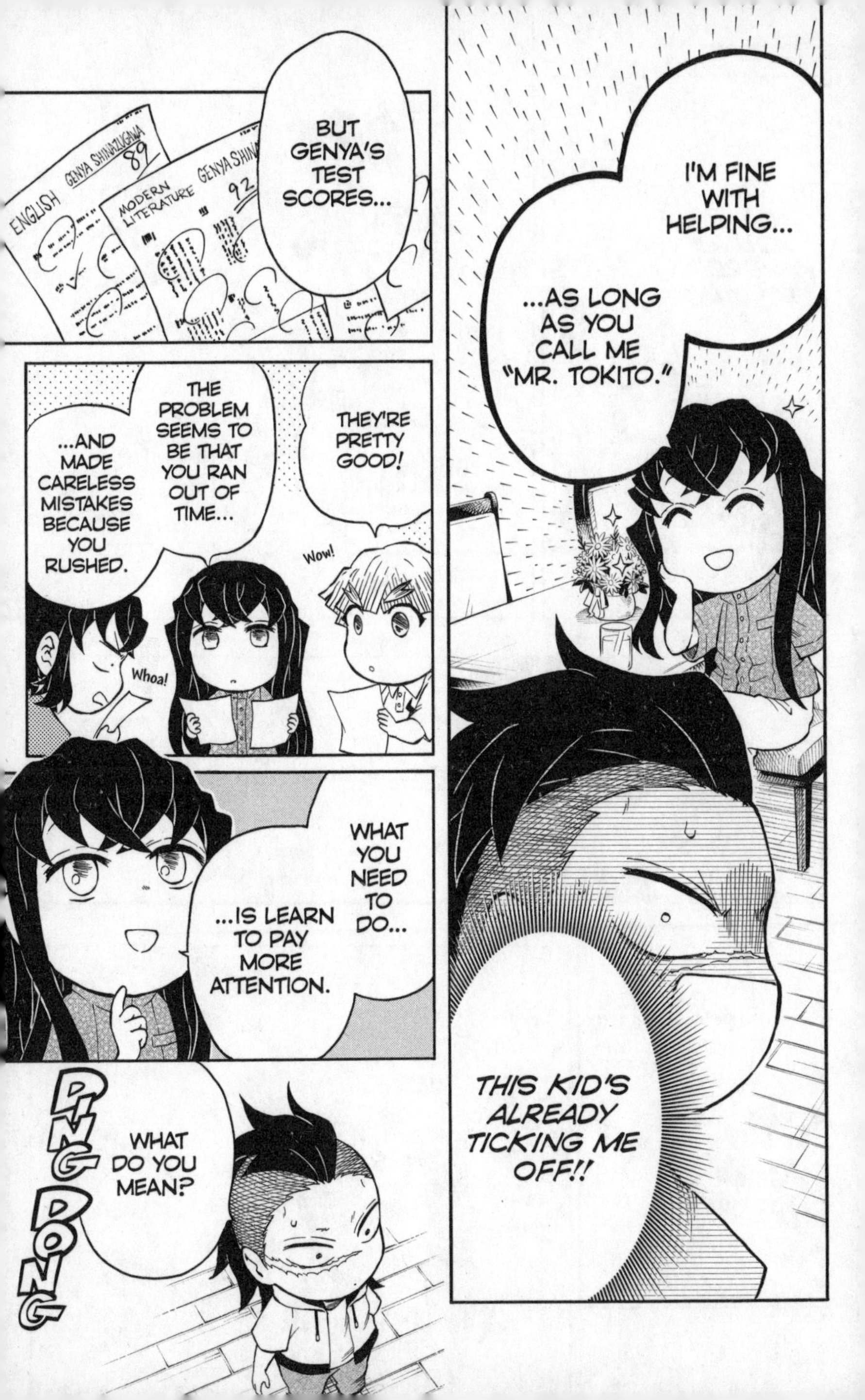
I'M FINE WITH HELPING...
...AS LONG AS YOU CALL ME "MR. TOKITO."
THIS KID'S ALREADY TICKING ME OFF!!
ENGLISH GENYA SHINAZUGAWA 89
MODERN LITERATURE GENYA SHINA
BUT GENYA'S TEST SCORES...
THEY'RE PRETTY GOOD!
Wow!
THE PROBLEM SEEMS TO BE THAT YOU RAN OUT OF TIME...
...AND MADE CARELESS MISTAKES BECAUSE YOU RUSHED.
Whoa!
WHAT YOU NEED TO DO...
...IS LEARN TO PAY MORE ATTENTION.
WHAT DO YOU MEAN?
DING DONG

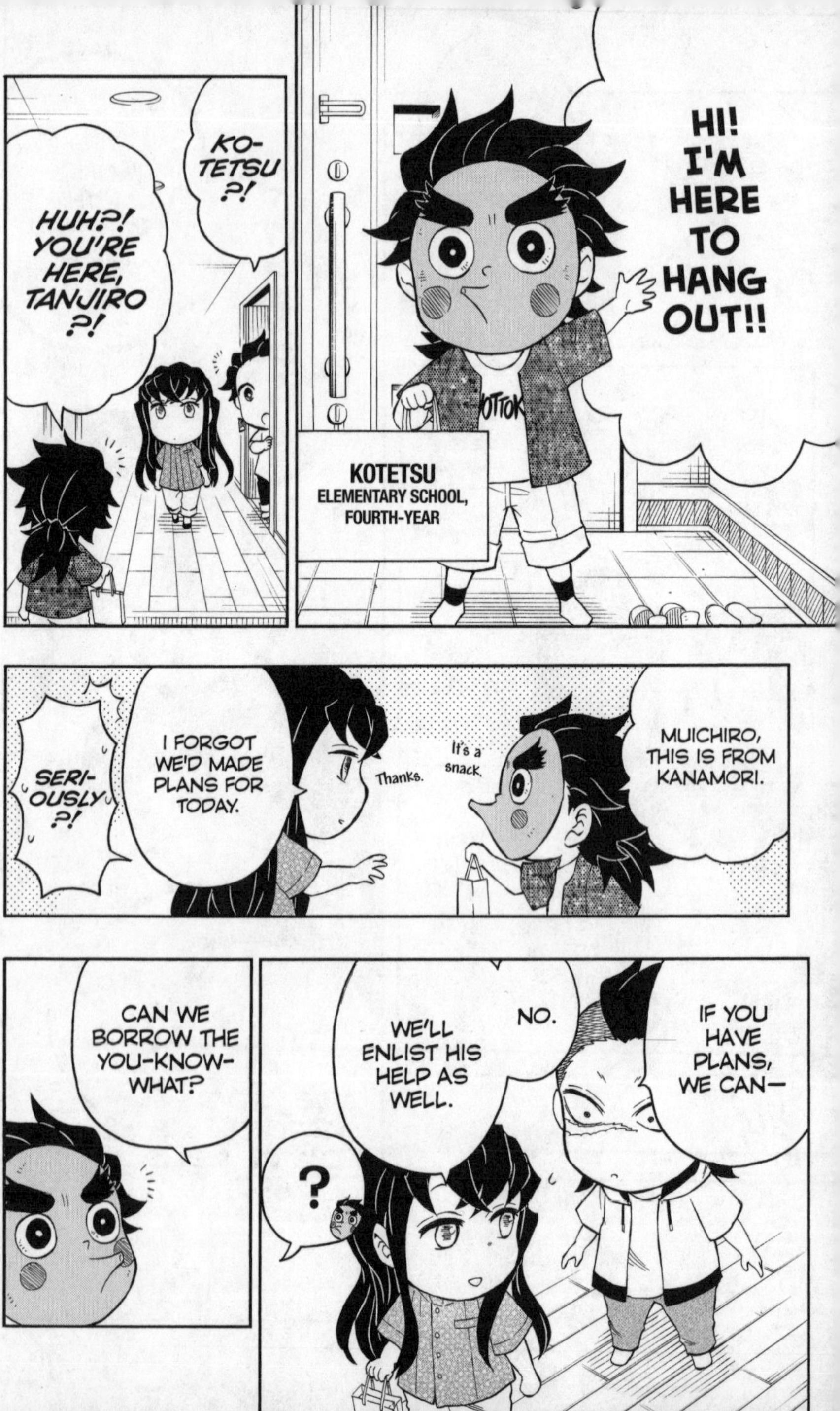
HI! I'M HERE TO HANG OUT!!
KOTETSU
ELEMENTARY SCHOOL, FOURTH-YEAR
KO-TETSU?!
HUH?! YOU'RE HERE, TANJIRO?!
MUICHIRO, THIS IS FROM KANAMORI.
It's a snack.
Thanks.
I FORGOT WE'D MADE PLANS FOR TODAY.
SERI-OUSLY?!
IF YOU HAVE PLANS, WE CAN—
NO.
WE'LL ENLIST HIS HELP AS WELL.
?
CAN WE BORROW THE YOU-KNOW-WHAT?

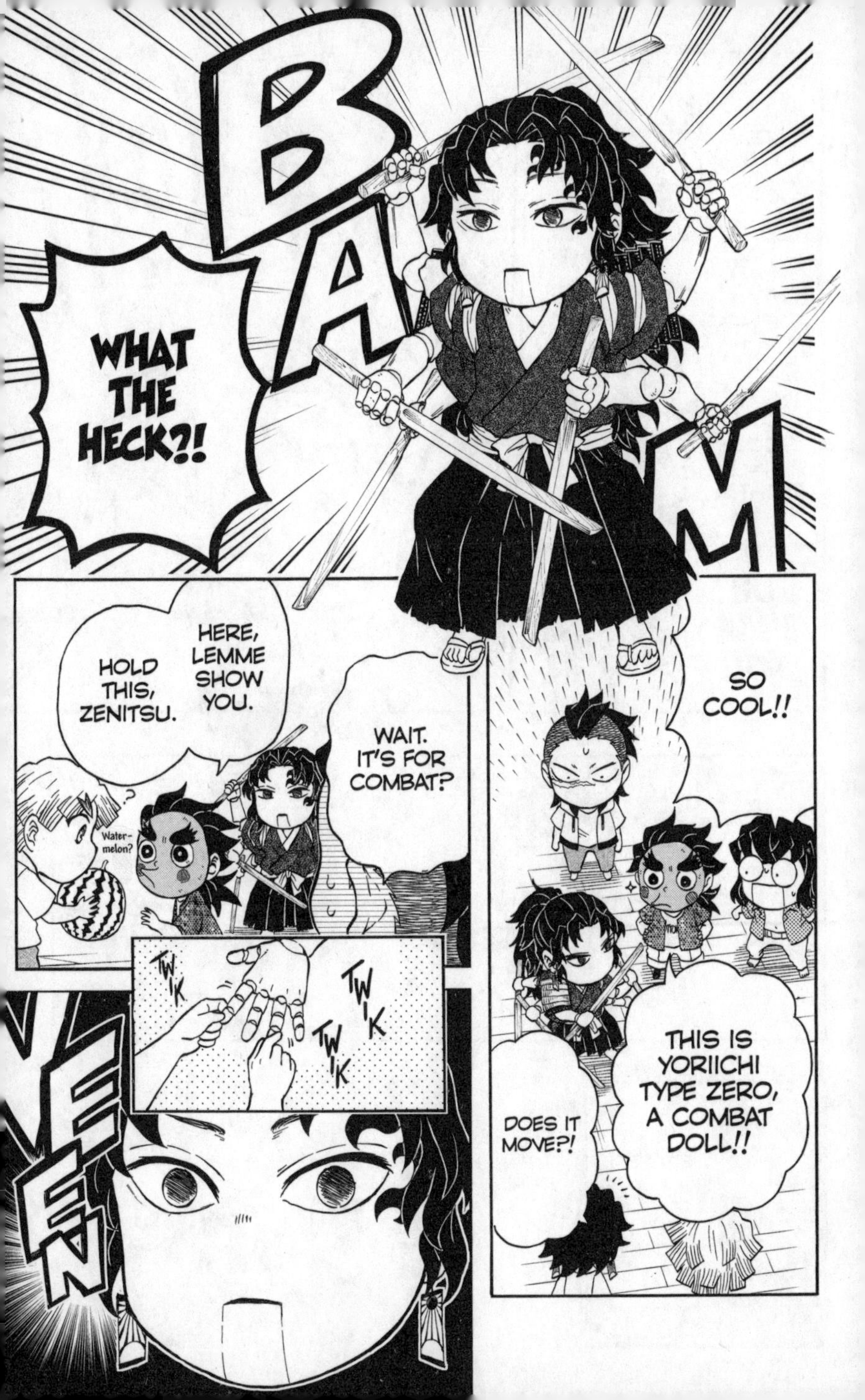
BAM
WHAT THE HECK?!
SO COOL!!
THIS IS YORIICHI TYPE ZERO, A COMBAT DOLL!!
DOES IT MOVE?!
WAIT. IT'S FOR COMBAT?
HERE, LEMME SHOW YOU.
HOLD THIS, ZENITSU.
?
Water-melon?
TWIK
TWIK
TWIK
VEEN

CHOP
AAAIIEEE!!
TOO CLOSE!
ZEN-ITSU!!
HE'S GOT A GOOD SWING, RIGHT?
OH HECK NO!!
HOW'S THIS THING SUPPOSED TO HELP ME STUDY?!
I'VE GOT A BAD FEELING ABOUT THIS!
BUT IT'S PERFECT FOR BUILDING ... ... ACCURACY AND SPEED.
I'LL READ A QUESTION ... ...AND YOU ANSWER ...
...WHILE YORIICHI STANDS BEHIND YOU.
IF YOU'RE TOO SLOW OR YOU GET IT WRONG...

I'D BE DEAD!!!

IT'S GOOD FOR MOTI-VATION.

※ WATERMELON

...THAT'LL BE YOUR HEAD.

THAT WOULD KILL ME!!

AND WHAT'D YOU DO TO ITS HANDS?!

THAT'S NOT JUST A DOLL, THEN!

YOU PROGRAM IT?!

TAK TAK TAK TAK

I'LL PROGRAM IT TO STOP FOR CORRECT ANSWERS.

HOW IS THAT GONNA MOTIVATE ME?!

I have plenty.

WE'LL JUST HAVE IT SPLIT ANOTHER WATERMELON INSTEAD.

FROM TETSUIDO

OH, OKAY.

TOKITO, I THINK THIS IS A LITTLE TOO DANGER-OUS.

...AFTER THE DOLL SPLITS THE WATERMELON...

...I'LL HAVE NO CHOICE BUT TO THROW AWAY THE LEFTOVERS.

OKAY, IN THAT CASE...

CHOMP MUNCH CHOMP

AT THAT POINT YOU'RE JUST WASTING WATERMELON!!

LOVES WATERMELON

IF THAT'S ALL IT TAKES, WHY'RE WE EVEN USING THAT THING?!

GRAAAAAH

I CAN'T LET THAT HAPPEN!!

THAT'D BE TERRIBLE!!

UM...

SHOULDN'T YOU THREE...

...BE STUDYING TOO?

HUH?

DOESN'T THAT WORRY YOU?

YOUR GRADES ARE WORSE THAN HIS, RIGHT?

YOU GET BAD GRADES WHEN YOU'RE LAZY.

HARSH

TICK TICK TICK

YOU HAVE 20 SECONDS!!

$$y = -3(x-1)^2 + 5$$
$$-3 \leqq x \leqq -1$$

FIND THE MAXIMUM AND MINIMUM VALUES FOR THIS EQUATION!!

FIRST QUESTION!!

W-WELL, UM...

UM...X=-3 FOR A MINIMUM OF -43 AND X=-1 FOR A MAX OF -7!!!
COR-RECT!
SHING
...
DURING SUMMER BREAK IT IS WISE TO STUDY HARD BUT WHO WOULD BOTHER?
—A SUMMER HAIKU BY THREE NINCOMPOOPS
TING
TING
GENYA'S DEDI-CATED!
BESIDES, YORIICHI IS BUSY WITH GENYA.
GAH!
CHOP
NO WORRIES! I'VE GOT ANOTHER ONE!!
I DIALED IT DOWN TO GOOSE-EGG MODE.
GAH!
I'M NOT GETTING PUNCHED BY THAT THING!
NO WAY!

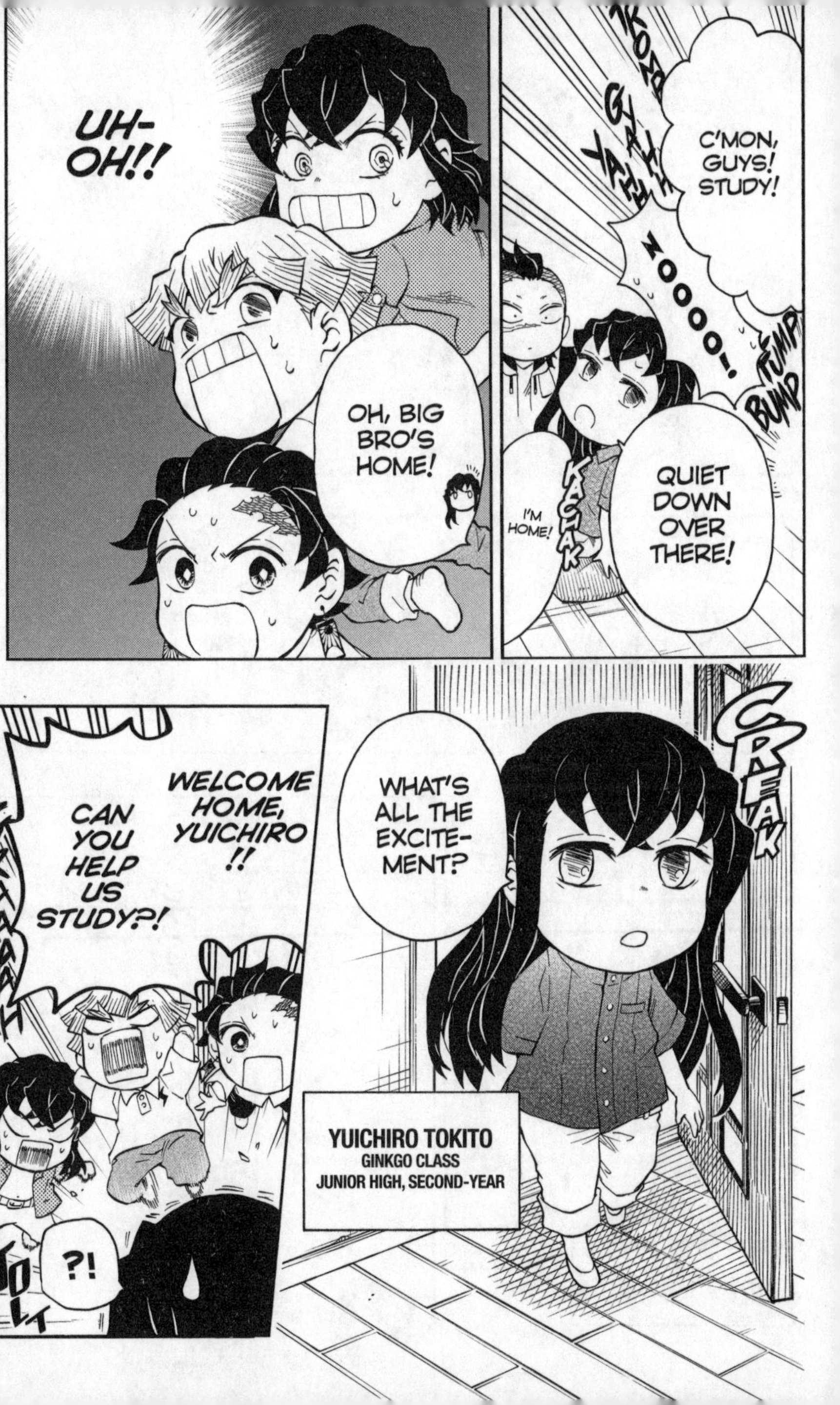
C'MON, GUYS! STUDY!
ZOOOOO!
THUMP BUMP
QUIET DOWN OVER THERE!
KACHAK
I'M HOME!
UH-OH!!
OH, BIG BRO'S HOME!
CREAK
WHAT'S ALL THE EXCITEMENT?
YUICHIRO TOKITO
GINKGO CLASS
JUNIOR HIGH, SECOND-YEAR
WELCOME HOME, YUICHIRO!!
CAN YOU HELP US STUDY?!
GRAAAAAH
?!
JOLT

JUST USE YORIICHI TYPE ZERO!!
NAH, YUICHIRO WILL TEACH US!!
GETTING PUNCHED BY HIM WOULD HURT A LOT LESS!
YOU'RE FINE WITH THAT, RIGHT?!
HUH?
IN THE END...
...TANJIRO AND FRIENDS STUDIED...
CHOP
WATERMELOOON!!
AAAAGH!
...AT THE TOKITOS' HOUSE WHILE THEIR PARENTS WERE AWAY.
We're traveling!
Don't you understand this?
SI--GH

I WAS HOPING I COULD SPEND THE NIGHT TONIGHT...
...SO ABOUT TOMORROW'S BREAD...
REALLY? THANKS, MOM!
PIP
RATTL
TAKING A BREAK, GENYA?
YEAH.
WE'RE GONNA ORDER PIZZA.
KOTETSU'S RELATIVES RUN A PIZZA JOINT.
Part-time delivery girl Mitsuru
SOUNDS GREAT!!
BLEH...

DON'T WORRY! YOU'LL GET YOUR VOUCHERS BACK!!
LET'S ALL DO OUR BEST!!
Y-YEAH...
I KNOW THAT'S THE RIGHT ATTITUDE, BUT...
?
...I CAN'T BELIEVE THAT TOKITO...
...ALREADY KNOWS ALL THIS.
HE'S LIKE AN INFORMATION SPONGE.
YOU THINK SO?
CHATTER
C'mon! Just try it!
Goose-egg mode
STAY BACK!
YIIIKES!
CHATTER
Come on already!
You try it!
IF I WAS GIFTED LIKE TOKITO...

...THEN MY BROTHER WOULDN'T GET MAD AT ME...
...FOR BEING A LOSER.
SPARKL
HE MUST BE ASHAMED OF ME.
CONTEMPLATIVE
GENYA...
...YOU'RE NOT A LOSER.
HE GETS ANGRY BECAUSE HE CARES ABOUT YOU.
YOU'RE HIS FAVORITE!
HIS FAVO-RITE?!

I'VE NEVER SEEN HIM SCOLD ANYONE ELSE FOR THEIR GRADES...
...BUT HE'S SUPER HARD ON YOU.
THAT'S A KIND OF FAVORITISM ...
...ISN'T IT?
YOU REALLY THINK THAT, HUH?
IF YOU DO WELL, I BET HE'LL EVEN REWARD YOU!!!
NOT A CHANCE.
BUT IF YOU DO...
...HAVE A PROBLEM WITH WHAT HE DOES...
...THEN YOU SHOULD TELL HIM.
I'LL BACK YOU UP.
GYAH!
AH HA HA HA!

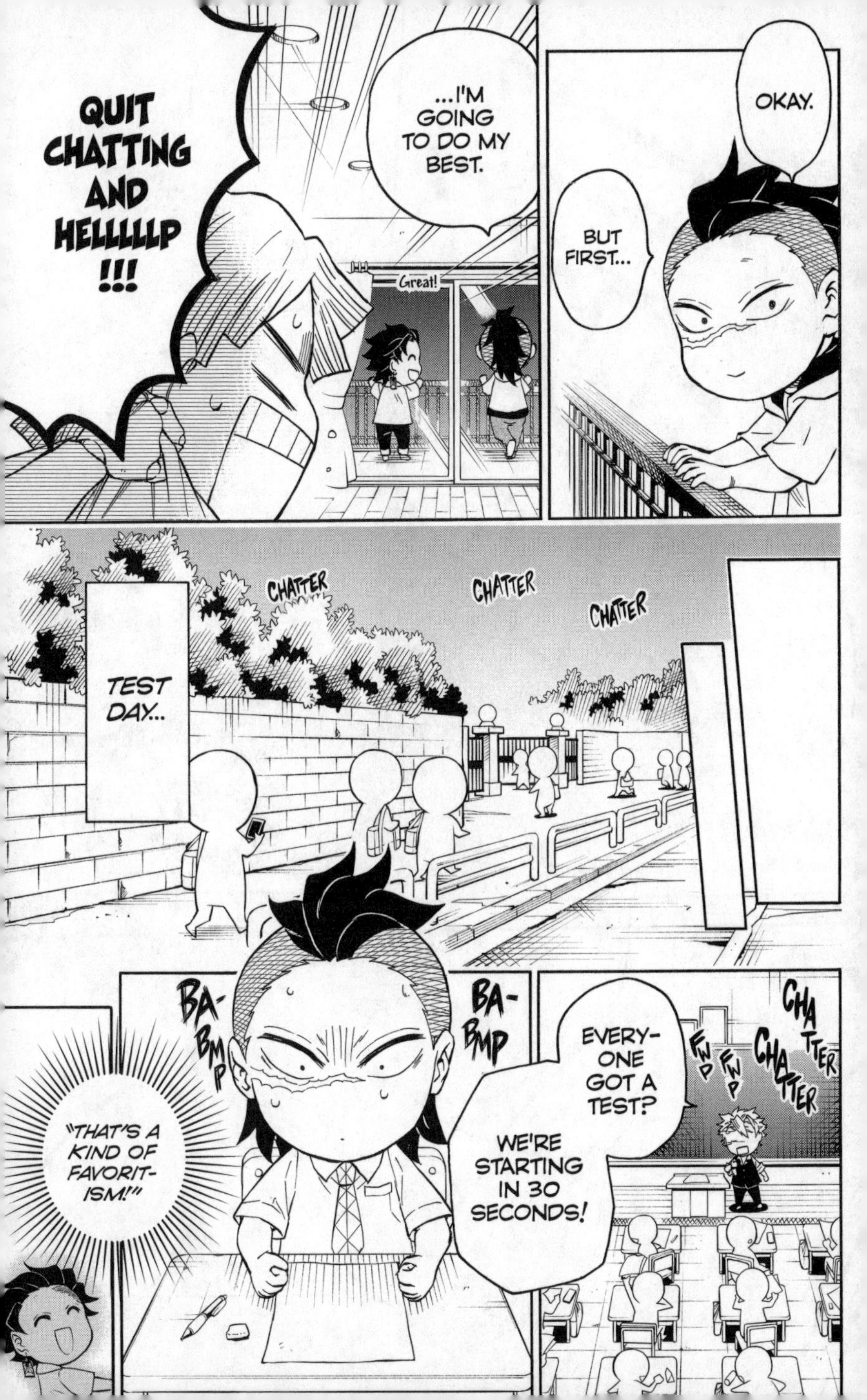
OKAY.
BUT FIRST...
...I'M GOING TO DO MY BEST.
Great!
QUIT CHATTING AND HELLLLLP!!!
CHATTER
CHATTER
CHATTER
TEST DAY...
CHATTER
CHATTER
FWP
FWP
EVERY-ONE GOT A TEST?
WE'RE STARTING IN 30 SECONDS!
BA-BMP
BA-BMP
"THAT'S A KIND OF FAVORIT-ISM!"

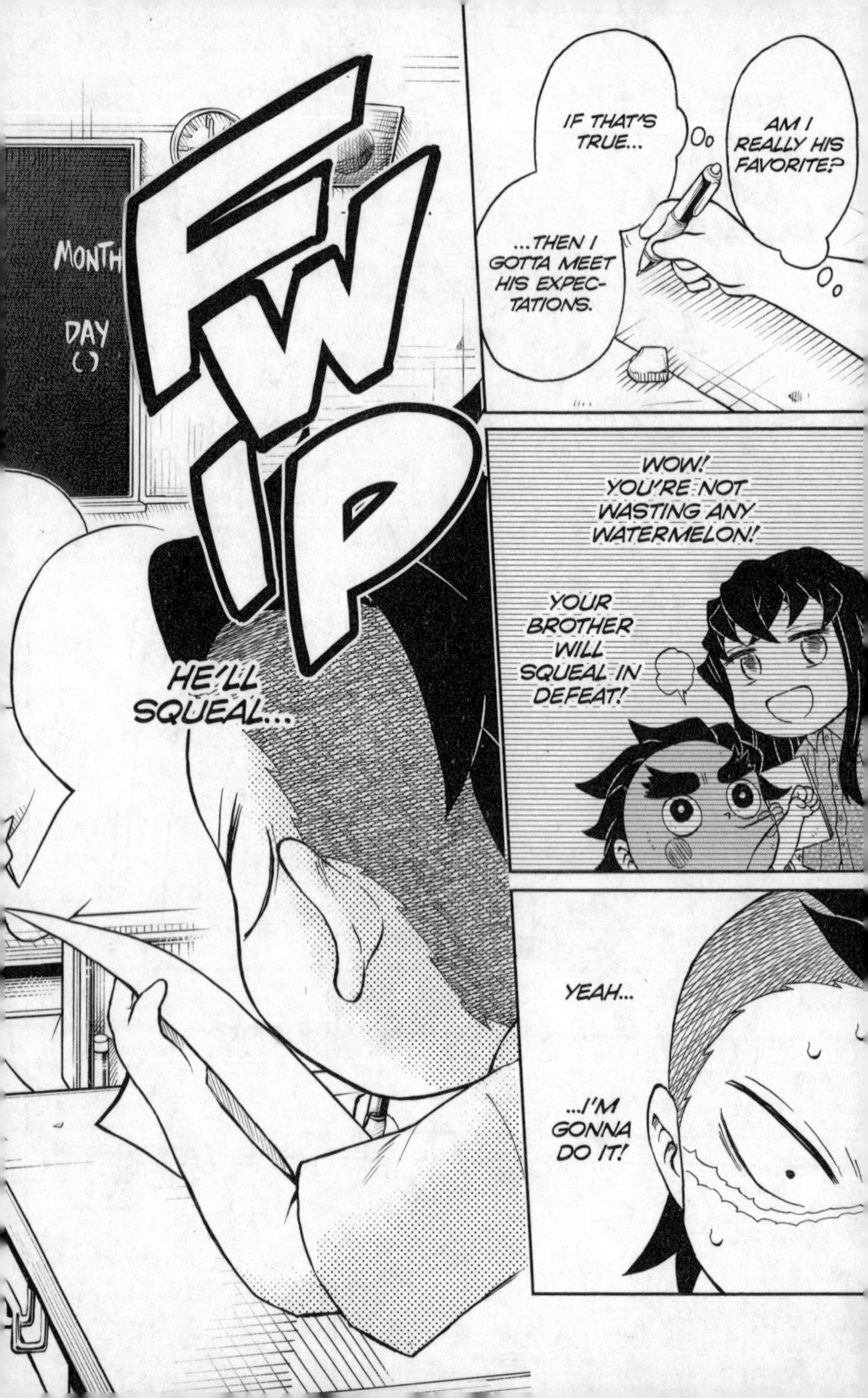
AM I REALLY HIS FAVORITE?
IF THAT'S TRUE...
...THEN I GOTTA MEET HIS EXPECTATIONS.
WOW! YOU'RE NOT WASTING ANY WATERMELON!
YOUR BROTHER WILL SQUEAL IN DEFEAT!
YEAH...
...I'M GONNA DO IT!
MONTH
DAY
( )
FWIP
HE'LL SQUEAL...

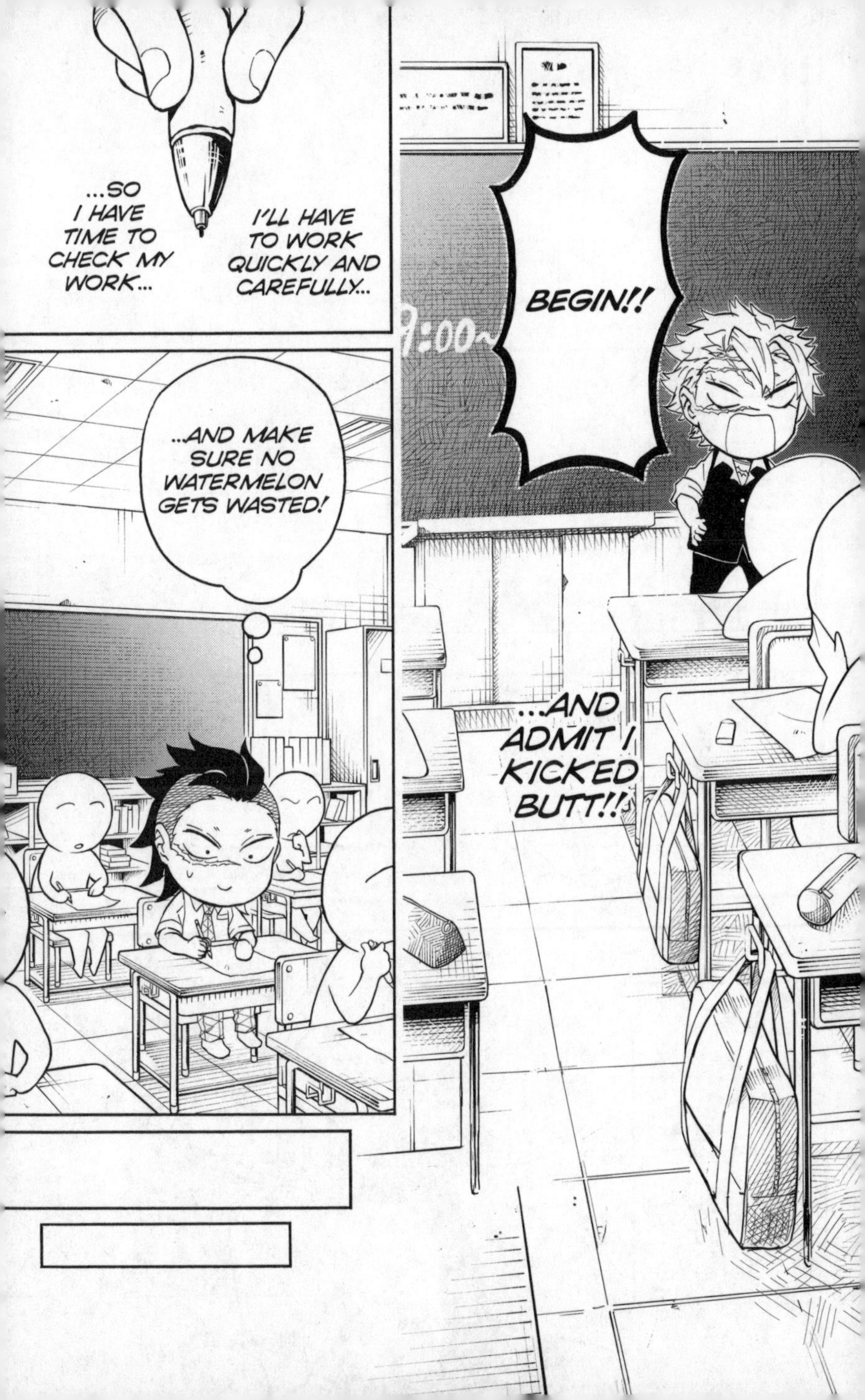
BEGIN!!
...AND ADMIT I KICKED BUTT!!
I'LL HAVE TO WORK QUICKLY AND CAREFULLY...
...SO I HAVE TIME TO CHECK MY WORK...
...AND MAKE SURE NO WATERMELON GETS WASTED!

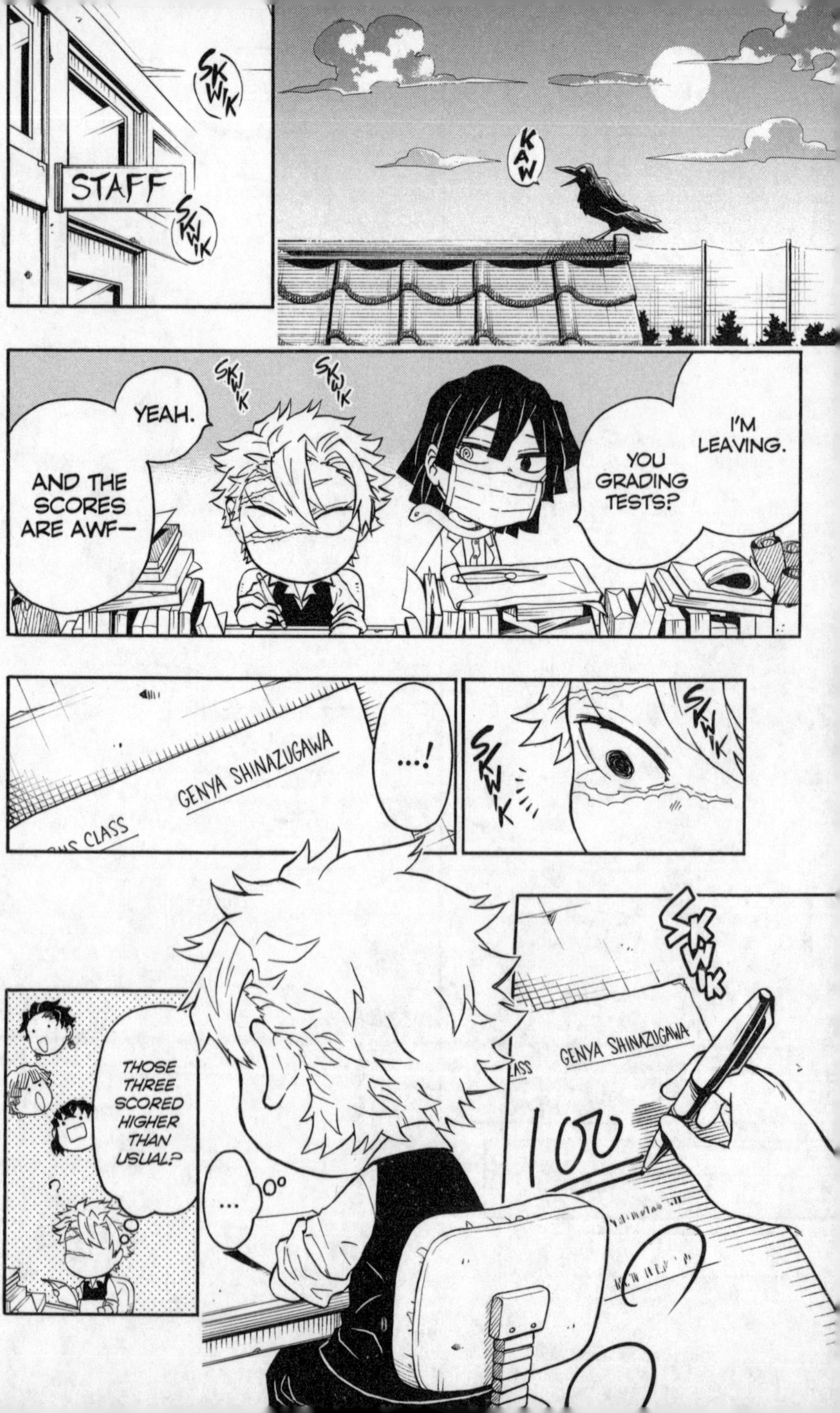
KAW
SKWIK
STAFF
SKWIK
I'M LEAVING.
YOU GRADING TESTS?
SKWIK
SKWIK
YEAH.
AND THE SCORES ARE AWF—
SKWIK
SKWIK
...!
GENYA SHINAZUGAWA
CLASS
SKWIK
GENYA SHINAZUGAWA
CLASS
100
...
THOSE THREE SCORED HIGHER THAN USUAL?

A FEW DAYS LATER ...
... OUTSIDE THE SHINAZUGAWA RESIDENCE ...
A HUNDRED POINTS!!
I DIDN'T KNOW THAT WAS POSSIBLE!
IT'S NOT JUST A MYTH?!
Holy moly!
STOP GAWKING AT MY TEST!
NOW GO INSIDE...
...AND GET YOUR VOUCHERS BACK!
URK!
HURRY!! WE'RE HEADIN' TO THE FESTIVAL!!
Move it, Genya!
SHUT UP!
KA-CHAK
WILL HE...
...REALLY GIVE THEM BACK?
KREEK
I'M HOME...
ARE YOU HERE ...?
BDMP
BDMP
BIG BRO?
AH!

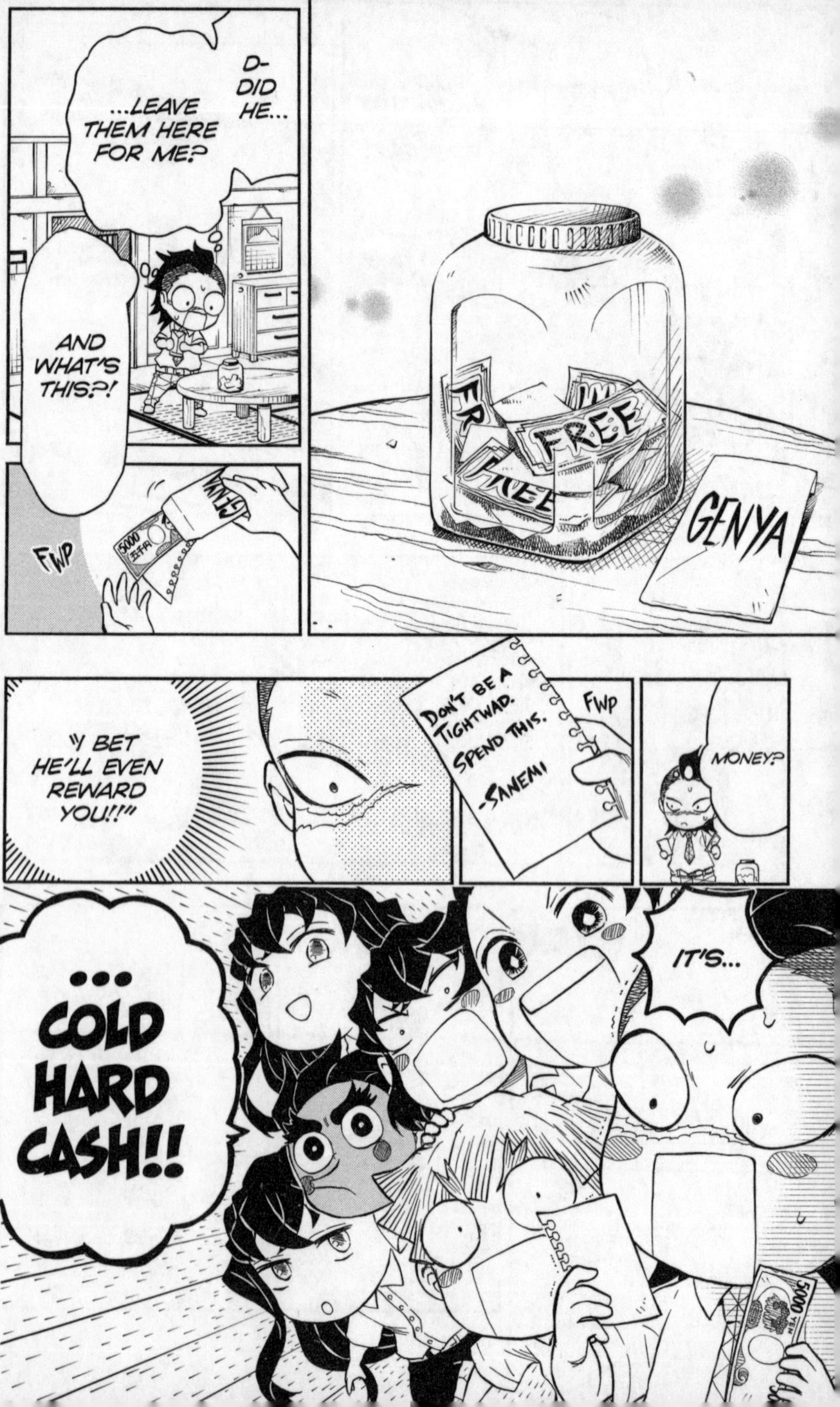
FREE
GENYA
D-DID HE...
...LEAVE THEM HERE FOR ME?
AND WHAT'S THIS?!
FWP
GENYA
MONEY?
DON'T BE A TIGHTWAD. SPEND THIS. -SANEMI
FWP
"I BET HE'LL EVEN REWARD YOU!!"
IT'S...
...COLD HARD CASH!!
5000 YEN

CANDIED APPLES!

CHATTER

GENYA! I WANT TAKOYAKI!

CHATTER

GAH! WHAT THE?!

YAKI-SOBA!

SHAVED ICE!!

STOP DROOLING OVER MY VOUCHERS!!

LET'S GO TO THE FESTIVAL!

WHY'RE YOU UP HERE, SANEMI?

SIGH...

AH HA HA HA! AH HA HA HA!

Let's go!

OKAY, OKAY...

THE GUY RUNNING THE MARKSMANSHIP GAME IS THE ONE WHO REALLY WON HERE.

PLAYING AGAIN? THAT'S 300 YEN!

WA HA HA HA

YOU'RE GONNA TAKE ALL THE PRIZES AT THIS RATE!

TOKITOS

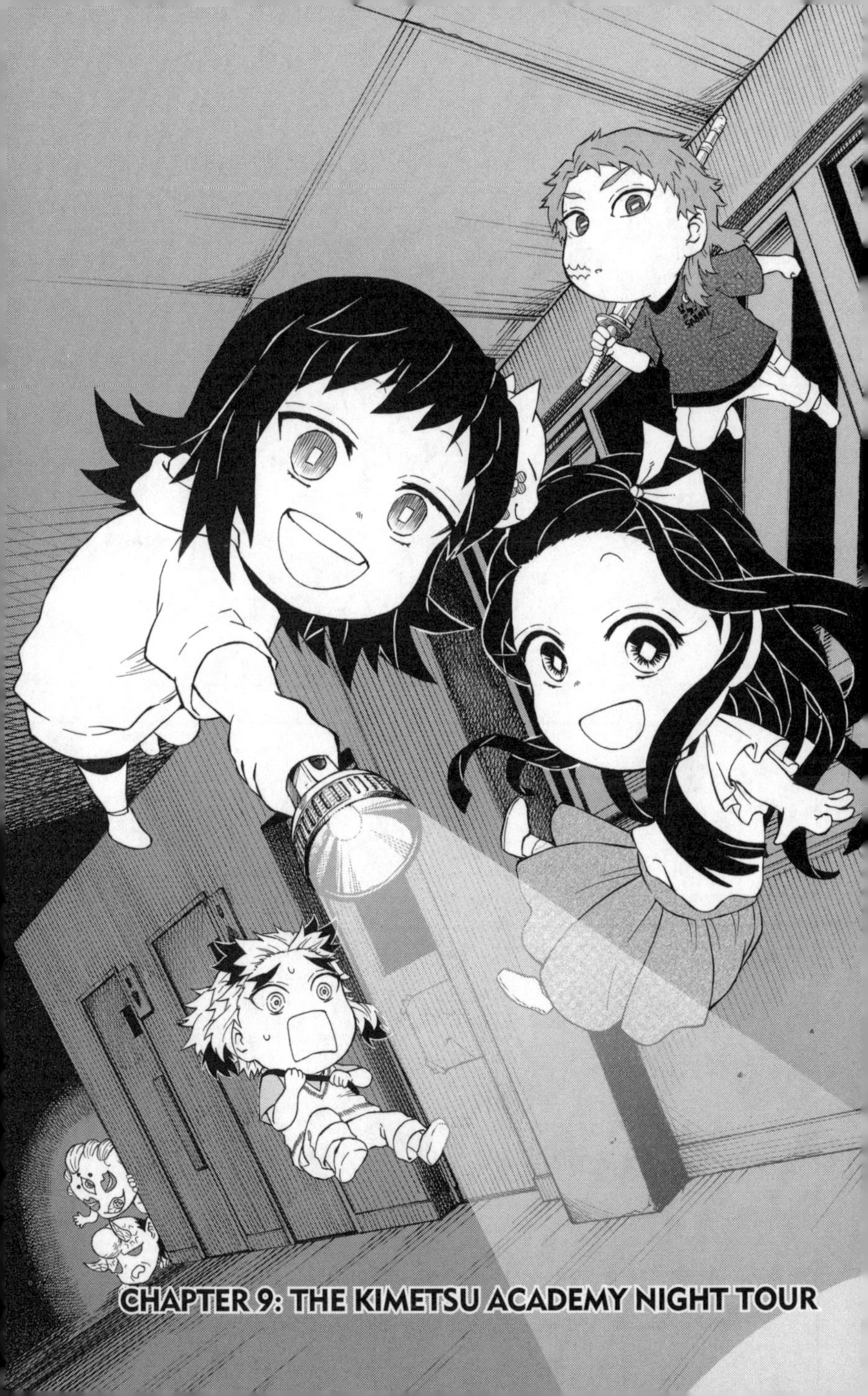

CHAPTER 9: THE KIMETSU ACADEMY NIGHT TOUR

IDEAS FOR THE SCHOOL'S SEVEN MYSTERIES?
YEAH! THE SCHOOL PAPER...
...PUT OUT A CALL FOR IDEAS!
IT SAYS, UM...
"LIKE OTHER SCHOOLS, KIMETSU ACADEMY SHOULD HAVE SEVEN MYSTERIOUS HAUNTINGS ..."
"...SO WE'RE LOOKING FOR YOUR SPOOKY STORIES."
"ONCE WE HAVE SEVEN, WE'LL ANNOUNCE THE CHOSEN MYSTERIES."
Cool!
SPOOKY STORIES, HUH?

I'VE NEVER HEARD ANYTHING SPOOKY ABOUT THIS SCHOOL.
I BET WE COULD COME UP WITH SOME THINGS!
THE TERRIFYING BOAR-MAN UNDER THE FLOOR!!
SNORT
THE LEMON-HEADED LUNATIC STALKER!!
HUFF... HUFF... WHERE'S NEZUKO?
WHAT'D YOU CALL ME?!
GRAAAH
I CAN'T WAIT TO SEE WHAT PEOPLE COME UP WITH!
THE JUNIOR HIGH'S GOING TO GET IN ON THIS TOO, RIGHT?

THE JUNIOR HIGH...
TARO CLASS SECOND-YEAR
LET'S VISIT THE SCHOOL AT NIGHT TO GET IDEAS!!
MAKOMO TARO CLASS JUNIOR HIGH, SECOND-YEAR
IDEAS FOR WHAT?
NEZUKO KAMADO TARO CLASS JUNIOR HIGH, SECOND-YEAR
WHAT ARE YOU TALKING ABOUT?
DIDN'T YOU SEE THE SCHOOL PAPER?
WE NEED A GOOD STORY TO SUBMIT!
SO WE'LL SNEAK INTO SCHOOL AT NIGHT...
...FOR A GHOST-HUNTING ADVENTURE!

ADVEN-TURE...
YAY
WAIT, WE CAN'T!
THERE'S NO WAY THE TEACHERS OR OUR PARENTS WOULD LET US!
THAT'S WHY WE'LL KEEP IT A SECRET!
TELL YOUR PARENTS YOU'RE SLEEPING OVER AT MY HOUSE!
BRING A FLASHLIGHT AND JUNK FOOD!
HMMM
WILL IT BE DANGER-OUS?
COULD BE!
THAT'S WHY WE'LL NEED A BODY-GUARD!
...
SABITO
TARO CLASS JUNIOR HIGH, SECOND-YEAR

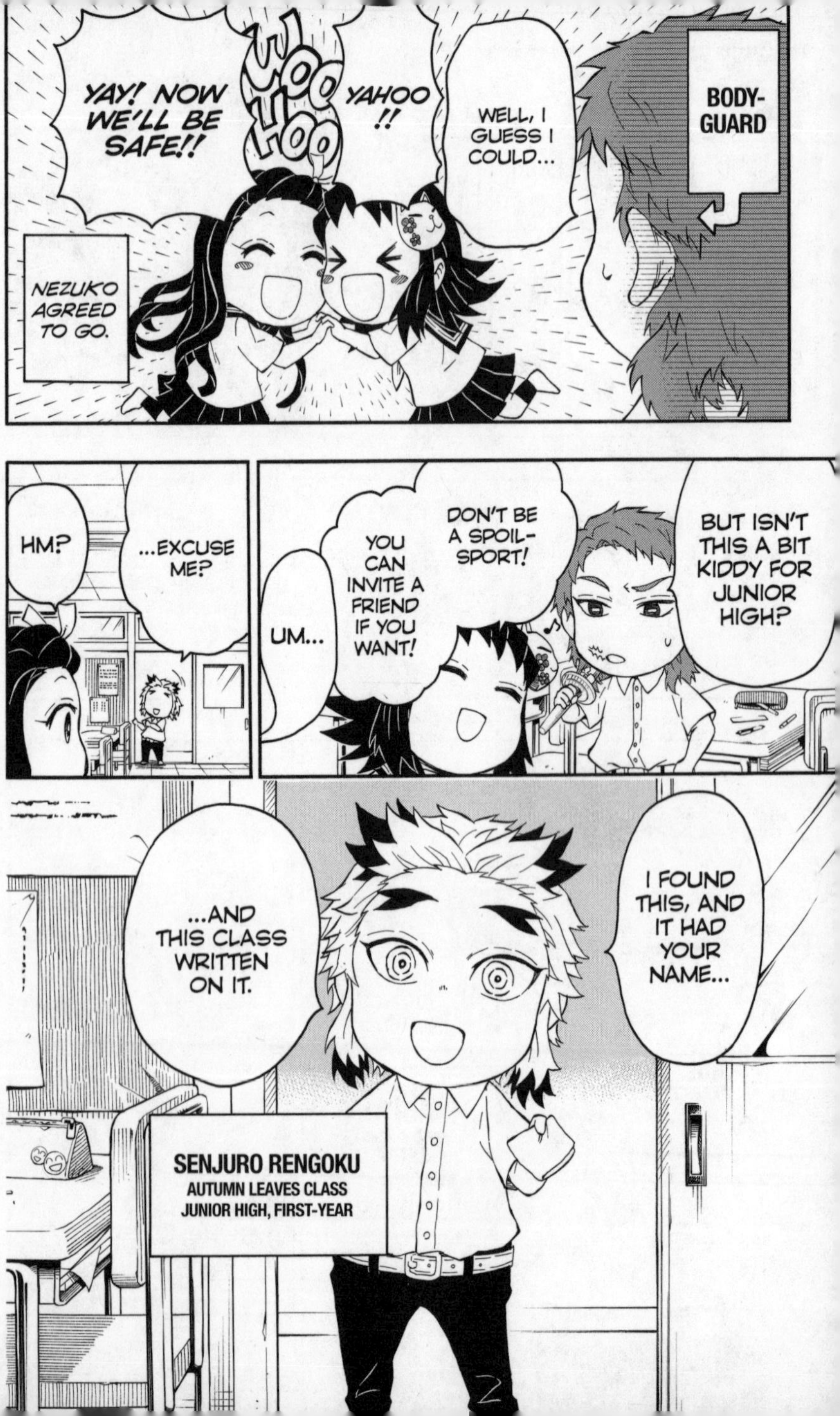
BODY-GUARD
WELL, I GUESS I COULD...
YAHOO!!
WOO HOO
YAY! NOW WE'LL BE SAFE!!
NEZUKO AGREED TO GO.
BUT ISN'T THIS A BIT KIDDY FOR JUNIOR HIGH?
DON'T BE A SPOIL-SPORT!
YOU CAN INVITE A FRIEND IF YOU WANT!
UM...
...EXCUSE ME?
HM?
I FOUND THIS, AND IT HAD YOUR NAME...
...AND THIS CLASS WRITTEN ON IT.
SENJURO RENGOKU
AUTUMN LEAVES CLASS
JUNIOR HIGH, FIRST-YEAR

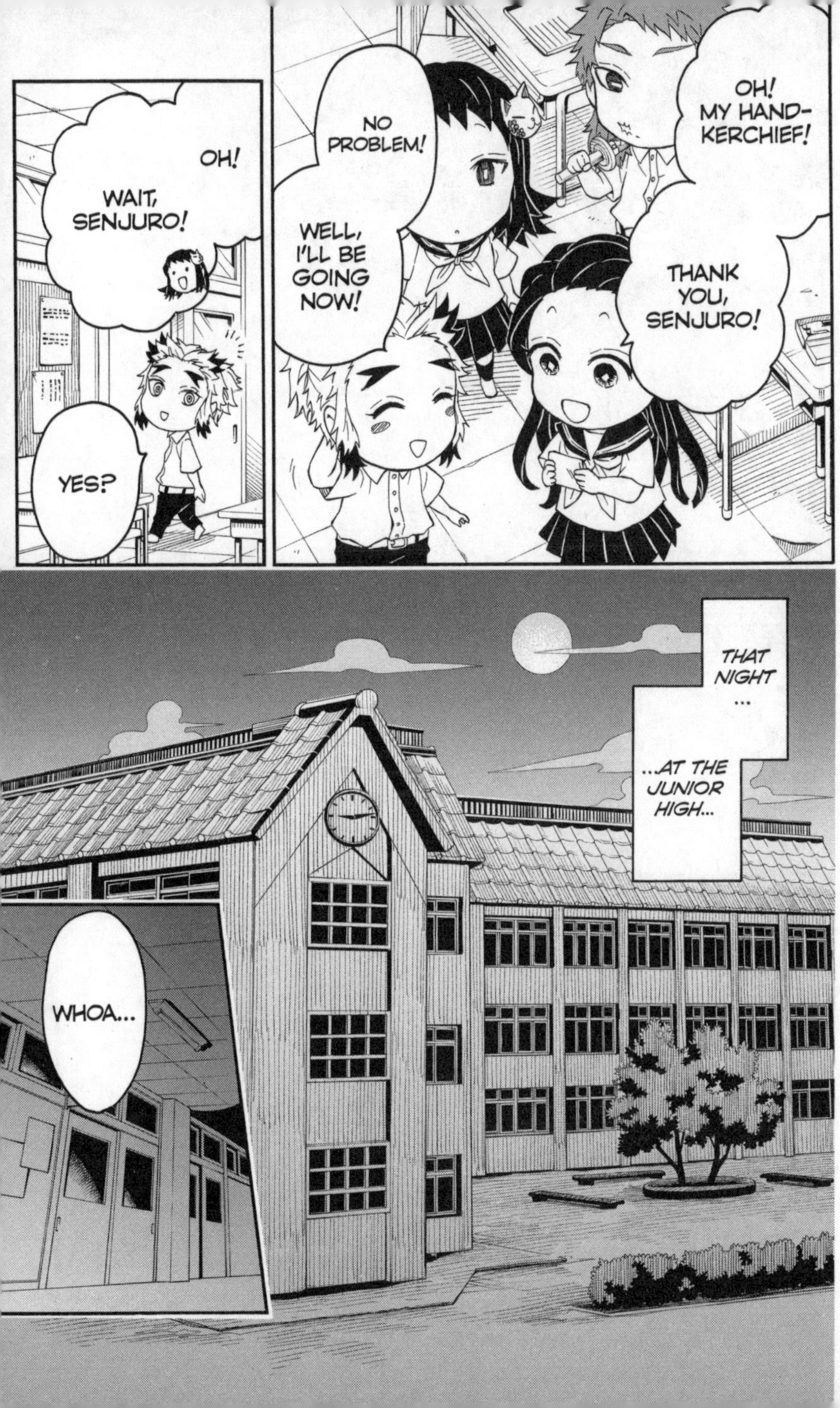
OH! MY HAND-KERCHIEF!
THANK YOU, SENJURO!
NO PROBLEM!
WELL, I'LL BE GOING NOW!
OH!
WAIT, SENJURO!
YES?
THAT NIGHT...
...AT THE JUNIOR HIGH...
WHOA...

THE SCHOOL FEELS...
...TOTALLY DIFFERENT AT NIGHT.
MAYBE THERE REALLY ARE GHOSTS!
BDMP BDMP
WELL, THE SCHOOL IS PRETTY OLD!
IF YOU SEE ONE, MAKE SURE YOU SNAP A PIC!
SHOULD I ASK PERMISSION FIRST?
OH, RIGHT!
I GUESS EVEN GHOSTS HAVE RIGHTS!
WE CAN ASK FOR TWO SELFIES!
AH HA HA HA
...

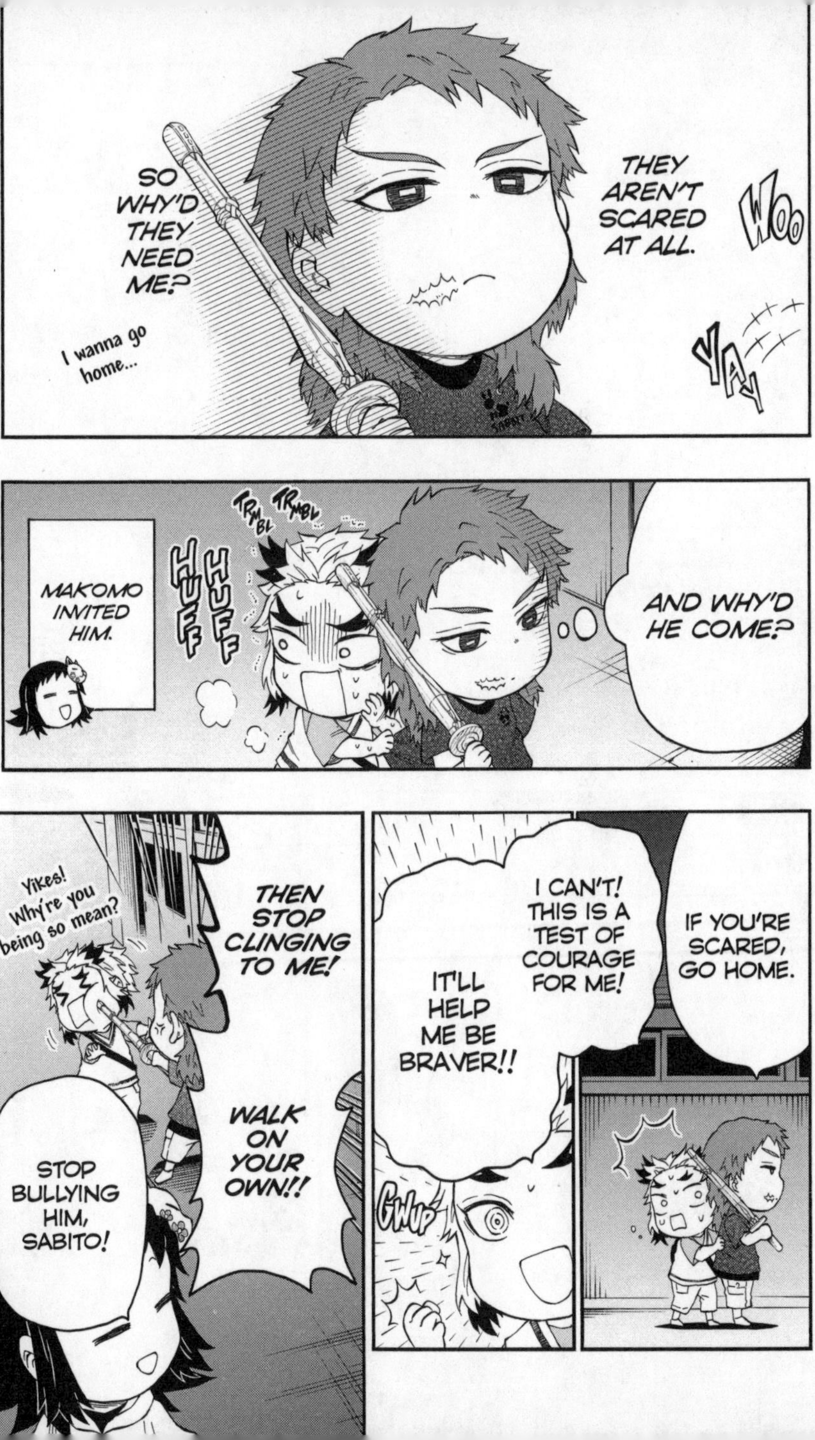
THEY AREN'T SCARED AT ALL.
WOO
YAY
SO WHY'D THEY NEED ME?
I wanna go home...
AND WHY'D HE COME?
TRMBL TRMBL
HUFF HUFF
MAKOMO INVITED HIM.
IF YOU'RE SCARED, GO HOME.
I CAN'T! THIS IS A TEST OF COURAGE FOR ME!
IT'LL HELP ME BE BRAVER!!
GWUP
THEN STOP CLINGING TO ME!
Yikes! Why're you being so mean?
WALK ON YOUR OWN!!
STOP BULLYING HIM, SABITO!

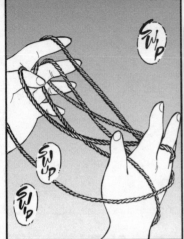

SO! WHERE SHOULD WE LOOK?
MAYBE THE SCIENCE ROOM?
!
SHH!
SWIP
SWUP
SWIP
WHAT'S WRONG, SABITO?
SOME-ONE'S IN THE CLASS-ROOM!
WHAT ?!
LOOK!
SWUP
SWIP
NO ONE ELSE SHOULD BE HERE THIS LATE!
TH- THEN IS THAT...
...A G-G-GHOST?
AH!
WHERE?

PIPE DOWN.
YEEEEEK!
AIEEE!
UWAAAH!
GYAAAH!
PHEW!
THAT WAS SCARY.
ARE YOU ALL RIGHT, SENJURO?
M-MY LEGS GAVE OUT...
SO WHO'S THAT KID?
UM, HE'S...

...MY CLASSMATE *RUI AYAKI!*
RUI AYAKI
AUTUMN LEAVES CLASS
JUNIOR HIGH, FIRST-YEAR
WHAT ARE YOU DOING HERE AT NIGHT?
I JUST DO THIS SOME-TIMES.
WHAT'RE *YOU* DOING HERE?
DO WHAT?
HANG OUT AT SCHOOL AT NIGHT.
BUT UNLIKE YOU, I DON'T MAKE A BUNCH OF NOISE.
I ENJOY PRACTICING CAT'S CRADLE...
...IN A NICE, QUIET, PEACEFUL ENVIRON-MENT!
VEEN

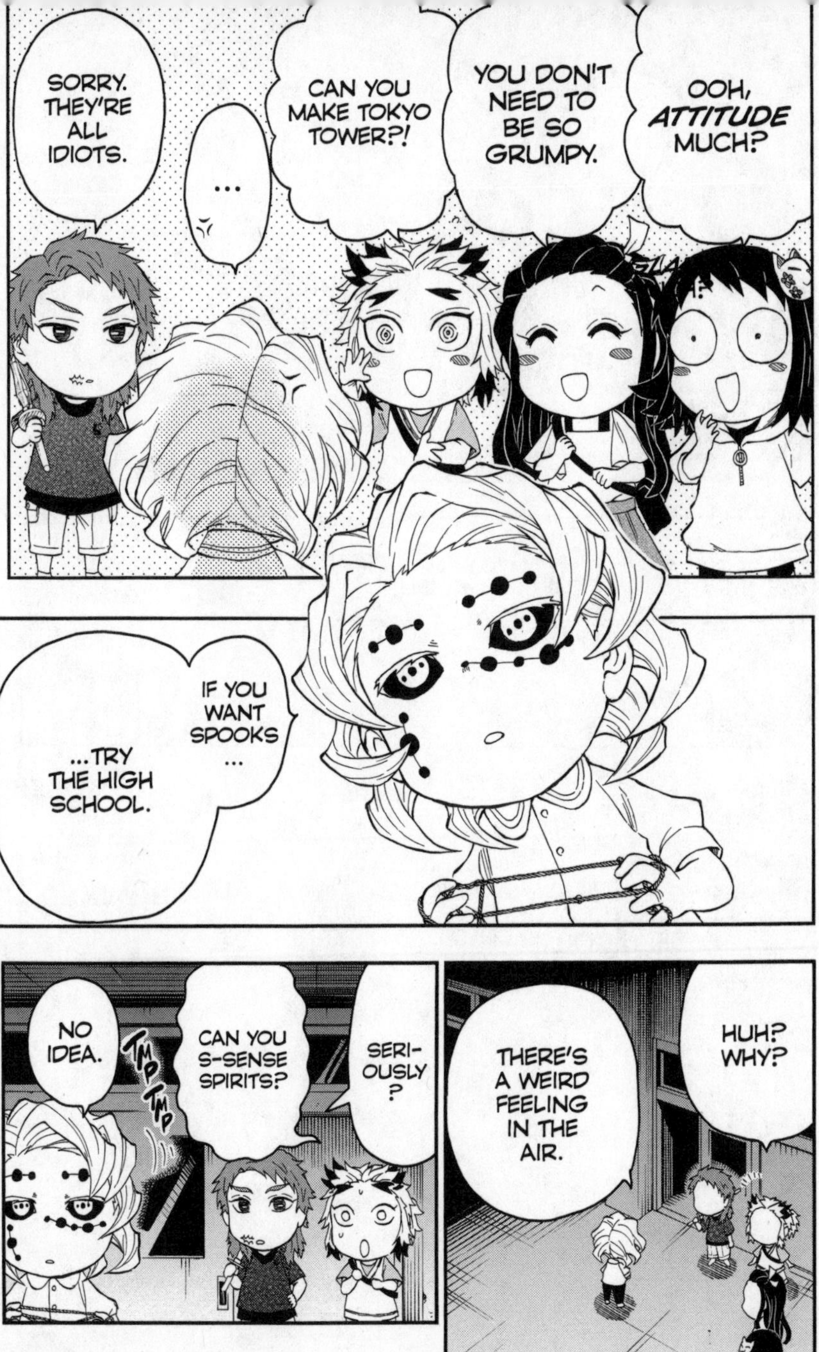
OOH, *ATTITUDE* MUCH?
YOU DON'T NEED TO BE SO GRUMPY.
CAN YOU MAKE TOKYO TOWER?!
...
SORRY. THEY'RE ALL IDIOTS.
IF YOU WANT SPOOKS ...
...TRY THE HIGH SCHOOL.
HUH? WHY?
THERE'S A WEIRD FEELING IN THE AIR.
SERI-OUSLY?
CAN YOU S-SENSE SPIRITS?
NO IDEA.
TMP TMP

SHALL WE CHECK IT OUT?
COME WITH US, RUI!
NO.
AW, C'MON!
WE'LL GIVE YOU SNACKS!
DON'T NEED 'EM.
...
FUMP
RUI'S KINDA WEIRD, HUH?
HE'S KIMETSU TOWN'S CAT'S CRADLE CHAMP!
NICE!
THE HIGH SCHOOL

HERE WE ARE, BUT...
PICKING UP ANY VIBES, SABITO?
WHY ASK ME?
I WAS ABLE TO LEAVE ONE OF THE JUNIOR HIGH'S WINDOWS UNLOCKED ...
...BUT THE HIGH SCHOOL'S GONNA BE LOCKED UP TIGHT.
Hmm...
I NEVER CONSID-ERED THAT!
What should we do?
CHAK
HM? WHAT WAS THAT?
WHAT'S WRONG, NEZUKO?
HEY! THIS WINDOW'S UNLOCKED!
LUCKY US!
RATL
DID SOMEONE JUST OPEN IT?

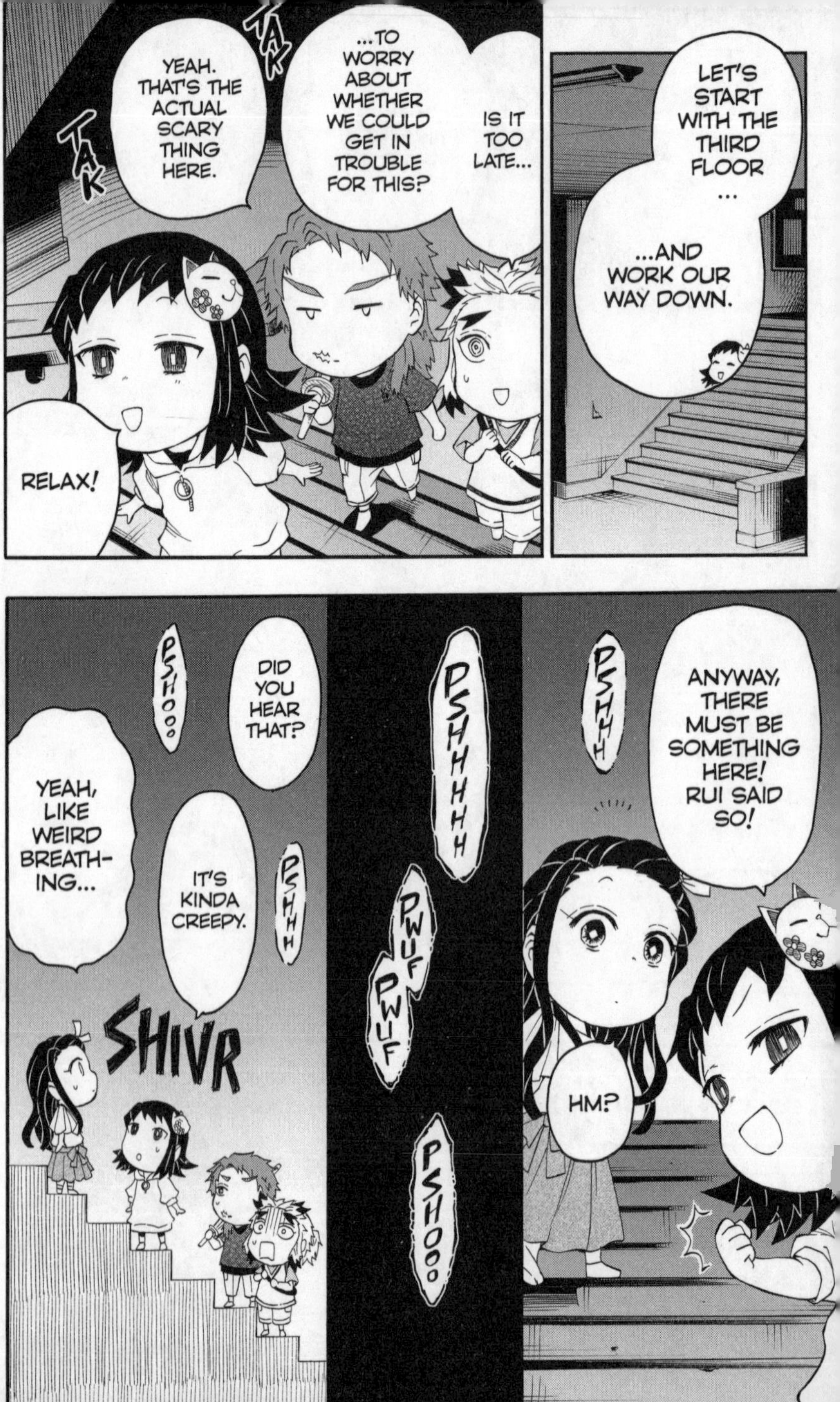
LET'S START WITH THE THIRD FLOOR ...
...AND WORK OUR WAY DOWN.
IS IT TOO LATE...
...TO WORRY ABOUT WHETHER WE COULD GET IN TROUBLE FOR THIS?
TAK
YEAH. THAT'S THE ACTUAL SCARY THING HERE.
TAK
RELAX!
PSHHH
ANYWAY, THERE MUST BE SOMETHING HERE! RUI SAID SO!
HM?
PSHHHHHH
PWUF
PWUF
PSHOOO
DID YOU HEAR THAT?
PSHOOO
YEAH, LIKE WEIRD BREATH-ING...
PSHHH
IT'S KINDA CREEPY.
SHIVR

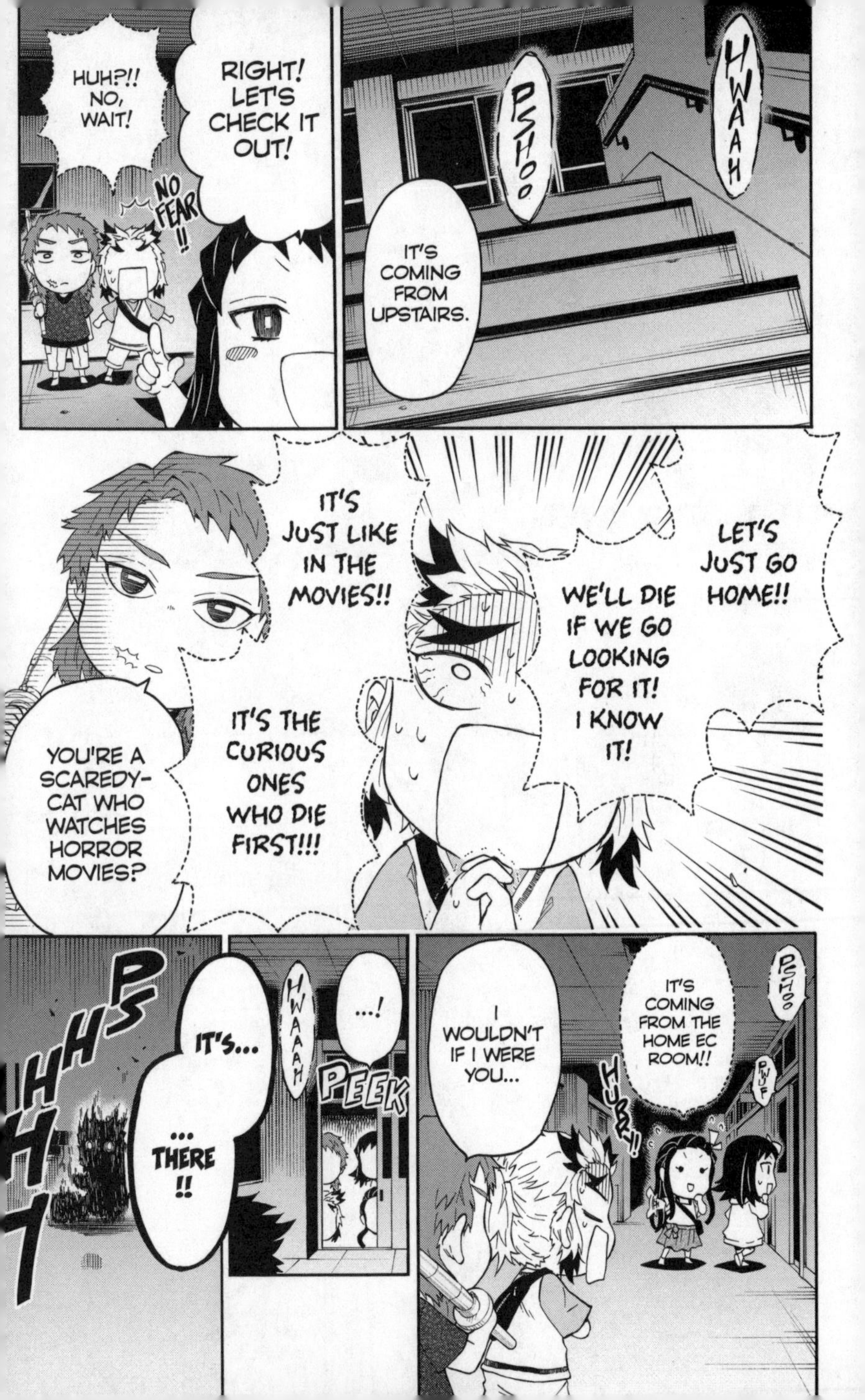
HWAAH
PSHOO
IT'S COMING FROM UPSTAIRS.
RIGHT! LET'S CHECK IT OUT!
NO FEAR!!
HUH?!! NO, WAIT!
LET'S JUST GO HOME!!
WE'LL DIE IF WE GO LOOKING FOR IT! I KNOW IT!
IT'S JUST LIKE IN THE MOVIES!!
IT'S THE CURIOUS ONES WHO DIE FIRST!!!
YOU'RE A SCAREDY-CAT WHO WATCHES HORROR MOVIES?
PSHOO
IT'S COMING FROM THE HOME EC ROOM!!
PWUF
HURRY!
I WOULDN'T IF I WERE YOU...
...!
HWAAAH
PEEK
PSHHHH
IT'S...
...THERE!!

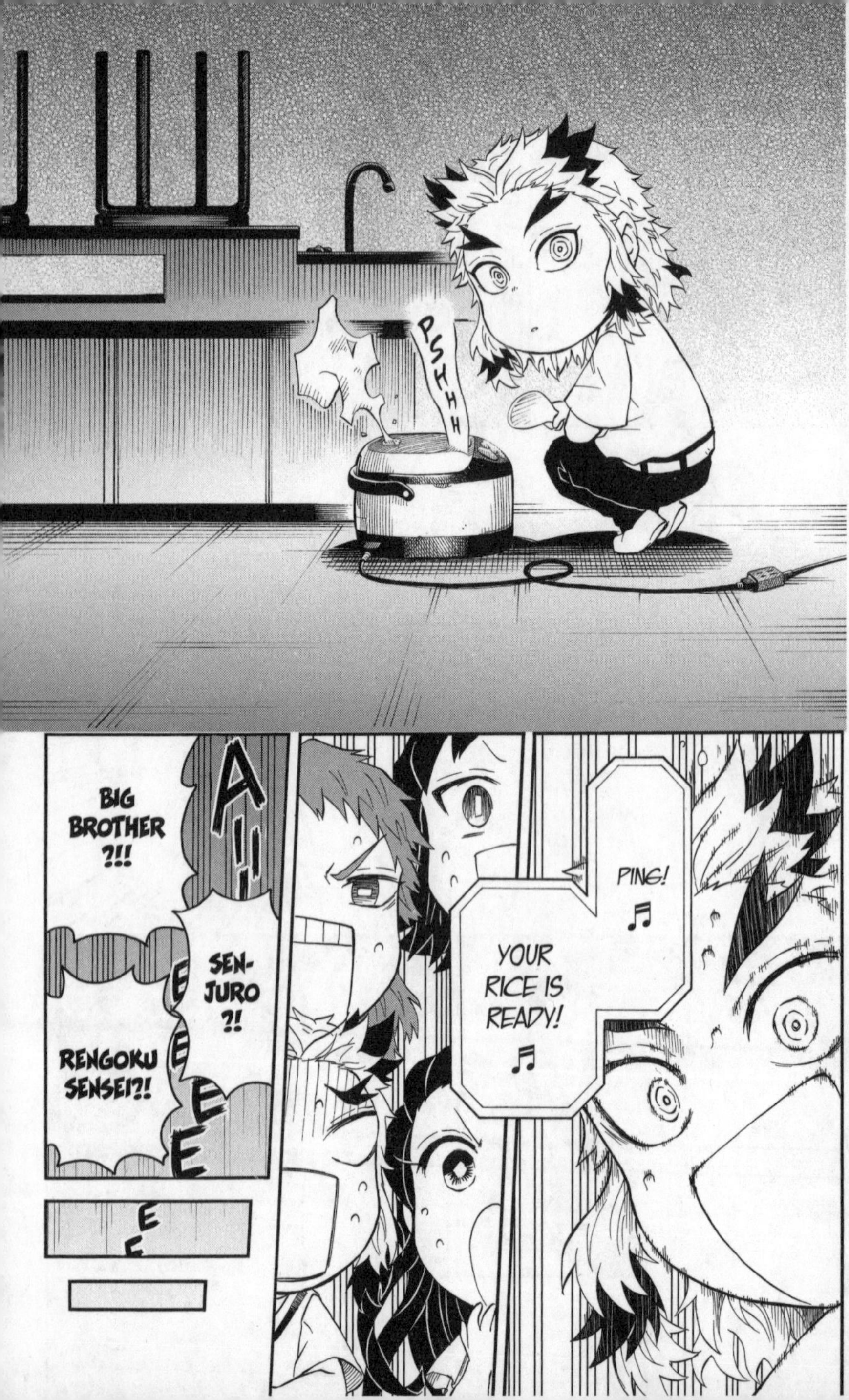
PSHHH
PING! ♬ YOUR RICE IS READY! ♬
AIIEEEEE
BIG BROTHER?!!
SEN-JURO?!
RENGOKU SENSEI!?!
EE

FWOOO
OH DEAR...
KYOJURO RENGOKU
HISTORY TEACHER
(SENJURO'S OLDER BROTHER)
WHAT ARE YOU DOING HERE AT THIS HOUR?!
IS HE GONNA LECTURE US?!
YOU'RE HERE TOO, BIG BRO...
HERE FOR A LATE-NIGHT SNACK?
YEP!! I'VE GOT THE MUNCHIES!
SKIR
SKIR
BUT WHY SNACK AT SCHOOL?
CAN I TAKE A PIC FOR THE SCHOOL PAPER?
The steamy specter...
...who reaps rice in the home ec room!
PLEASE DON'T, YOUNG MAN!

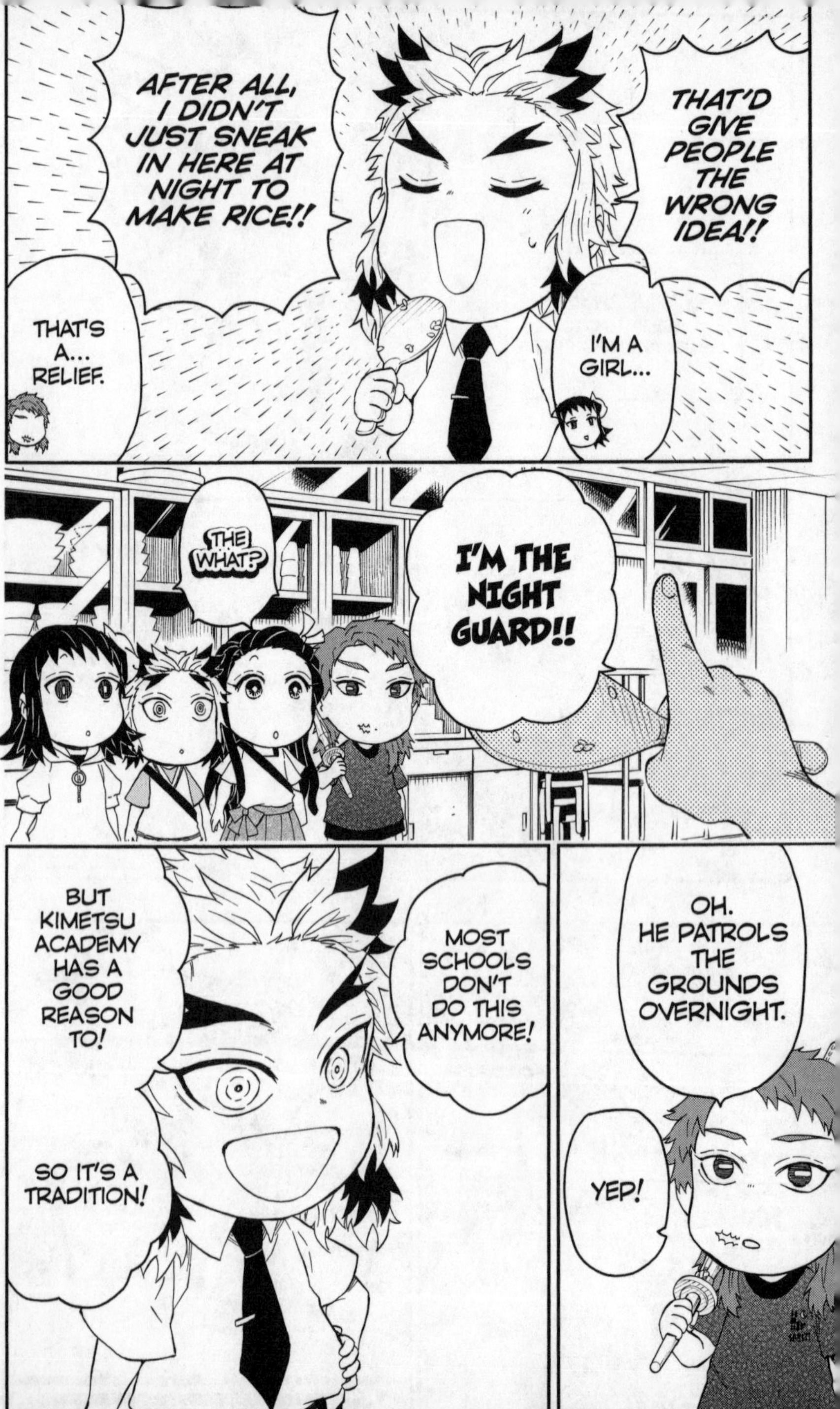
THAT'D GIVE PEOPLE THE WRONG IDEA!!
AFTER ALL, I DIDN'T JUST SNEAK IN HERE AT NIGHT TO MAKE RICE!!
I'M A GIRL...
THAT'S A... RELIEF.
I'M THE NIGHT GUARD!!
THE WHAT?
OH. HE PATROLS THE GROUNDS OVERNIGHT.
YEP!
MOST SCHOOLS DON'T DO THIS ANYMORE!
BUT KIMETSU ACADEMY HAS A GOOD REASON TO!
SO IT'S A TRADITION!

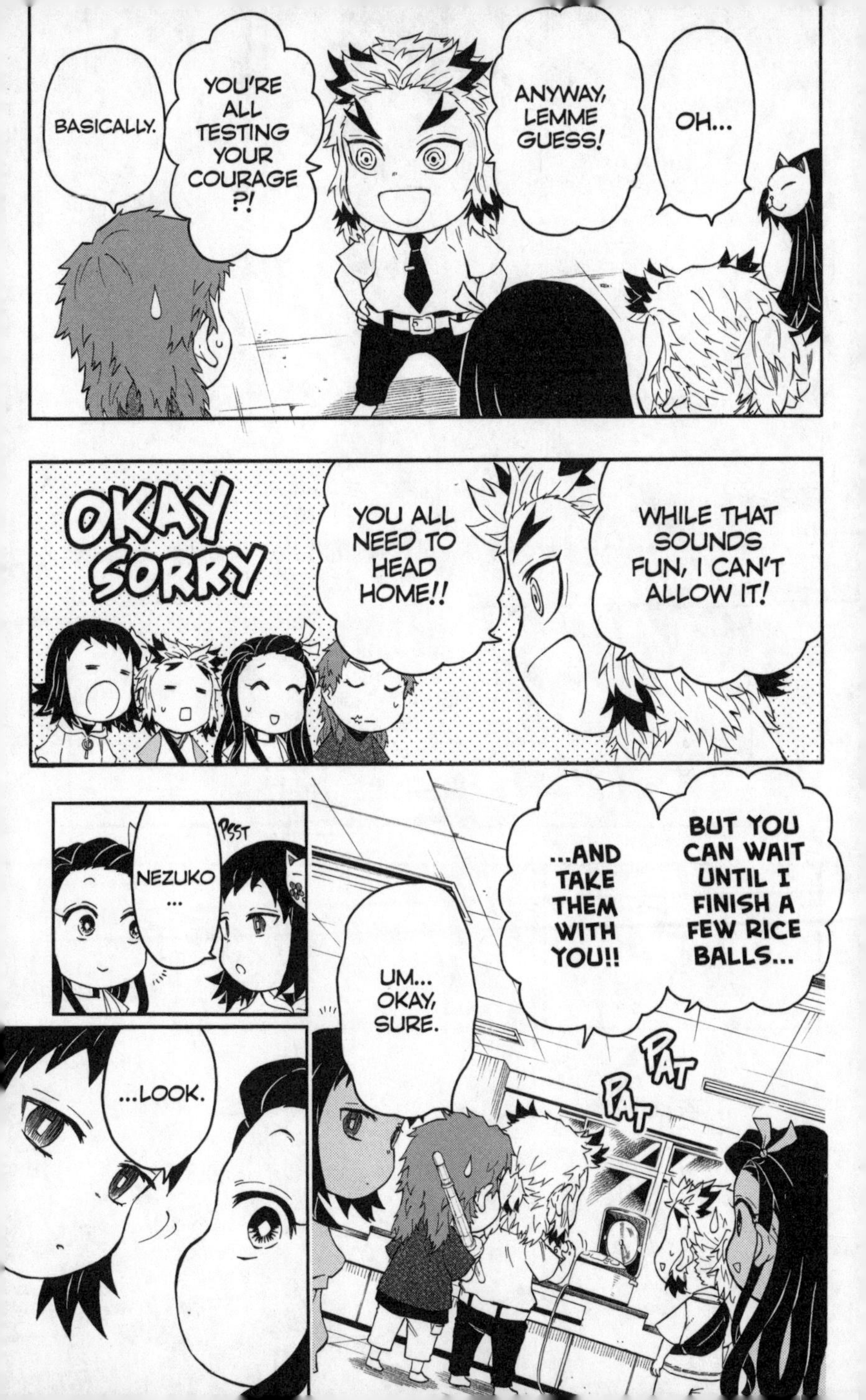
OH...
ANYWAY, LEMME GUESS!
YOU'RE ALL TESTING YOUR COURAGE?!
BASICALLY.
WHILE THAT SOUNDS FUN, I CAN'T ALLOW IT!
YOU ALL NEED TO HEAD HOME!!
OKAY SORRY
BUT YOU CAN WAIT UNTIL I FINISH A FEW RICE BALLS...
...AND TAKE THEM WITH YOU!!
UM... OKAY, SURE.
PAT
PAT
PSST
NEZUKO...
...LOOK.

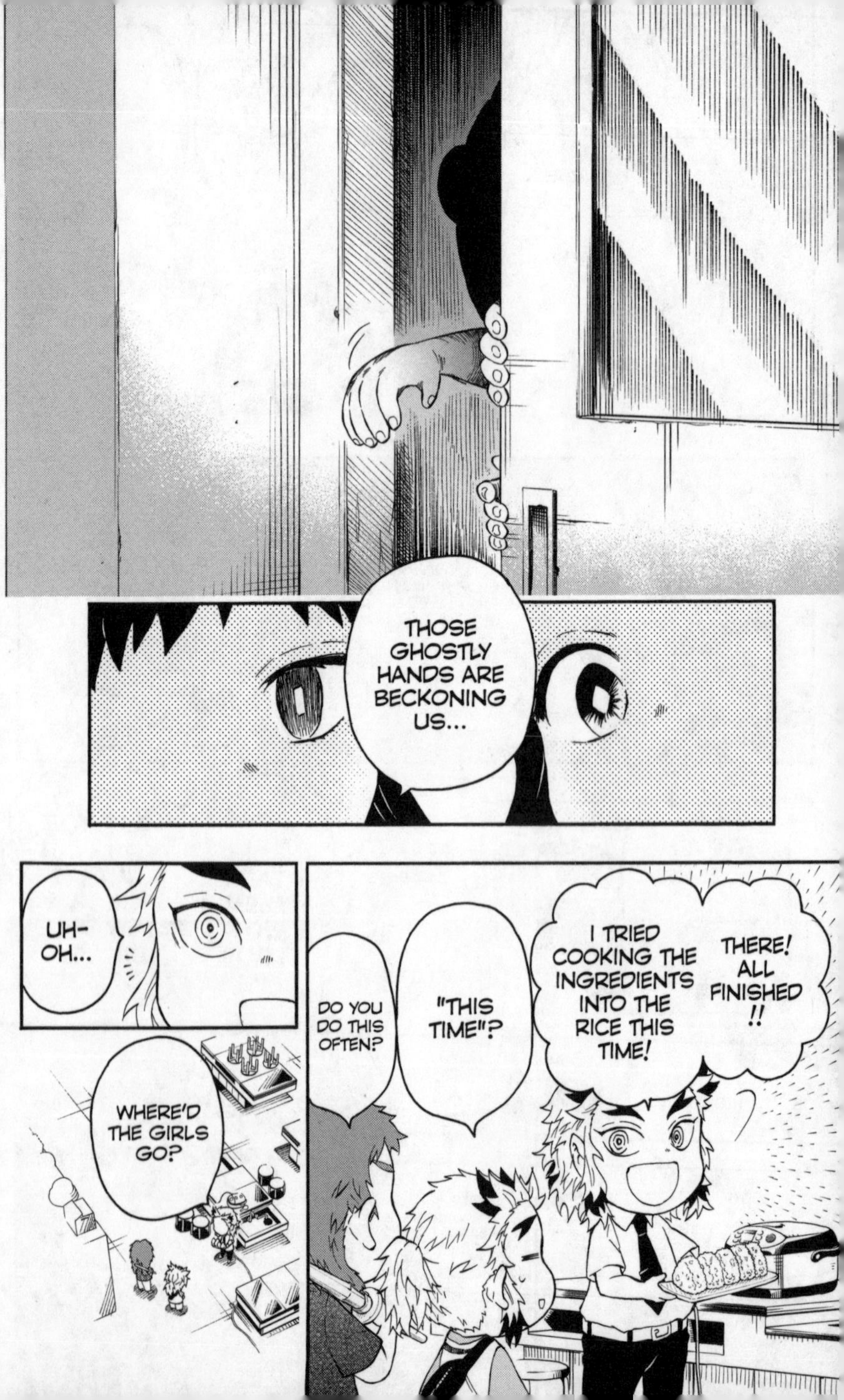
THOSE GHOSTLY HANDS ARE BECKONING US...
THERE! ALL FINISHED!!
I TRIED COOKING THE INGREDIENTS INTO THE RICE THIS TIME!
"THIS TIME"?
DO YOU DO THIS OFTEN?
UH-OH...
WHERE'D THE GIRLS GO?

BIOLOGY
HYO HYO!
YOU GALS HAVE FALLEN INTO MY HANDS!
TREMBLE IN FEAR!!
FOR I AM KIMETSU ACADEMY'S GREATEST HORROR!!
I'LL DRAG YOU INTO THIS FINE VASE OF MINE!!
GYOKKO
SCHOOL HORROR
*EYES: UPPER/FIVE
EEP!
A MONSTER!!!
HYO HYO!
YES! TREMBLE IN FEAR!!

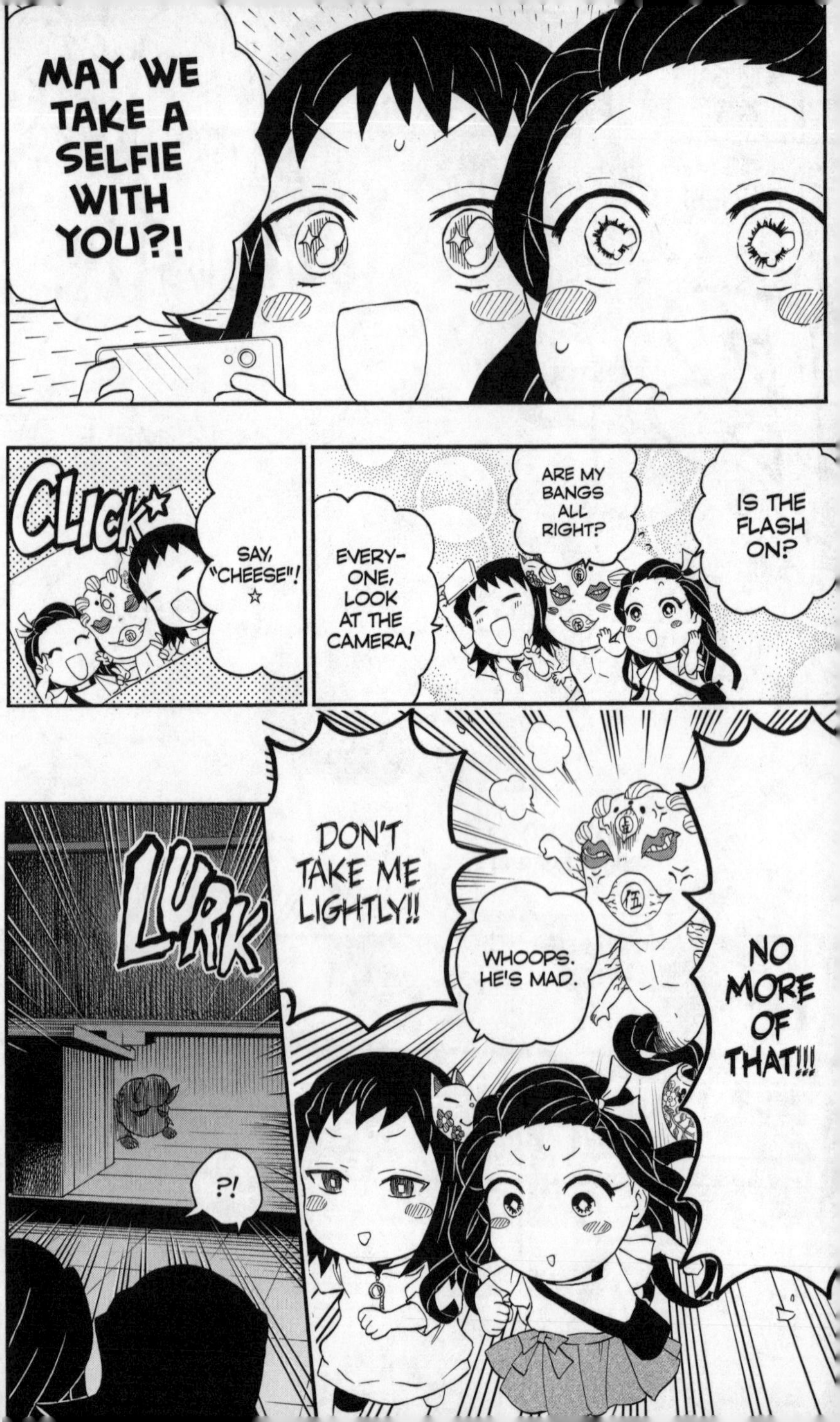
MAY WE TAKE A SELFIE WITH YOU?!
IS THE FLASH ON?
ARE MY BANGS ALL RIGHT?
EVERY-ONE, LOOK AT THE CAMERA!
SAY, "CHEESE"! ☆
CLICK☆
NO MORE OF THAT!!!
DON'T TAKE ME LIGHTLY!!
WHOOPS. HE'S MAD.
LURK
?!

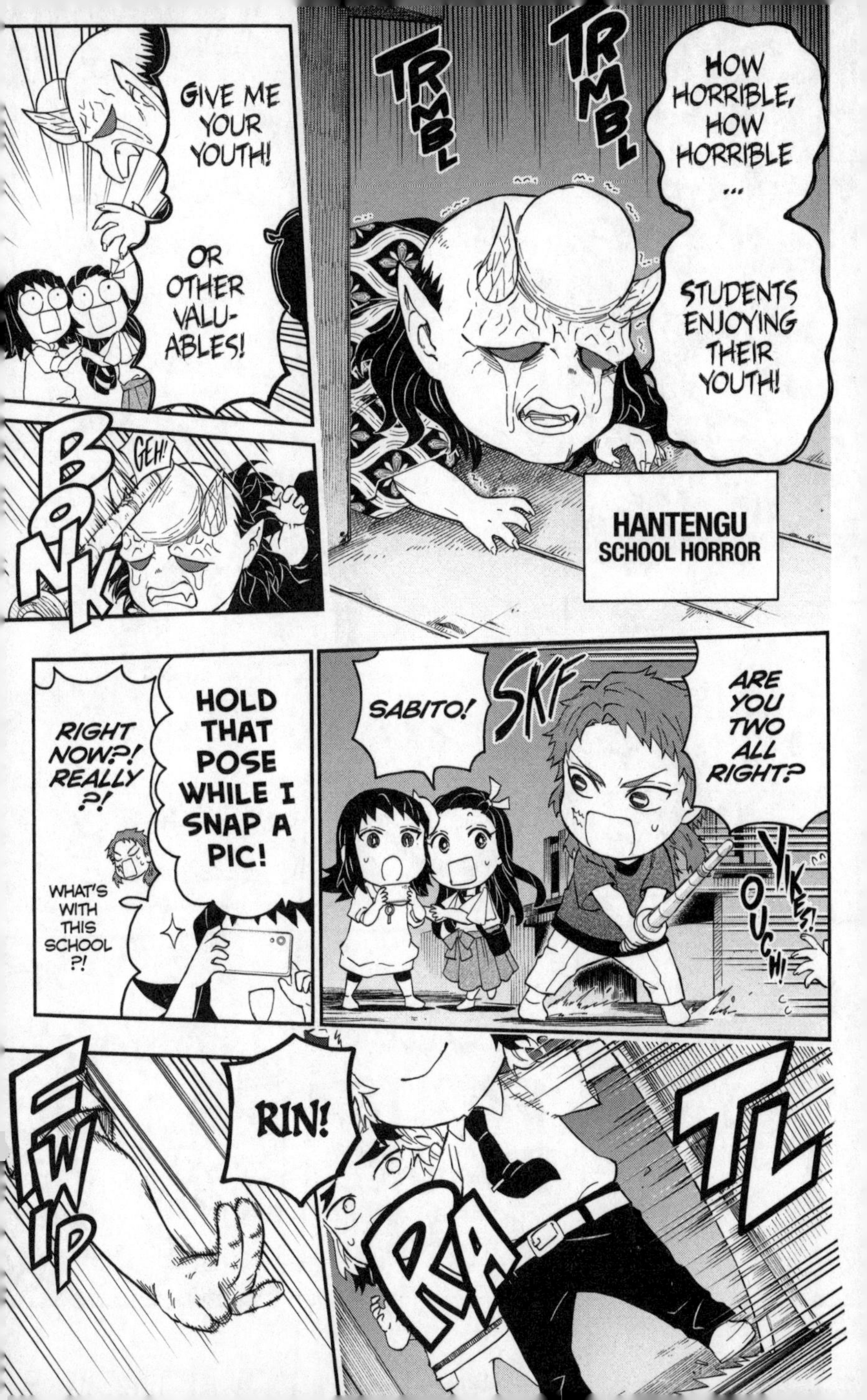
HOW HORRIBLE, HOW HORRIBLE ...
STUDENTS ENJOYING THEIR YOUTH!
TRMBL TRMBL
HANTENGU SCHOOL HORROR
GIVE ME YOUR YOUTH!
OR OTHER VALU-ABLES!
GEH!
BONK
ARE YOU TWO ALL RIGHT?
SKF
SABITO!
YIKES!
OUCH!
HOLD THAT POSE WHILE I SNAP A PIC!
RIGHT NOW?! REALLY ?!
WHAT'S WITH THIS SCHOOL ?!
TL
RIN!
PRA
FWIP

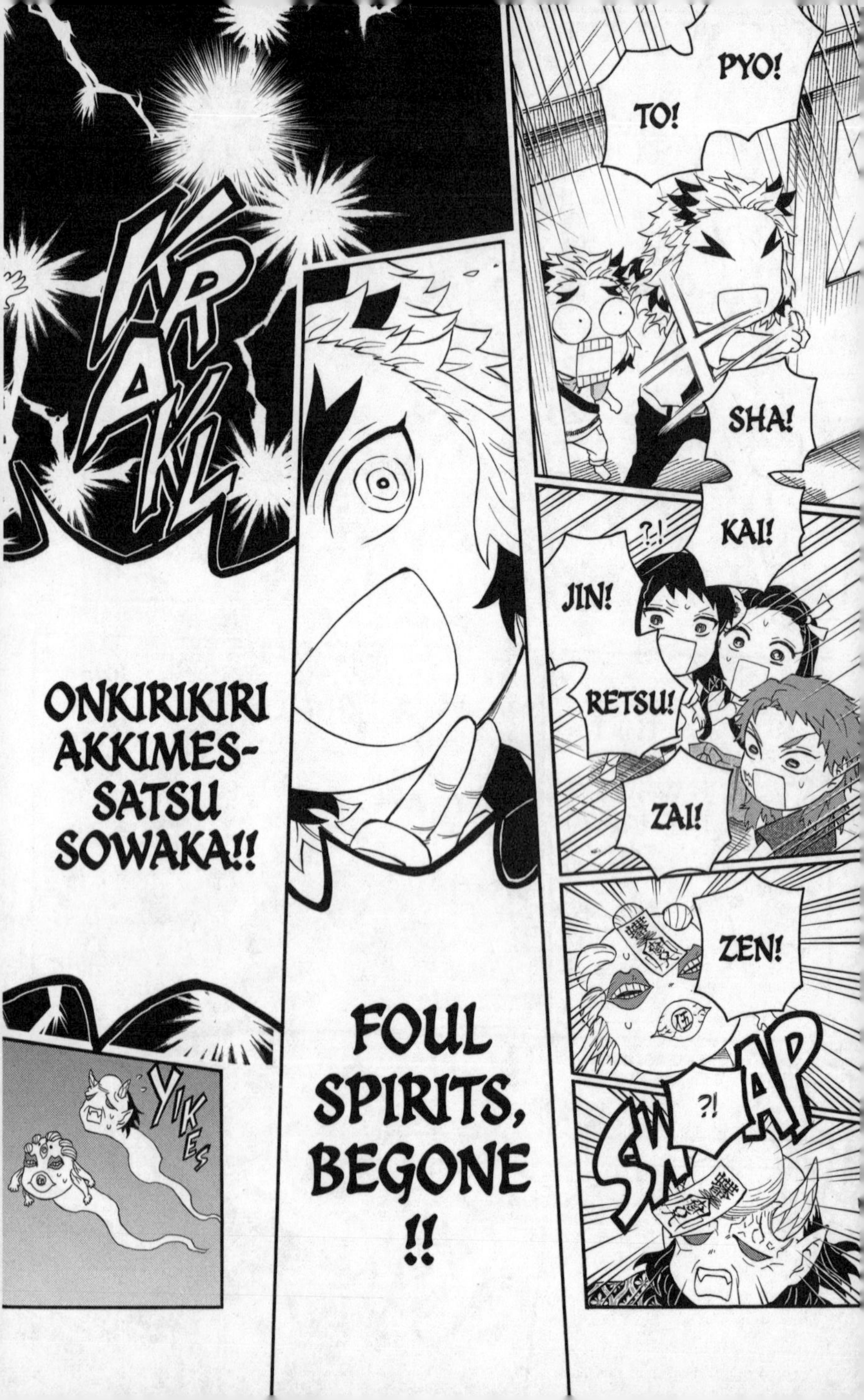
PYO!
TO!
SHA!
KAI!
?!
JIN!
RETSU!
ZAI!
ZEN!
SNAP
?!
FOUL SPIRITS, BEGONE!!
KRAAK
ONKIRIKIRI AKKIMES-SATSU SOWAKA!!
YIKES

KRAK
GYAAAAAAH!!
...
SWOO

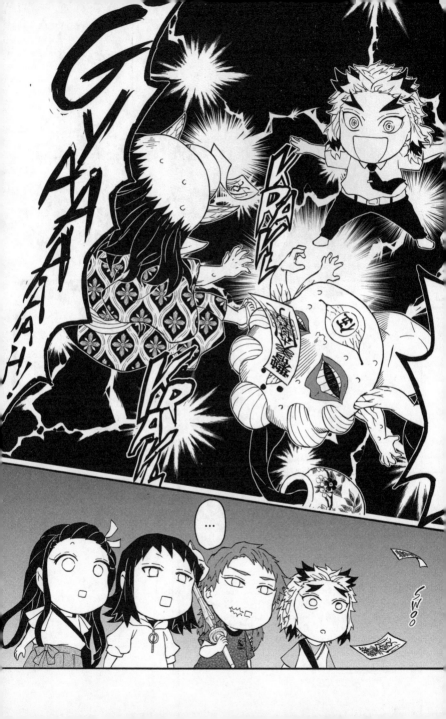

WHAT...
...THE HECK?!?!
WHAT JUST HAPPENED?
OH!
FWIP
THOSE CREEPS ALWAYS SHOW UP HERE AT NIGHT.
THE NIGHT GUARD'S JOB IS TO ERASE 'EM!!
LIKE SCRIBBLES ON A BLACKBOARD?!

YOU CAN DO EXORCISMS?!
ALL THE HIGH SCHOOL TEACHERS CAN!!
THEY ALL CAN?!
R-REALLY?!
ALL OF THEM?!
YOU ALL JUST GO AROUND EXORCISING GHOSTS AND GHOULS?!
GYAAAH
YEP! THAT'S RIGHT!
TO BE HONEST, THOUGH ...
...ANYONE CAN SLAP ON A SEAL ON SOME SPOOKS!
And chant somethin'!
THESE SEALS ARE THAT POWER-FUL?
THE SHOCK-ING TRUTH COMES OUT.
I had no idea.
YEAH, I CAN'T SUBMIT THAT.

THAT WAS FUN!
SOMEDAY, I WANNA DO AN EXORCISM!
YEAH! A REAL ADVEN-TURE!
YOU DON'T LEARN, DO YOU?
WHERE DO THE SEALS COME FROM?
WELL, UM...
...I DON'T ACTUALLY KNOW!!
HELP YOURSELF
The night duty room has 'em!!
LIKE FREE SNACKS?!
THEY MUST BE FROM A FAMOUS SHRINE!
Wow!
THUS, THANKS TO MAKOMO...
..."THE CREEPY OLD BABY GUY" AND "THE GUY IN A POT"...
...WERE ENSHRINED AS TWO OF THE SCHOOL'S SEVEN MYSTERIES.
SEVEN SCHOOL
THEY KEPT THE NIGHT GUARD SECRET, THOUGH.
STAFF
KOCHO SENSEI!

YES?
KANAE KOCHO
BIOLOGY TEACHER
ARE YOU USING THE COPY MACHINE?
VRRR
VRRR
YES, I AM.
DO YOU NEED TO USE IT?
NO, BUT...
...
VRRR
VRRR
GWOOOO
...WHAT ARE YOU COPYING?
VRRR
OH, THAT?
VRRR
TEE HEE!
IT BEATS WRITING THEM BY HAND!
Right?
??
THE SOURCE OF THE SEALS WAS CLOSE AT HAND.

LIFE IN TARO CLASS

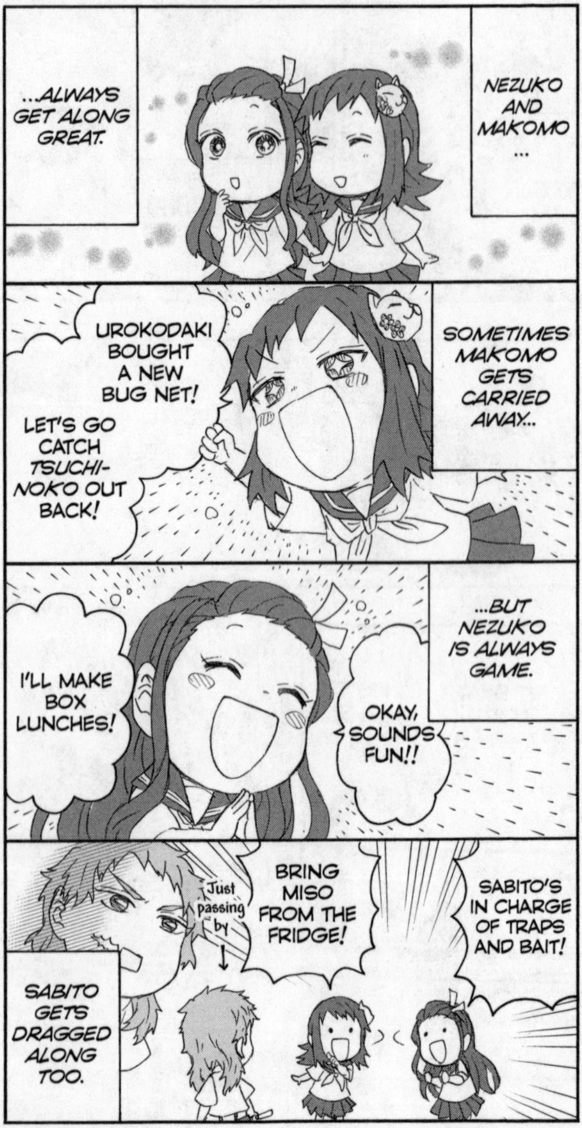
NEZUKO AND MAKOMO ...
...ALWAYS GET ALONG GREAT.
SOMETIMES MAKOMO GETS CARRIED AWAY...
UROKODAKI BOUGHT A NEW BUG NET!
LET'S GO CATCH TSUCHI-NOKO OUT BACK!
...BUT NEZUKO IS ALWAYS GAME.
OKAY, SOUNDS FUN!!
I'LL MAKE BOX LUNCHES!
SABITO'S IN CHARGE OF TRAPS AND BAIT!
BRING MISO FROM THE FRIDGE!
Just passing by
SABITO GETS DRAGGED ALONG TOO.

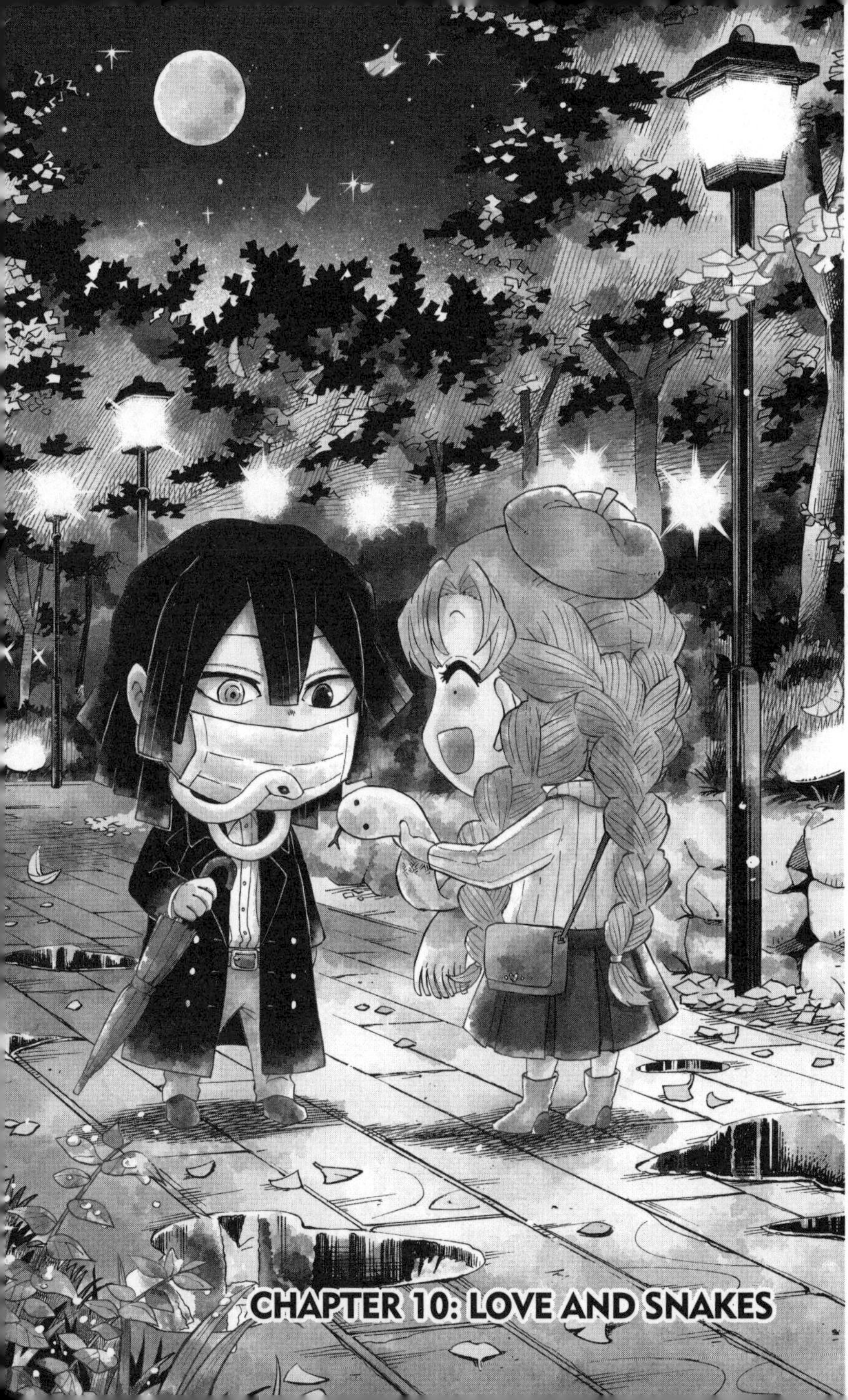
CHAPTER 10: LOVE AND SNAKES

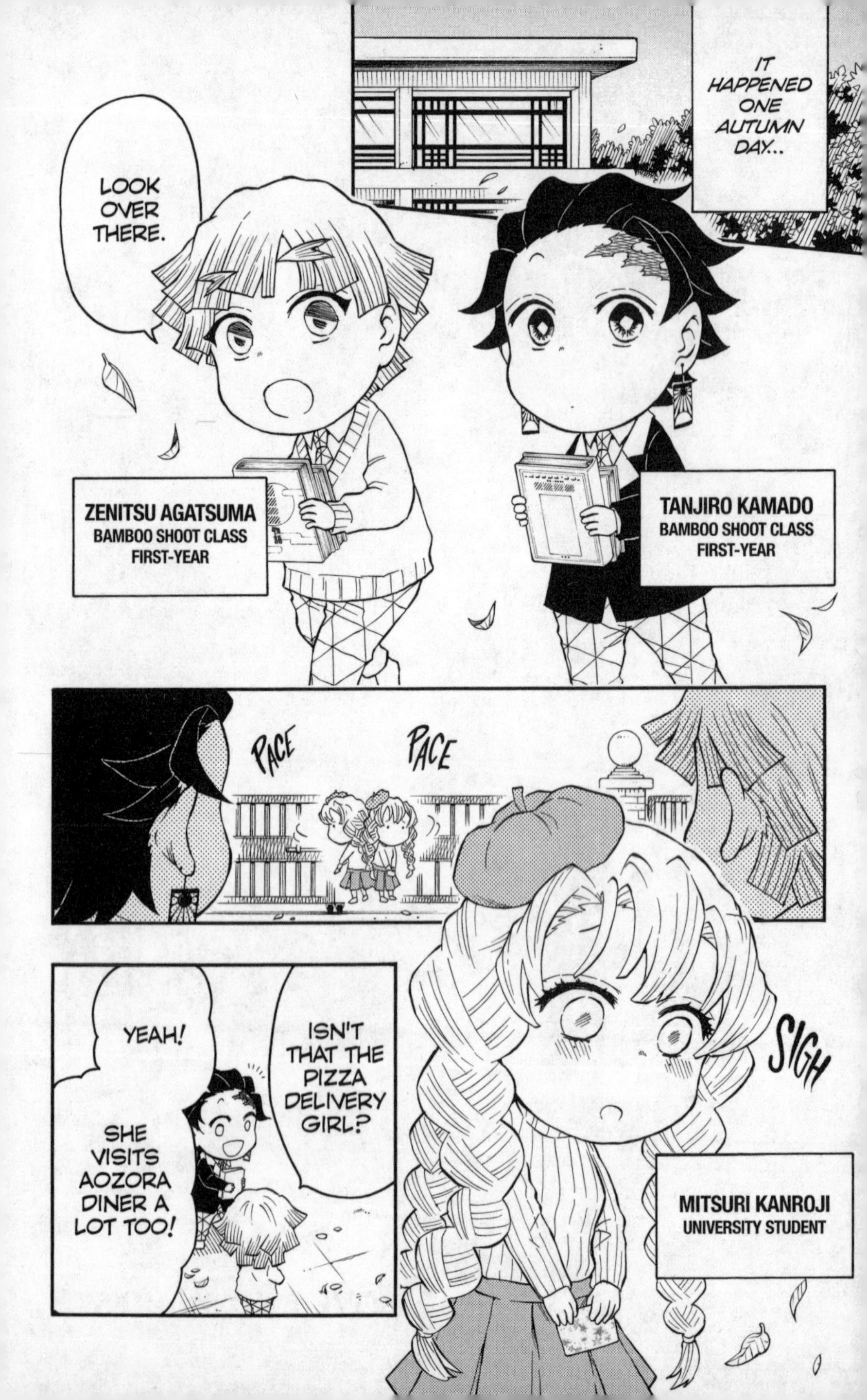
IT HAPPENED ONE AUTUMN DAY...
LOOK OVER THERE.
TANJIRO KAMADO
BAMBOO SHOOT CLASS FIRST-YEAR
ZENITSU AGATSUMA
BAMBOO SHOOT CLASS FIRST-YEAR
PACE
PACE
SIGH
MITSURI KANROJI
UNIVERSITY STUDENT
ISN'T THAT THE PIZZA DELIVERY GIRL?
YEAH!
SHE VISITS AOZORA DINER A LOT TOO!

WHATCHA HANGIN' AROUND HERE FOR?!
SHOUT
D'YOU NEED SOMETHIN'?!
GASP
KYAH!
I BET I LOOK SUSPICIOUS, HUH?!
BUT I GRAD-UATED FROM HERE!
Oh!
YOU DID?
WANT US TO GET SOME-ONE FOR YOU?
NO, I'M FINE. THANKS.
WHAT I REALLY NEED...
...IS A CROW TO DELIVER THIS LETTER FOR ME.

IT'S FOR...

CHEMISTRY

...OBANAI IGURO?! OUR CHEMISTRY TEACHER?!

NO FREAKING WAY...

NAG NAG

Oh, you forgot your homework?

Then why even bother coming?!

NOT A CHANCE!

WELL, I GUESS HE'S POPULAR!

HE'S A GLOOMY AND ANNOYING SNAKE!!

ROMANCE ISN'T A COMPETITION! BE STRONG, ZENITSU!

HE BEAT ME!!

I CAN'T BELIEVE IT!!

FINE, WHATEVER. BUT...

AFTER ALL...

HM?

...THAT GUY AND KANROJI?

I BET SHE'LL DUMP HIM!

HE'LL PROBABLY FROTH AT THE MOUTH AND COLLAPSE!

Mask

Ward against women? Kaburamaru (snake)

WOMAN

WOMAN

...HE'S BASICALLY ALLERGIC TO WOMEN!

HIS HEART POUNDS AND HE SWEATS BUCKETS!

...

ANYWAY, UM...

WELL, IT'S NOT OUR DECISION.

SO MAYBE IT'D BE BEST IF WE DIDN'T DELIVER THIS.

OBANAI IGURO
CHEMISTRY TEACHER

...THIS LETTER IS FOR YOU.
HISSSS
Keep that away from me!
CHOMP
HWIP
GOOD.
GRIP
THANK YOU FOR DELIVERING IT.
?!!

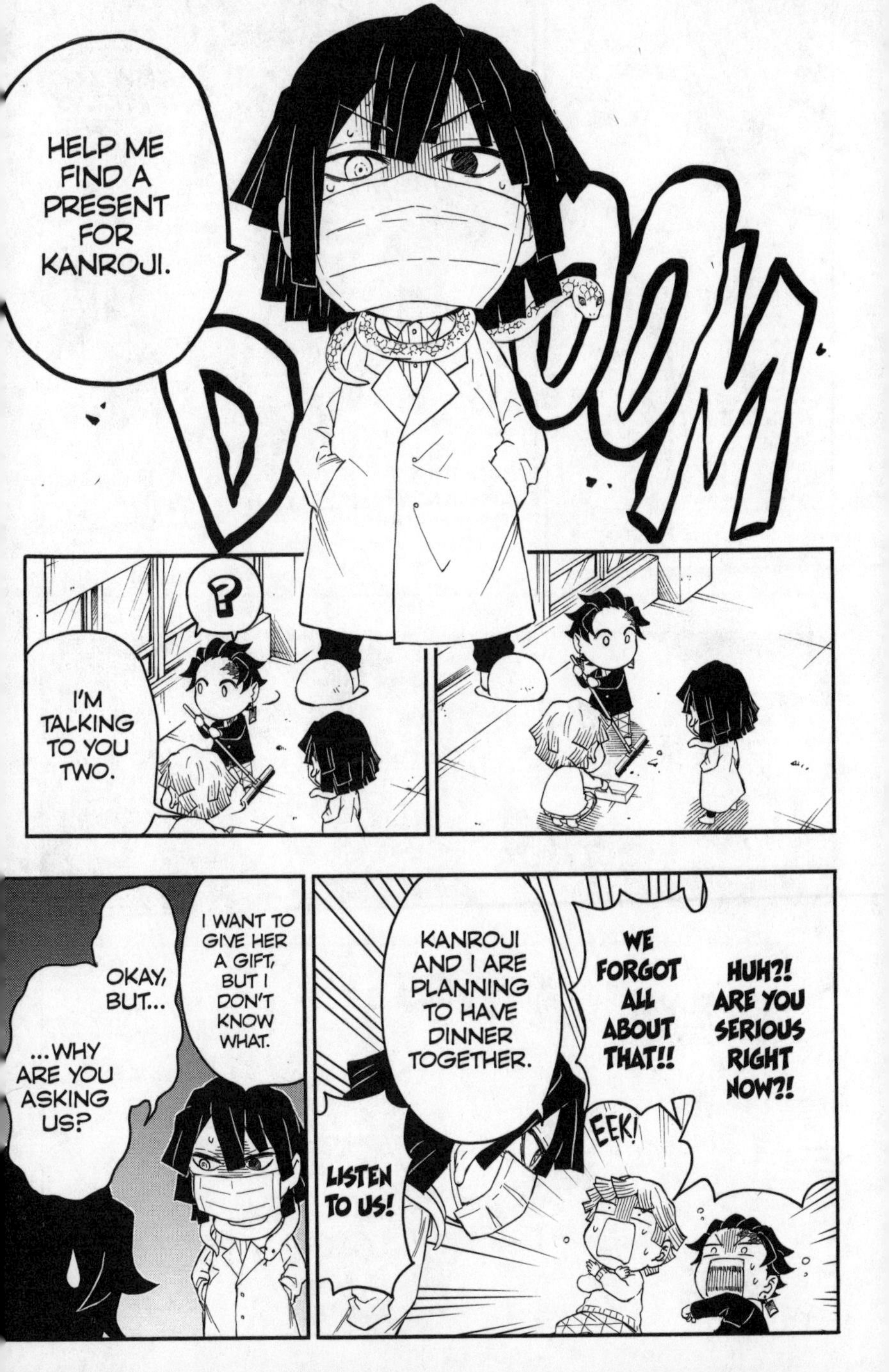
HELP ME FIND A PRESENT FOR KANROJI.
DOOM
?
I'M TALKING TO YOU TWO.
HUH?! ARE YOU SERIOUS RIGHT NOW?!
WE FORGOT ALL ABOUT THAT!!
KANROJI AND I ARE PLANNING TO HAVE DINNER TOGETHER.
EEK!
LISTEN TO US!
I WANT TO GIVE HER A GIFT, BUT I DON'T KNOW WHAT.
OKAY, BUT...
...WHY ARE YOU ASKING US?

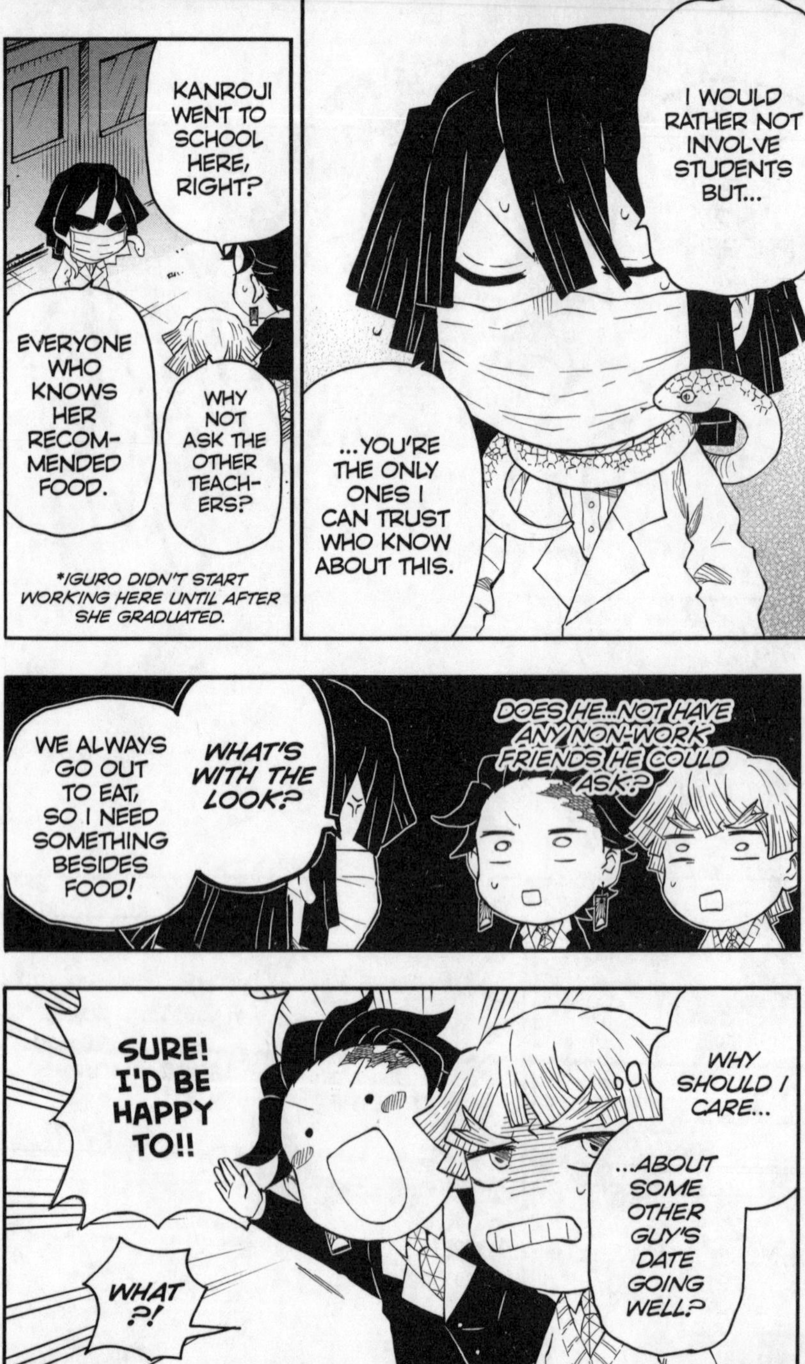
I WOULD RATHER NOT INVOLVE STUDENTS BUT...
...YOU'RE THE ONLY ONES I CAN TRUST WHO KNOW ABOUT THIS.
KANROJI WENT TO SCHOOL HERE, RIGHT?
WHY NOT ASK THE OTHER TEACHERS?
EVERYONE WHO KNOWS HER RECOMMENDED FOOD.
*IGURO DIDN'T START WORKING HERE UNTIL AFTER SHE GRADUATED.
DOES HE...NOT HAVE ANY NON-WORK FRIENDS HE COULD ASK?
WHAT'S WITH THE LOOK?
WE ALWAYS GO OUT TO EAT, SO I NEED SOMETHING BESIDES FOOD!
WHY SHOULD I CARE...
...ABOUT SOME OTHER GUY'S DATE GOING WELL?
SURE! I'D BE HAPPY TO!!
WHAT?!

REALLY?
YEAH!
ZENITSU WILL HELP TOO!!
I WILL ...?
WHAT'S THE PAY LIKE?
THEN WHY SHOULD I— UGH!
BONK
HE DOESN'T HAVE TO PAY US!!
HMM...
I SHOULD REPAY YOU SOMEHOW ...
HOW ABOUT I BUY YOU LUNCH?
But keep it secret.
RATTL
I'LL TREAT YOU TO WHATEVER YOU WANT.
FREE LUNCH? I'M IN!!
NO!!!
INOSUKE HASHIBIRA
BAMBOO SHOOT CLASS
FIRST-YEAR

THIS WEEKEND, RIGHT?!
NO ONE INVITED—
INOSUKE!!
JOLT
YOU PROMISED TO HELP OUT AT THE DINER THIS WEEKEND!!
TO PAY FOR ALL THE BROKEN DISHES!!
AOI KANZAKI
PERSIMMON CLASS
SECOND-YEAR
ULP! AOI...
YOU SHOULD KEEP YOUR PROMISE.
OR YOU'LL LOSE FREE REFILLS.
BUT... FOOD...
YOU CAN HAVE A FREE TEMPURA BOWL!
SORRY. SEE YA, DUDES.
WHY'D YOU EVEN BOTHER SHOWING UP?
AND SO THE MATTER WAS SETTLED.

THAT WEEK-END...
...AT THE TRAIN STATION ...
BAM
CHATTER
さぎりやま駅
Sagiriyama Station
CHATTER
SEN-SEI!!
GACK
I'VE GOTTA SAY, I HATE SEEING TEACHERS ON THE WEEKEND!!
KEEP IT TO YOURSELF.
UM, SEN-SEI?
WE DON'T REALLY KNOW WHAT COLLEGE GIRLS LIKE.
STILL, AS TEEN-AGERS, YOU'LL PICK SOME-THING...
...BETTER THAN I EVER COULD.
UH...
TMP
IS HE ALWAYS THIS INSECURE?
NOW LET'S START SHOPPING.

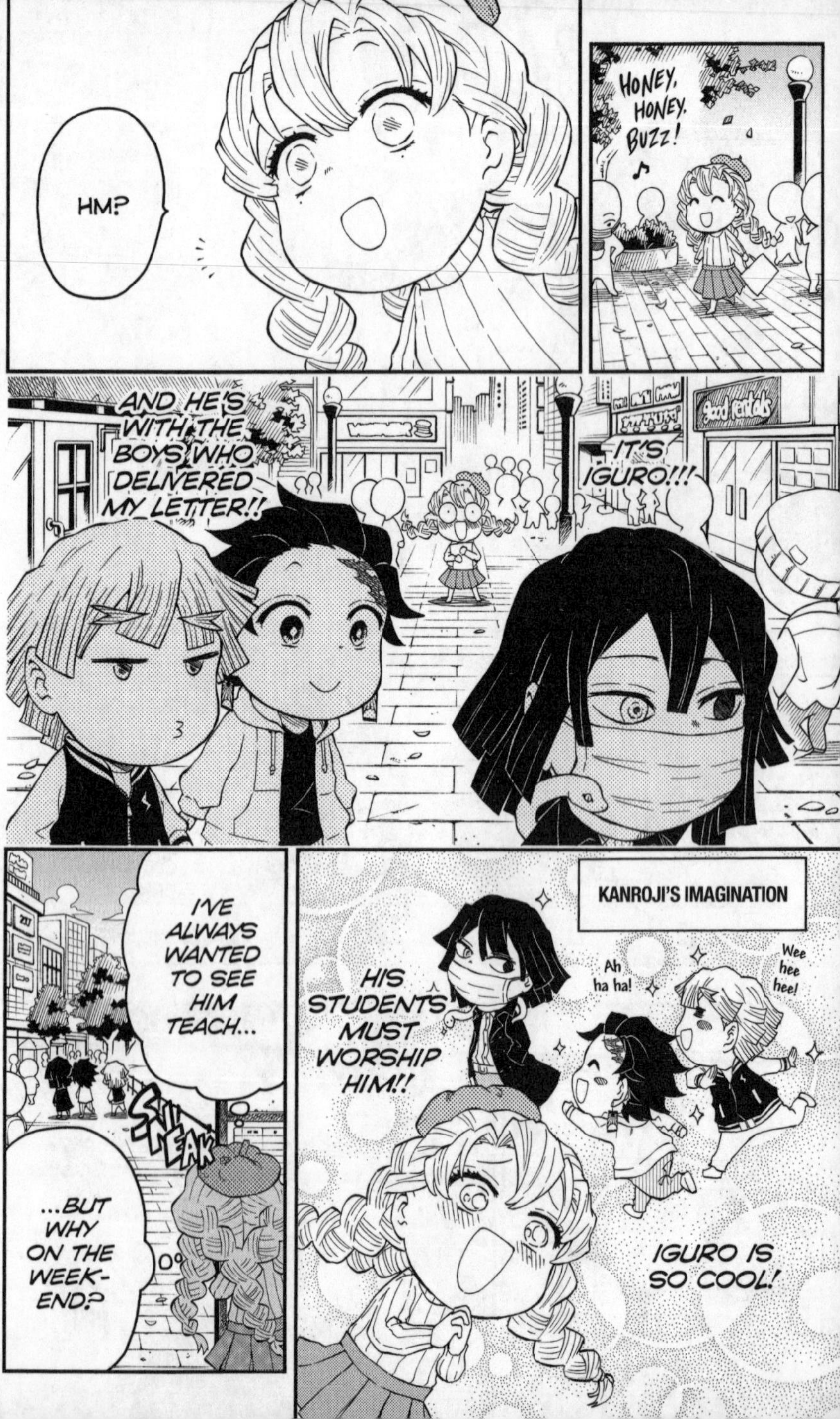
HONEY, HONEY, BUZZ! ♪
HM?
IT'S IGURO!!!
AND HE'S WITH THE BOYS WHO DELIVERED MY LETTER!!
KANROJI'S IMAGINATION
Wee hee hee!
Ah ha ha!
HIS STUDENTS MUST WORSHIP HIM!!
IGURO IS SO COOL!
I'VE ALWAYS WANTED TO SEE HIM TEACH...
SNEAK
...BUT WHY ON THE WEEK-END?

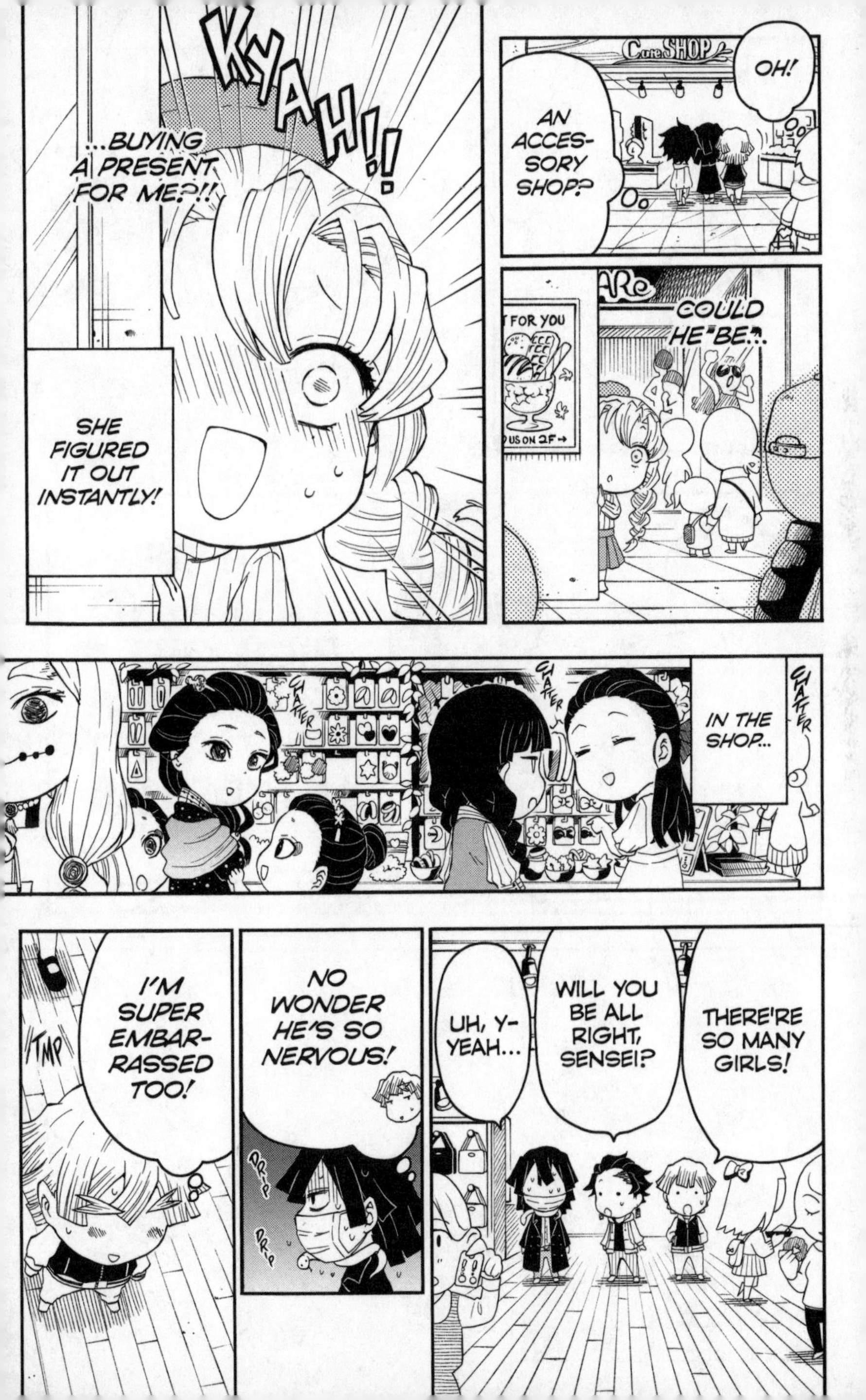
Cute SHOP
OH!
AN ACCESSORY SHOP?
FOR YOU
US ON 2F →
COULD HE BE...
KYAH!!
...BUYING A PRESENT FOR ME?!!
SHE FIGURED IT OUT INSTANTLY!
CHATTER
IN THE SHOP...
CHATTER
CHATTER
THERE'RE SO MANY GIRLS!
WILL YOU BE ALL RIGHT, SENSEI?
UH, Y-YEAH...
NO WONDER HE'S SO NERVOUS!
DRIP
DRIP
I'M SUPER EMBARRASSED TOO!
TMP

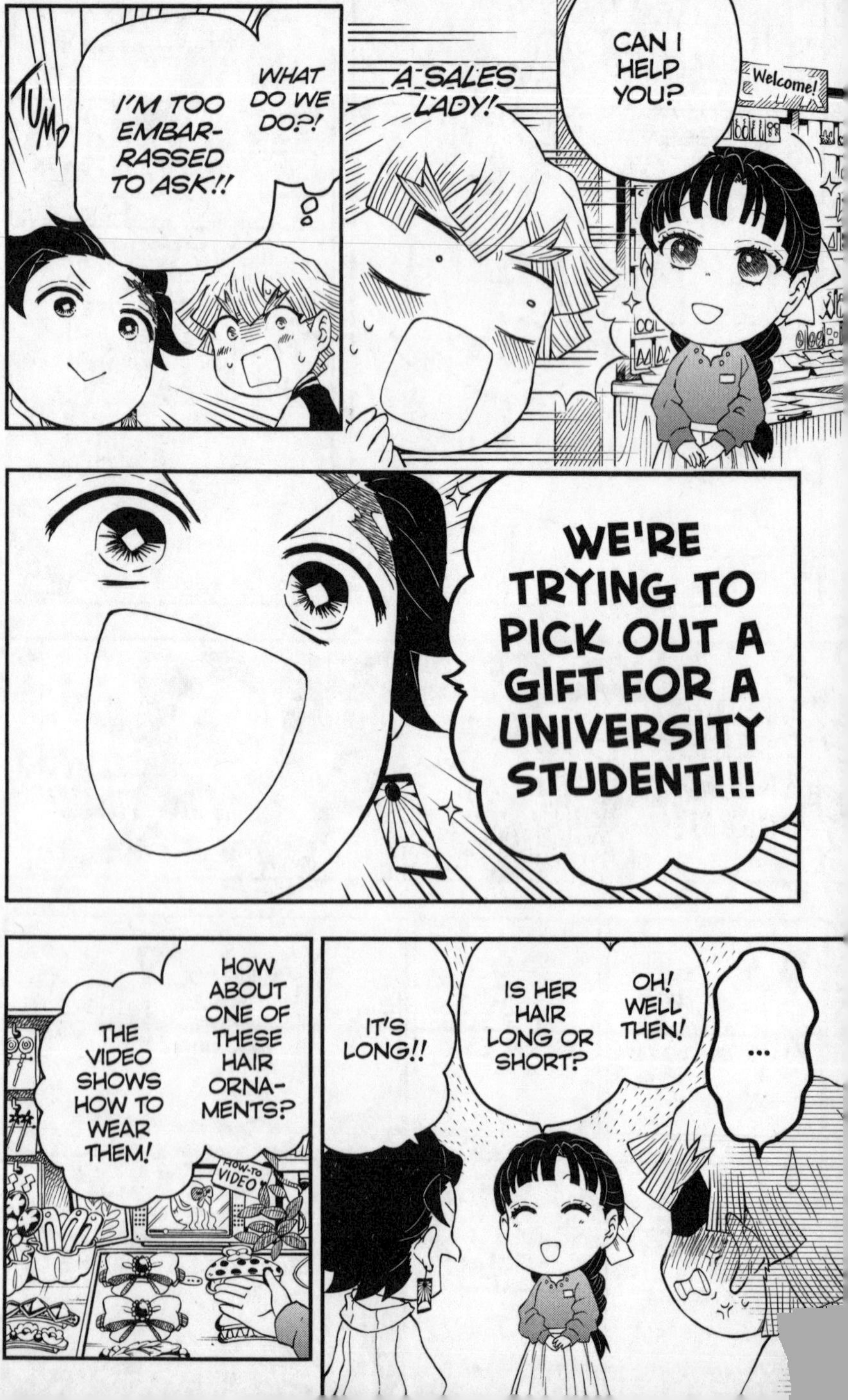
CAN I HELP YOU?
Welcome!
A SALES LADY!
WHAT DO WE DO?!
I'M TOO EMBARRASSED TO ASK!!
TUMP
WE'RE TRYING TO PICK OUT A GIFT FOR A UNIVERSITY STUDENT!!!
...
OH! WELL THEN!
IS HER HAIR LONG OR SHORT?
IT'S LONG!!
HOW ABOUT ONE OF THESE HAIR ORNAMENTS?
THE VIDEO SHOWS HOW TO WEAR THEM!
HOW-TO VIDEO

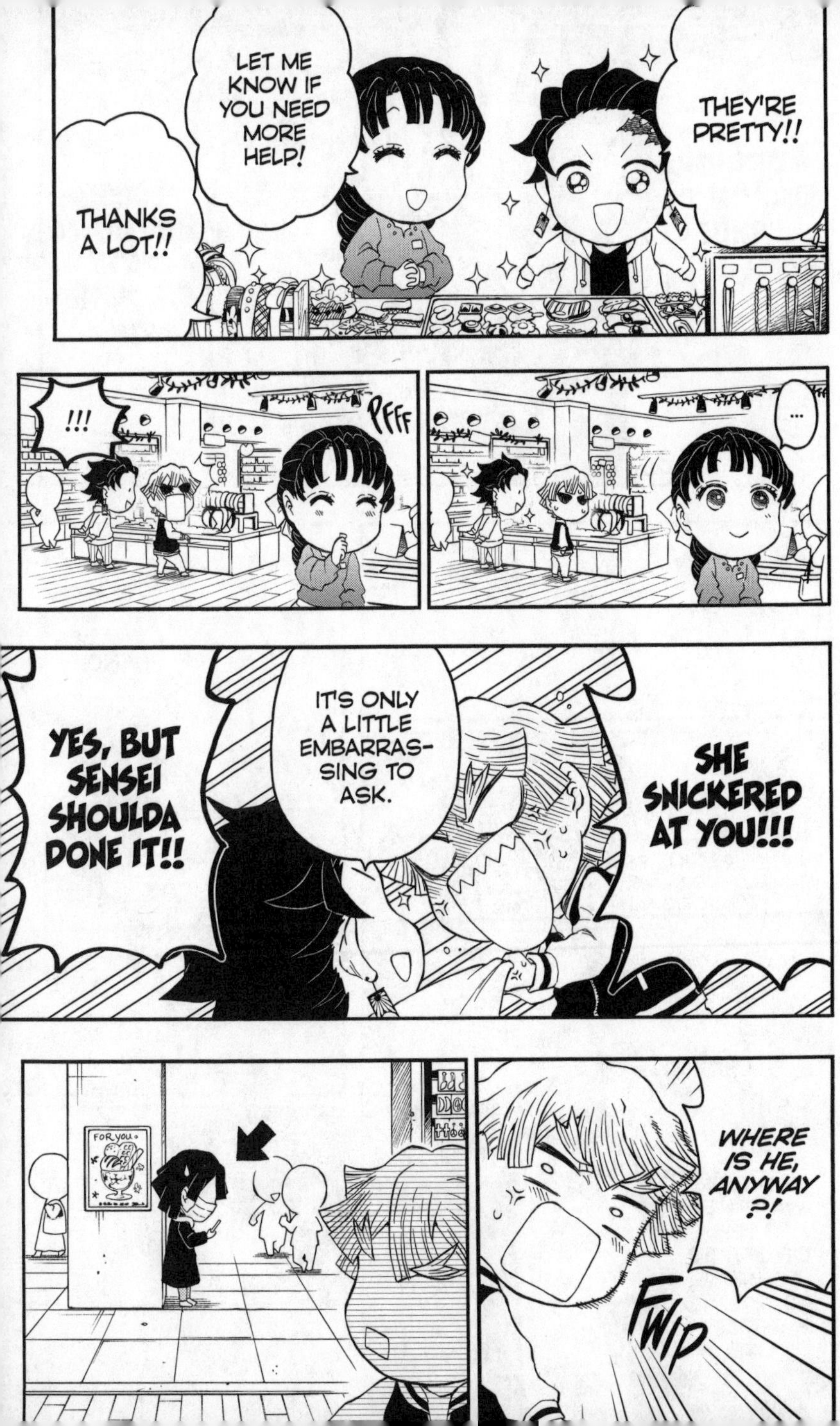
THEY'RE PRETTY!!
LET ME KNOW IF YOU NEED MORE HELP!
THANKS A LOT!!
...
PFFF
!!!
SHE SNICKERED AT YOU!!!
IT'S ONLY A LITTLE EMBARRAS-SING TO ASK.
YES, BUT SENSEI SHOULDA DONE IT!!
WHERE IS HE, ANYWAY ?!
FWIP
FOR YOU.

WE'RE HERE BECAUSE OF YOU!!

YOU'RE PRETENDING WE'RE STRANGERS?!!

GUH!

B*OOM*

HOWEVER...

THAT SETTLES IT! NOW—

HOW ABOUT A HAIR ORNAMENT, SENSEI?

HMM...

I BET THIS ONE'D LOOK GOOD ON KANROJI.

SHE'LL BE WEARING IT AROUND OTHER PEOPLE, SO IT'S MORE IMPORTANT...

...WHETHER IT'S TO HER TASTE.

I WOULDN'T WANT HER TO FEEL OBLIGATED TO WEAR SOMETHING SHE DIDN'T LIKE.

YES, IT WOULD...

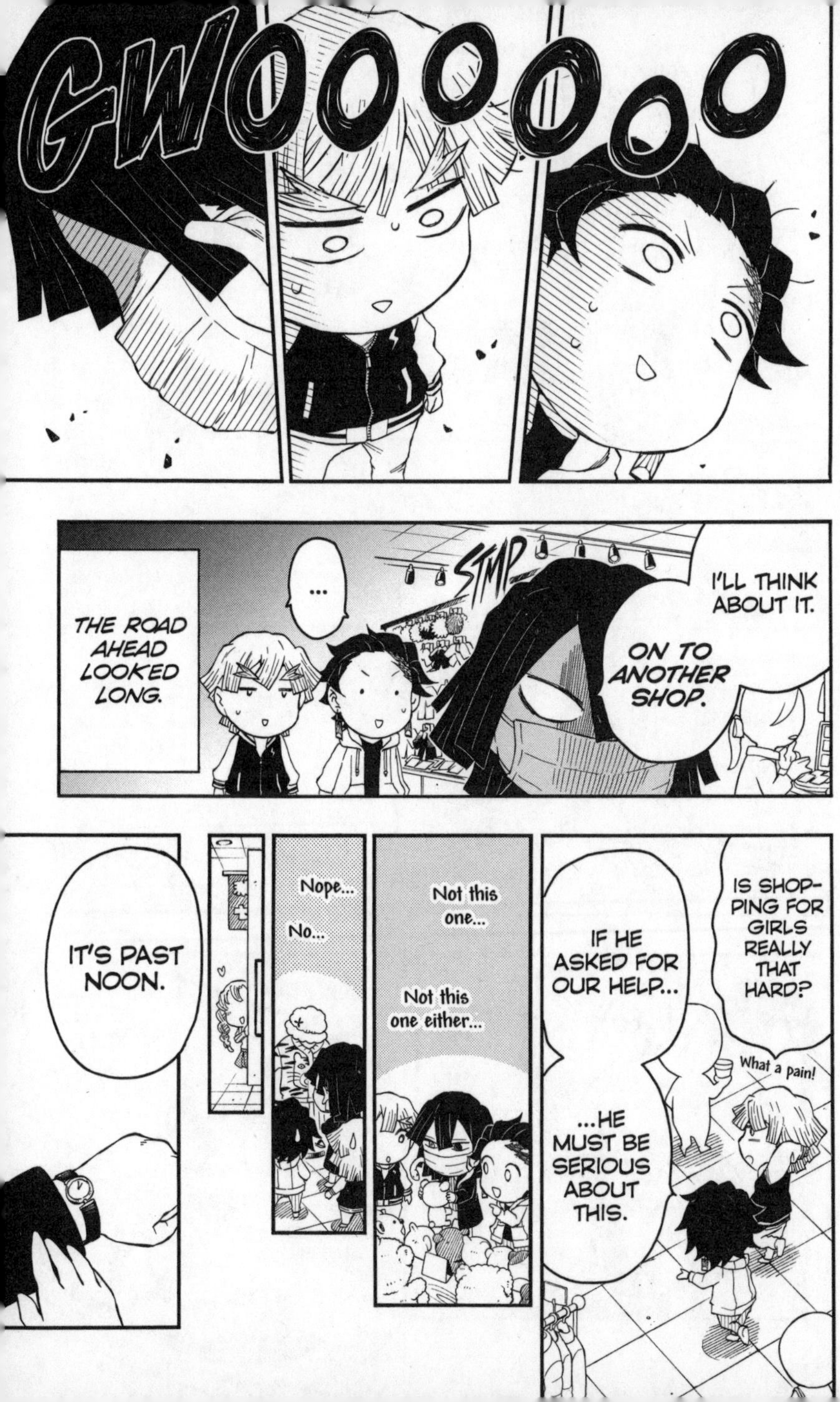
GWOOOOOO
I'LL THINK ABOUT IT.
ON TO ANOTHER SHOP.
STMP
...
THE ROAD AHEAD LOOKED LONG.
IS SHOP-PING FOR GIRLS REALLY THAT HARD?
What a pain!
IF HE ASKED FOR OUR HELP...
...HE MUST BE SERIOUS ABOUT THIS.
Not this one...
Not this one either...
Nope...
No...
IT'S PAST NOON.

SHALL WE BREAK FOR LUNCH?
ARE YOU EVEN TRYING?!
WE HAVEN'T MADE ANY PROGRESS ALL MORNING!
I'LL DECIDE THIS AFTER-NOON.
Welcome!
FAMILY RESTAURANT
FAMILY RESTAURANT
DOES THIS PLACE WORK FOR YOU?
YEAH! THE MENU'S GOT VARIETY!
HONESTLY, I PREFER FINER DINING...
HERE YOU GO!
HAMBURGER STEAK, GRILLED EEL, AND FRIED CHICKEN!
WHOA
LET'S DIG IN!!
MNCH MNCH
NOM NOM

Tastes great!
Yeah!
Yum!
Mm-mm!
...
HEY, SEN-SEI!
CAN WE ORDER PARFAITS TOO?!
SURE.
Heh...
ORDER WHATEVER YOU WANT.
PAPING
HE'S BEING SO NICE IT'S ACTUALLY KINDA CREEPY.
WOW! IGURO IN ACTION!
I WONDER WHAT THEY'RE TALKING ABOUT.
NOM NOM NOM NOM
NOM NOM NOM
GRAND MENU

HELLO? THIS IS KANROJI.
OH! HI, TECCHIN!!*
*HER BOSS
AHEM, MITSURI?
I TAKE IT YOU'VE FORGOT-TEN?
?
ABOUT WHAT?
YOUR SHIFT THIS AFTERNOON! ♡
OMIGOSH! S-SORRY! I GOT DISTRACTED!
FWOOOOSH
THAT'S ALL RIGHT.
TAKE CARE ON THE WAY HERE.
WELL, WHAT'S NEXT?
HMM...
AH HA HA HA!
KYA HA HA HA!
No WAY!
?

REALLY, HEBIKO?!
YEAH!! MY BOO BOUGHT THIS BAG FOR ME!!
NO WAY! IT'S HIDEOUS!
GUY'S GOT NO FASHION SENSE! WA HA HA!
WA HA HA
BWA HA HA
...!!
HE EVEN SAID HE SPENT ALL DAY PICKING IT OUT!!
DO THEY HAVE TO BE...
EW! CREEPY!!
...SO LOUD?
TITTER TITTER
GIGGLE GIGGLE
GUFFAW
UM, IGURO SENSEI?
DON'T WORRY.
HM?
I'M FINE.
KANROJI ISN'T LIKE THAT.
SSIP

WELL, IF YOU'RE SURE...
Thanks for coming in!
FAMILY RESTAURANT
...
BUT... AM I CREEPY TOO?
HM...
NO, NOT AT ALL!!!
YOU'RE DOING FINE!!
NO...
...I'M OVER-THINKING THINGS.
GLASSES
WHAT KANROJI LIKES IS OBVIOUS...
I love me...
...some eats!
...SO I SHOULD GET HER SOMETHING SWEET.

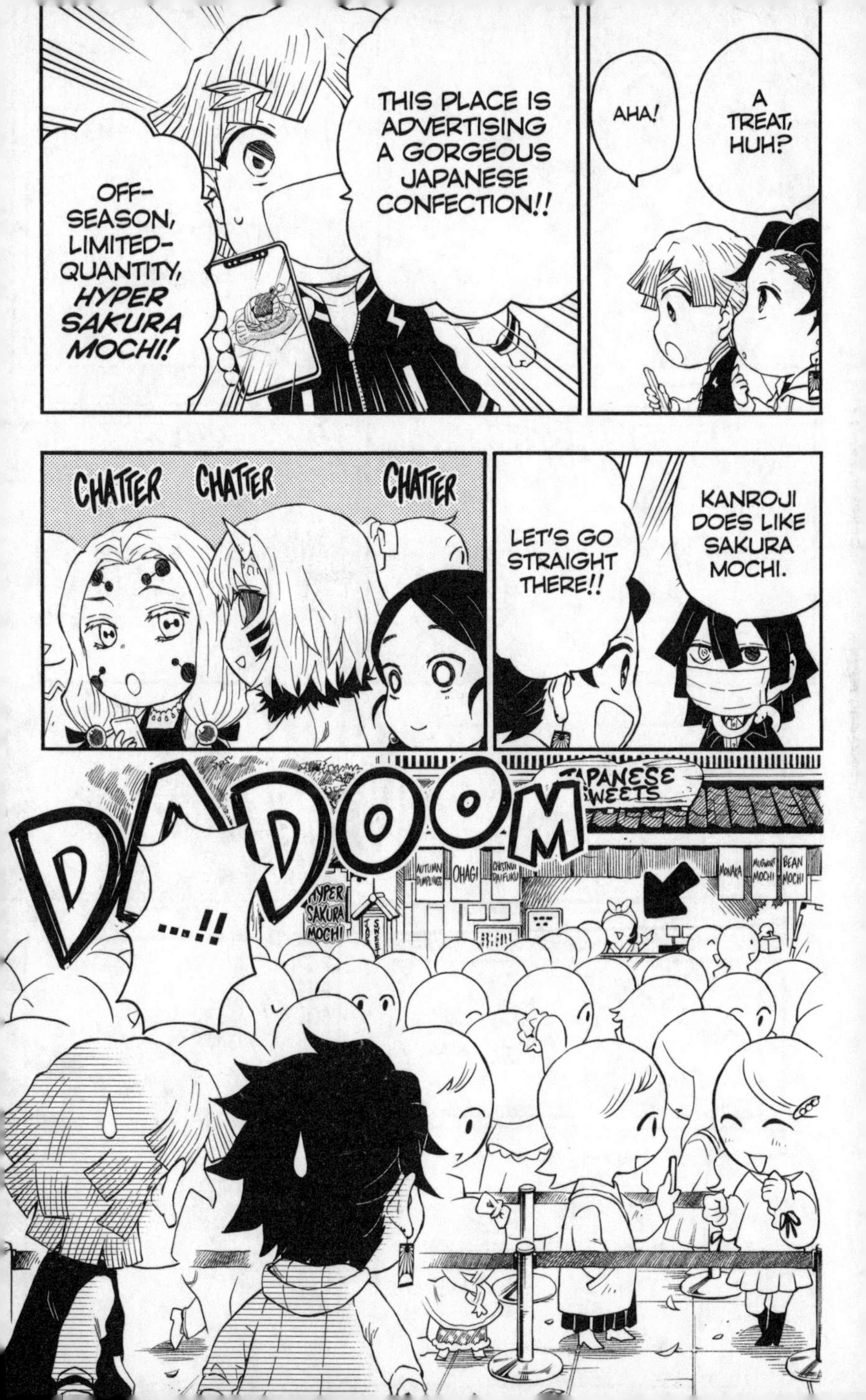
A TREAT, HUH?
AHA!
THIS PLACE IS ADVERTISING A GORGEOUS JAPANESE CONFECTION!!
OFF-SEASON, LIMITED-QUANTITY, *HYPER SAKURA MOCHI!*
KANROJI DOES LIKE SAKURA MOCHI.
LET'S GO STRAIGHT THERE!!
CHATTER
CHATTER
CHATTER
JAPANESE SWEETS
BEAN MOCHI
MUGWORT MOCHI
MONAKA
CHESTNUT DAIFUKU
OHAGI
AUTUMN DUMPLINGS
HYPER SAKURA MOCHI
DADOOM
...!!

BDMP

BDMP

SENSEI! CAN YOU DO IT?!

THE LINE IS NUTS!

AND THEY'RE ALL GIRLS!

...!!

WE'LL GET IN LINE FOR YOU, SENSEI!!

DASH

THEY'RE GONNA RUN OUT!

SHF

SHF

OH NO!

THE LINE'S GETTING EVEN LONGER!

WE'RE ALMOST THERE!

ONLY 20 MORE PEOPLE!

HUFF HUFF

YOU CAN DO IT, TEACH!

CLMP

NO...

...I HAVE TO DO THIS MYSELF!!

FIVE!

JUST TEN MORE!

WE'RE NEXT!!

SO CLMP

SWP

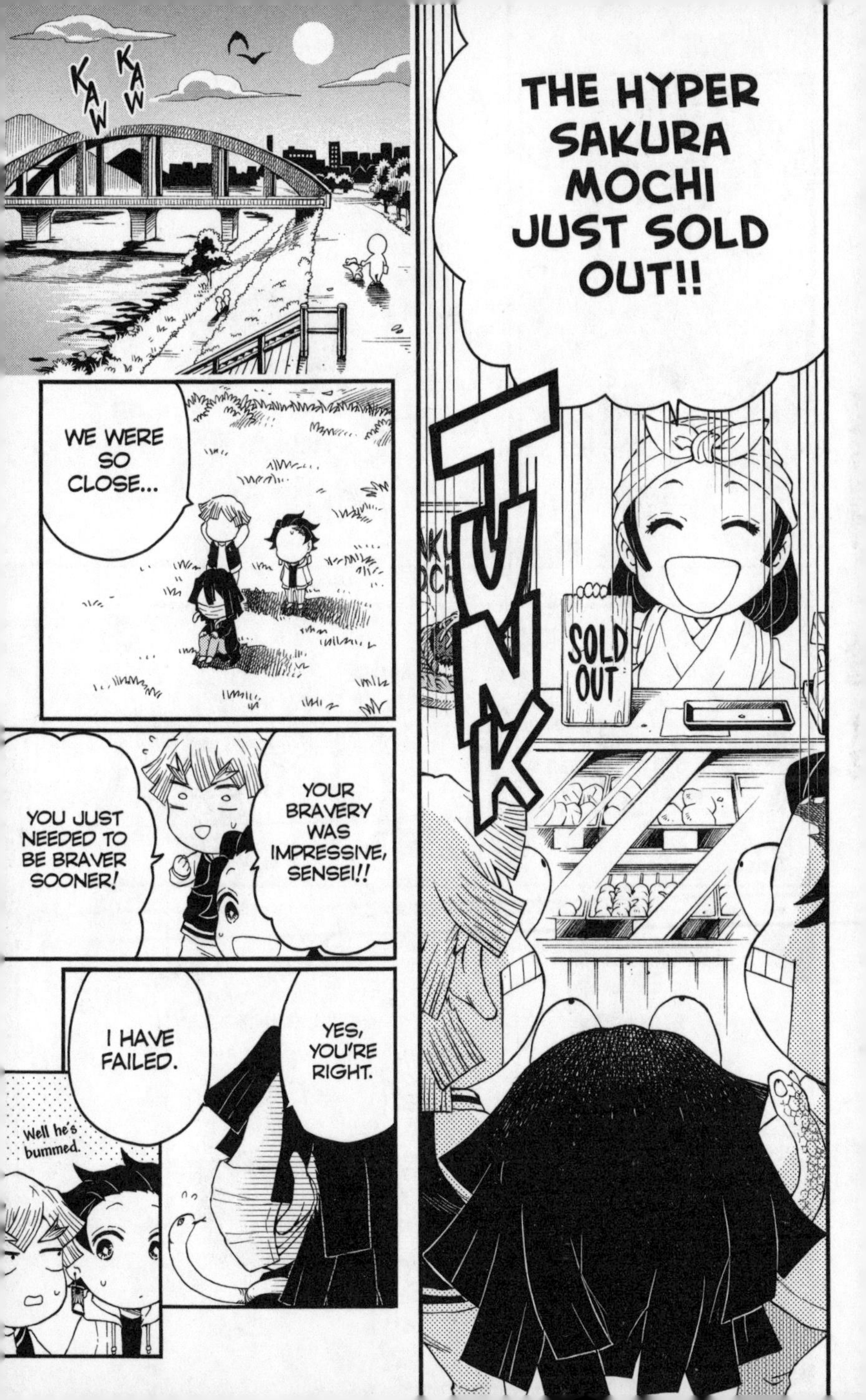
THE HYPER SAKURA MOCHI JUST SOLD OUT!!
JUNK
SOLD OUT
KAW KAW
WE WERE SO CLOSE...
YOUR BRAVERY WAS IMPRESSIVE, SENSEI!!
YOU JUST NEEDED TO BE BRAVER SOONER!
YES, YOU'RE RIGHT.
I HAVE FAILED.
Well he's bummed.

YOU'RE UNCOMFORTABLE AROUND GIRLS...
...BUT YOU'RE OKAY AROUND KANROJI?
YES. ISN'T THAT ODD?
I'M COMPLETELY FINE AROUND HER.
YEAH?
I'M AWARE OF HOW PATHETIC IT IS.
I GET ALL ANXIOUS AROUND OTHER GIRLS AND MAKE THEM UNCOMFORTABLE.
Oh my!
Sorry!
I COULD BARELY LINE UP TO BUY MOCHI.
BUT WHEN I'M WITH KANROJI...
...I FORGET ALL THAT AND JUST ENJOY MYSELF.
Nezukooo!

SNAKE SCARF
SHE GAVE ME A BIRTHDAY PRESENT THE OTHER DAY.
SHE GIVES ME SO MUCH...
...SO I WANTED TO DO THE SAME FOR HER.
...
OH WELL. LET'S GO HOME.
SWIP
HUH ?!
SORRY FOR BOTHERING YOU TWO WITH THIS.
BUT WHAT ABOUT A PRESENT ?!
THIS ISN'T A SPECIAL OCCASION.
I'LL GET HER SOMETHING SOME OTHER TIME.
IT WAS JUST SOMETHING I WANTED TO DO.
"IT WAS TASTY!"
"THANKS SO MUCH, ZENITSU!"

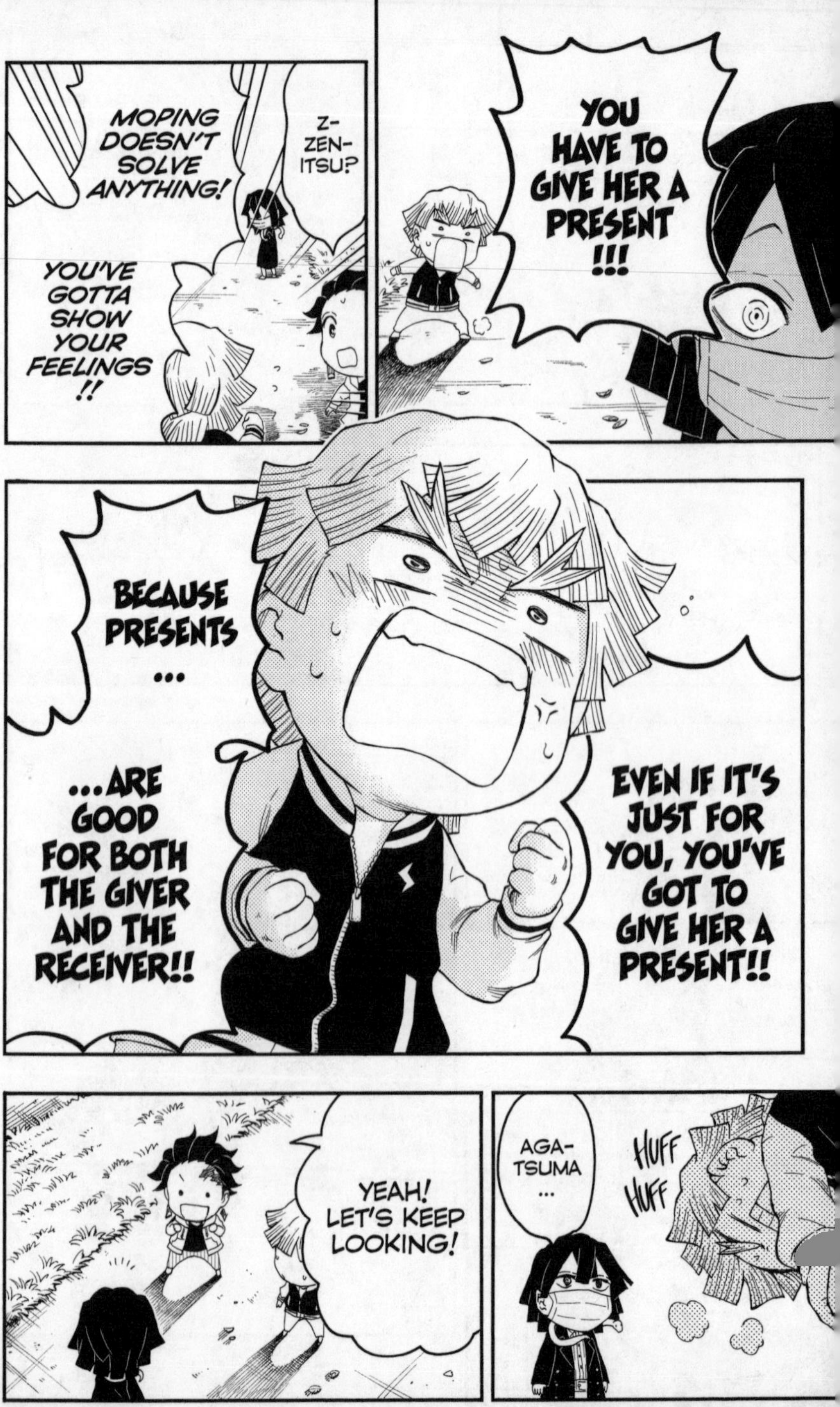
YOU HAVE TO GIVE HER A PRESENT !!!
Z-ZEN-ITSU?
MOPING DOESN'T SOLVE ANYTHING!
YOU'VE GOTTA SHOW YOUR FEELINGS !!
EVEN IF IT'S JUST FOR YOU, YOU'VE GOT TO GIVE HER A PRESENT!!
BECAUSE PRESENTS ...
...ARE GOOD FOR BOTH THE GIVER AND THE RECEIVER!!
HUFF HUFF
AGA-TSUMA ...
YEAH! LET'S KEEP LOOKING!

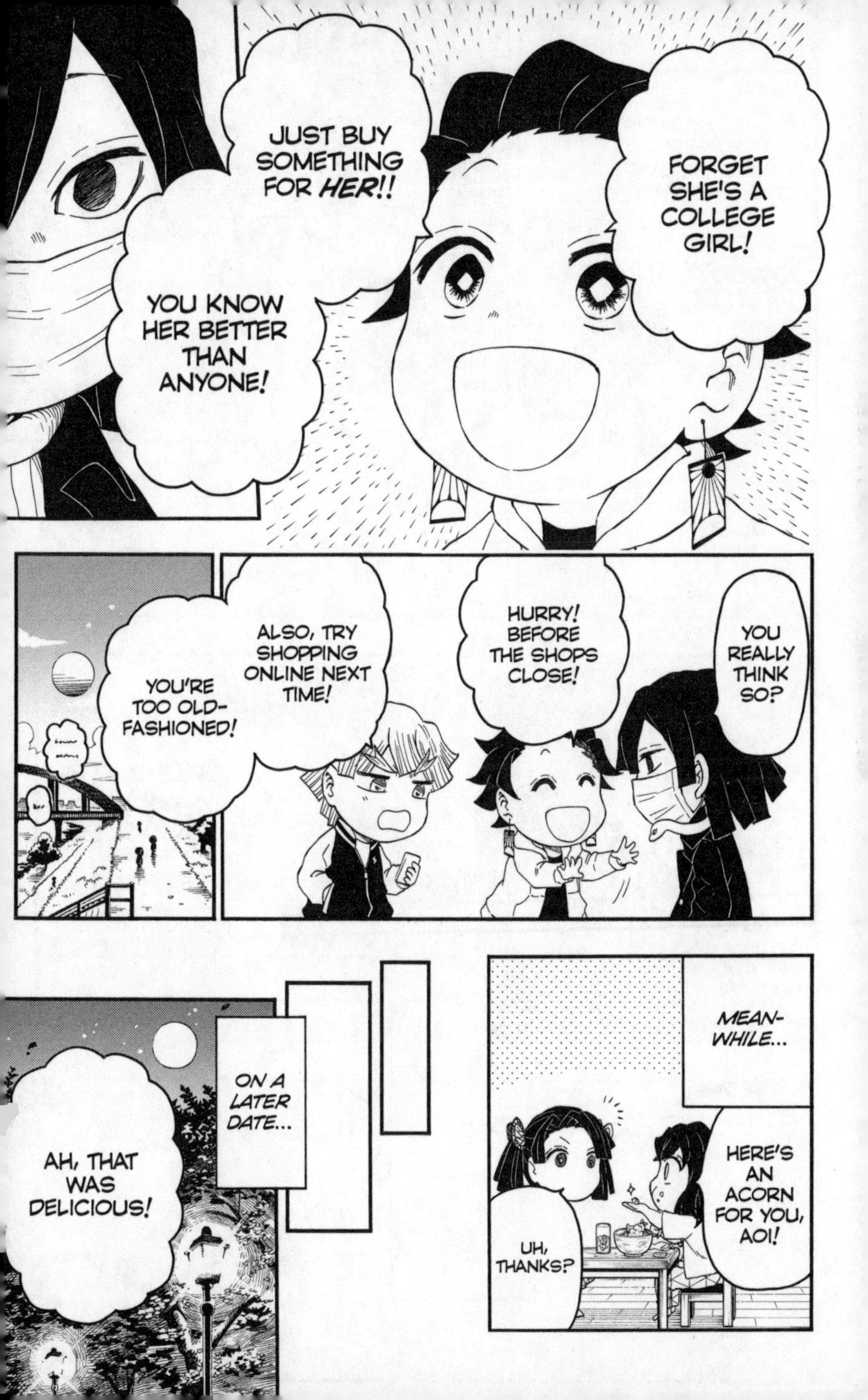
FORGET SHE'S A COLLEGE GIRL!
JUST BUY SOMETHING FOR *HER*!!
YOU KNOW HER BETTER THAN ANYONE!
YOU REALLY THINK SO?
HURRY! BEFORE THE SHOPS CLOSE!
ALSO, TRY SHOPPING ONLINE NEXT TIME!
YOU'RE TOO OLD-FASHIONED!
MEAN-WHILE...
HERE'S AN ACORN FOR YOU, AOI!
UH, THANKS?
ON A LATER DATE...
AH, THAT WAS DELICIOUS!

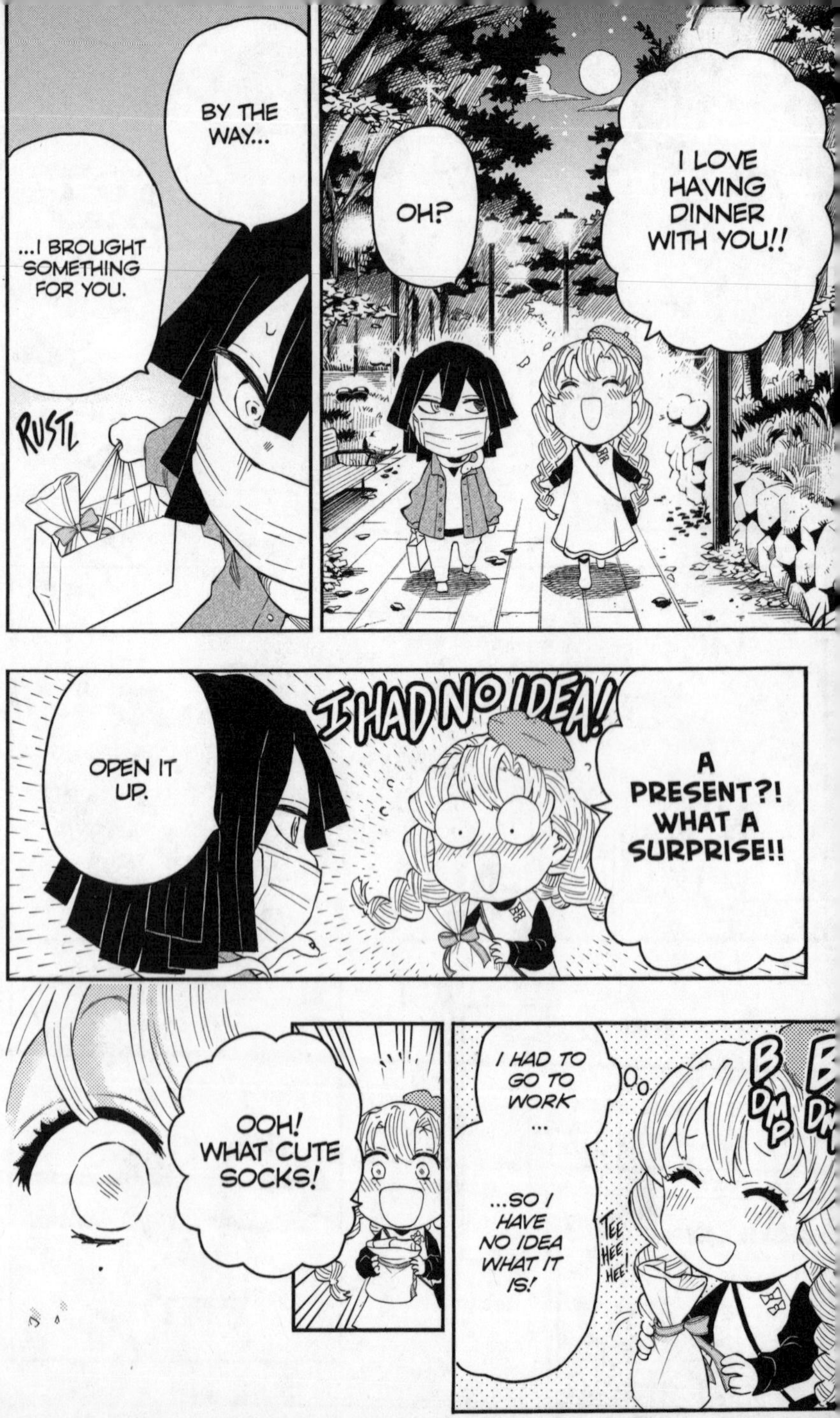
I LOVE HAVING DINNER WITH YOU!!
OH?
BY THE WAY...
...I BROUGHT SOMETHING FOR YOU.
RUSTL
A PRESENT?! WHAT A SURPRISE!!
I HAD NO IDEA!
OPEN IT UP.
BDMP
I HAD TO GO TO WORK ...
...SO I HAVE NO IDEA WHAT IT IS!
TEE HEE HEE!
OOH! WHAT CUTE SOCKS!

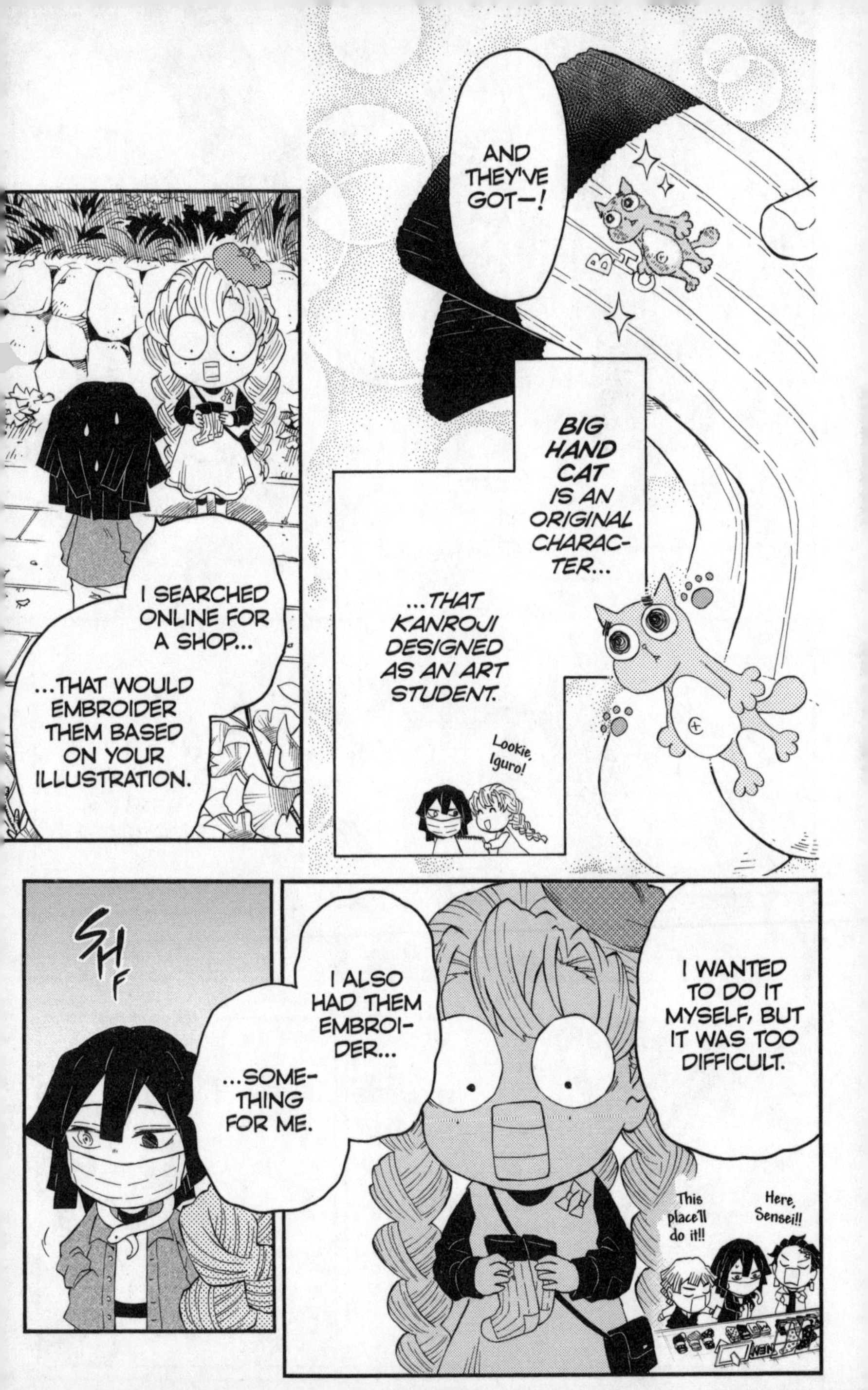
AND THEY'VE GOT—!
BIG HAND CAT IS AN ORIGINAL CHARAC-TER...
...THAT KANROJI DESIGNED AS AN ART STUDENT.
Lookie, Iguro!
I SEARCHED ONLINE FOR A SHOP...
...THAT WOULD EMBROIDER THEM BASED ON YOUR ILLUSTRATION.
I WANTED TO DO IT MYSELF, BUT IT WAS TOO DIFFICULT.
Here, Sensei!!
This place'll do it!!
I ALSO HAD THEM EMBROI-DER...
...SOME-THING FOR ME.
SHF

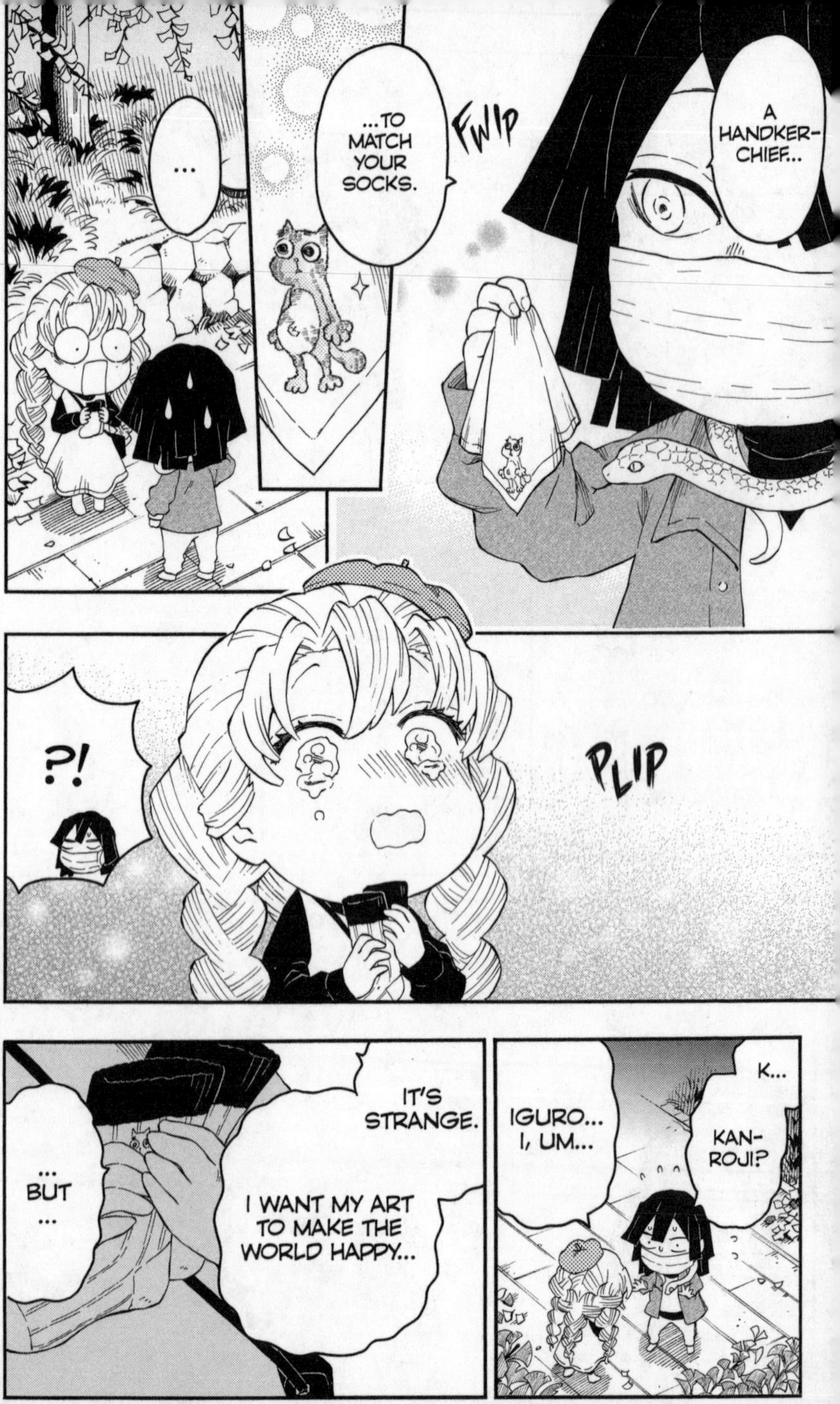
A HANDKERCHIEF...
FWIP
...TO MATCH YOUR SOCKS.
...
PLIP
?!
K...
KANROJI?
IGURO... I, UM...
IT'S STRANGE.
I WANT MY ART TO MAKE THE WORLD HAPPY...
... BUT ...

...RIGHT NOW...
...IT'S MAKING ME THE HAPPIEST OF ALL!
OH...
THAT'S GOOD.
I'M GLAD.
IGURO...
...WOULD GO ON TO BE MUCH KINDER TO TANJIRO AND ZENITSU.
JUST KIDDING!
NO NAP-PING IN CLASS!
BUT NOW WHEN THEY SEE...
...A CROW CARRYING A LOVE LETTER...
...THEY CAN'T HELP BUT SMILE.

CHAPTER 10 DELETED SCENES
USELESS TEACHERS

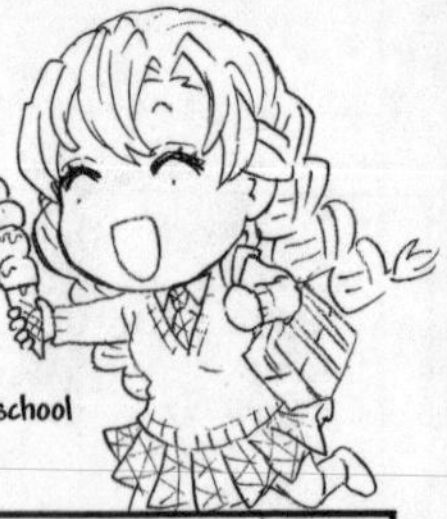

Kanroji in high school

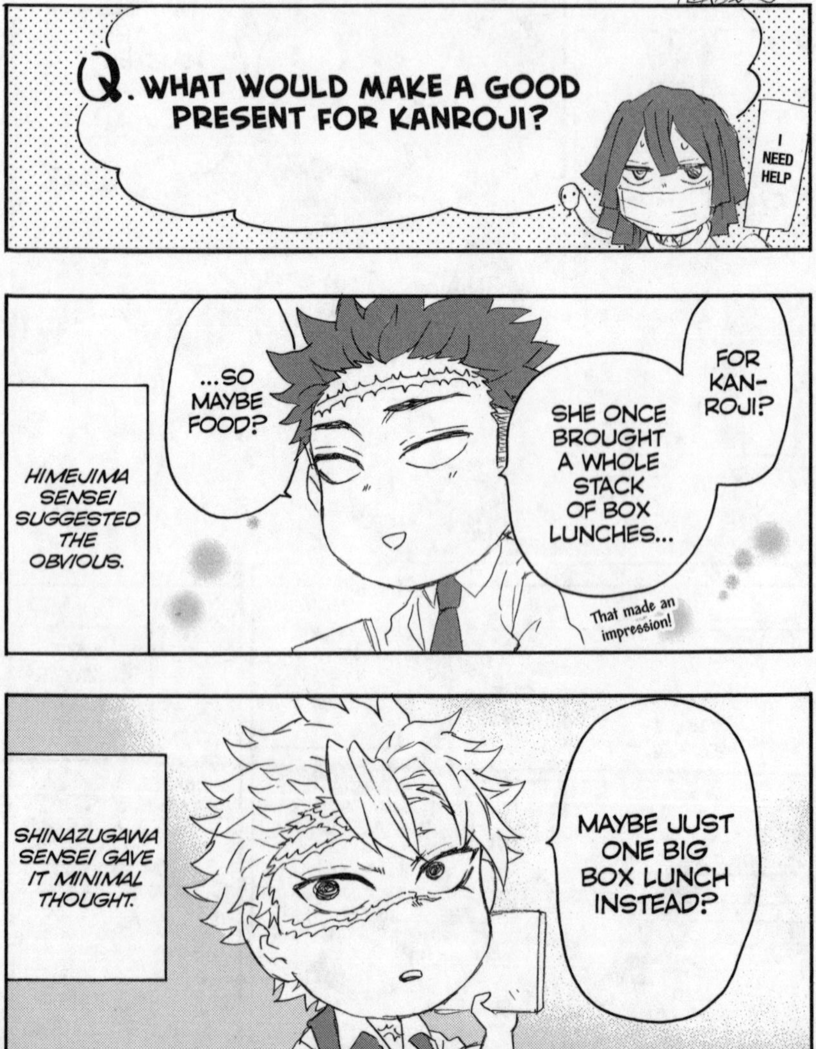
I NEED HELP
Q. WHAT WOULD MAKE A GOOD PRESENT FOR KANROJI?
FOR KAN-ROJI?
SHE ONCE BROUGHT A WHOLE STACK OF BOX LUNCHES...
...SO MAYBE FOOD?
That made an impression!
HIMEJIMA SENSEI SUGGESTED THE OBVIOUS.
MAYBE JUST ONE BIG BOX LUNCH INSTEAD?
SHINAZUGAWA SENSEI GAVE IT MINIMAL THOUGHT.

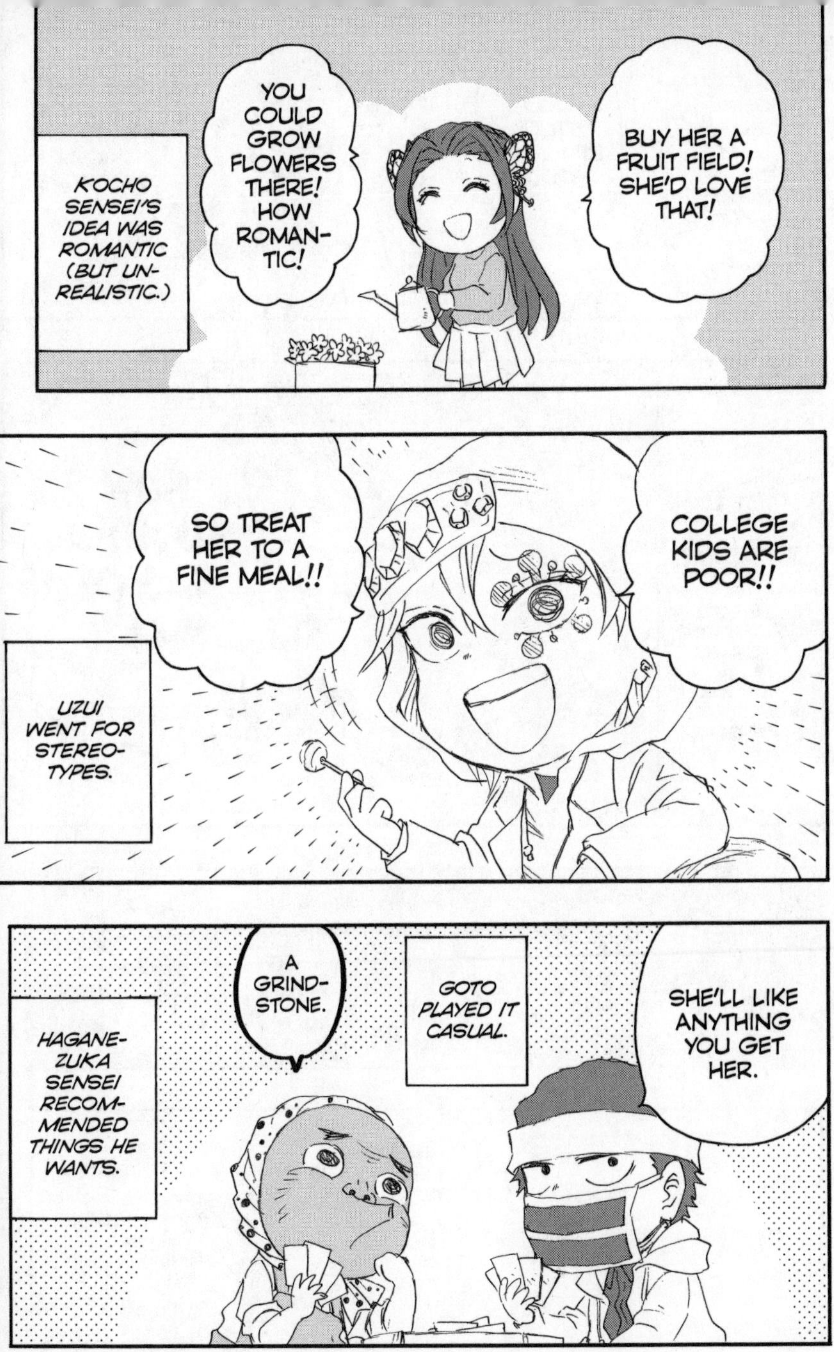
BUY HER A FRUIT FIELD! SHE'D LOVE THAT!
YOU COULD GROW FLOWERS THERE! HOW ROMAN-TIC!
KOCHO SENSEI'S IDEA WAS ROMANTIC (BUT UN-REALISTIC.)
COLLEGE KIDS ARE POOR!!
SO TREAT HER TO A FINE MEAL!!
UZUI WENT FOR STEREO-TYPES.
SHE'LL LIKE ANYTHING YOU GET HER.
GOTO PLAYED IT CASUAL.
A GRIND-STONE.
HAGANE-ZUKA SENSEI RECOM-MENDED THINGS HE WANTS.

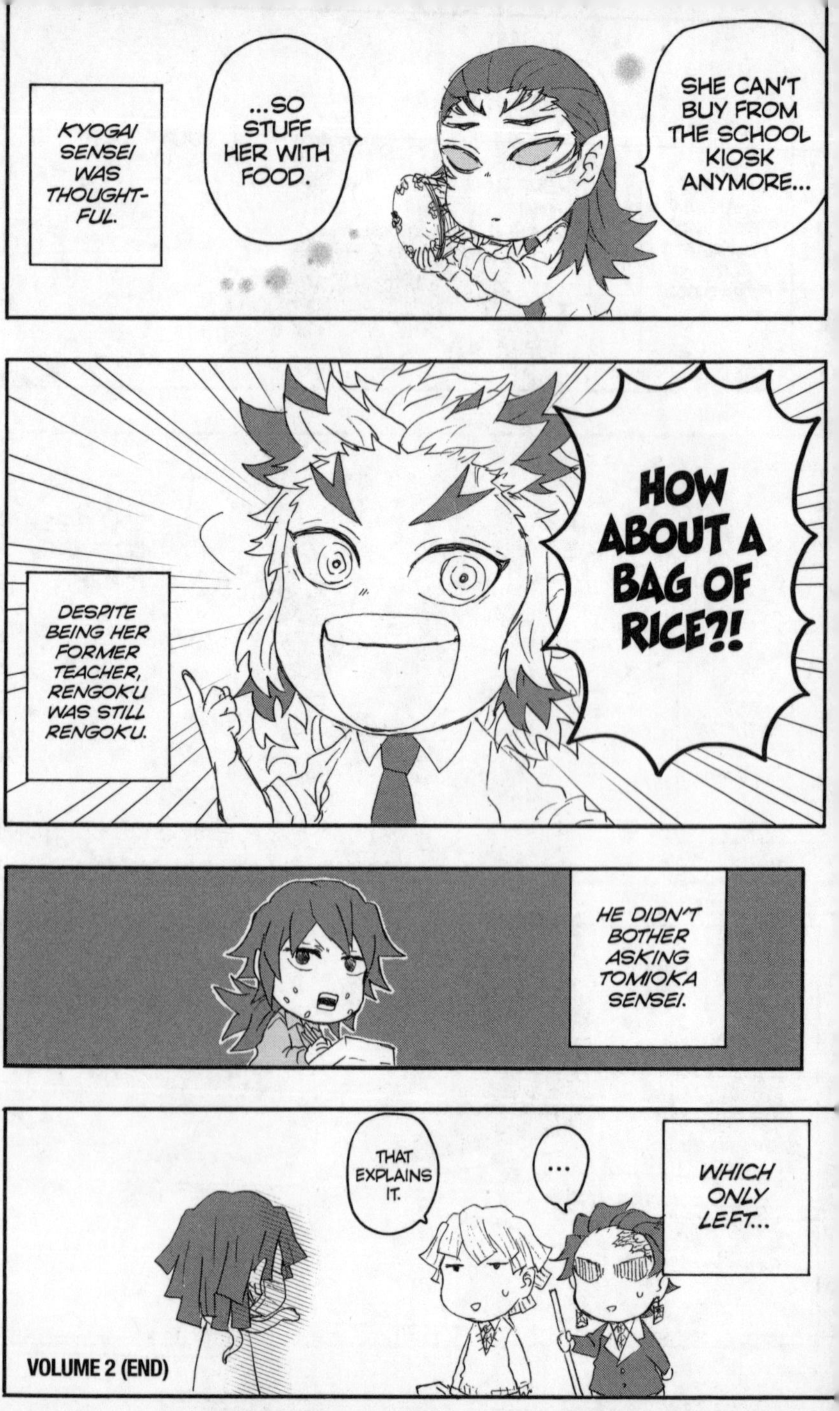
SHE CAN'T BUY FROM THE SCHOOL KIOSK ANYMORE...
...SO STUFF HER WITH FOOD.
KYOGAI SENSEI WAS THOUGHTFUL.
HOW ABOUT A BAG OF RICE?!
DESPITE BEING HER FORMER TEACHER, RENGOKU WAS STILL RENGOKU.
HE DIDN'T BOTHER ASKING TOMIOKA SENSEI.
WHICH ONLY LEFT...
...
THAT EXPLAINS IT.
VOLUME 2 (END)

EXIT
くもとり
KUMOTORI
THIS IS TAMIO ENMU.
TANJIRO ALWAYS CATCHES HIM MIS-BEHAVING ON THE TRAIN.*
HE'S A TRAIN GEEK WITH A CRIMINAL HABIT.
*SEE VOL. 1, CHAPTER 1.
♪
BONUS CHAPTER: KUMOTORI STATION, 7:30 A.M.
*EYES: LOWER ONE
TMP
TMP
くもとり
KUMOTORI
...
TMP
TMP
TMP

FOMP
GWOOOOOOOO
WHY DID YOU SIT NEXT TO ME?
SO I CAN NAB YOU WHEN YOU MOON PEOPLE!
HOW RUDE!
YOU MAKE ME SOUND LIKE A FLASHER!
WELL, AREN'T YOU?
YES, I AM.

CLOTHES COME BETWEEN ME AND THE TRAIN ...
...AND I CAN'T STAND IT.
BUT WHEN I STRIP DOWN...
YAY
I WEAR...
...THE TRAIN!!!
MAKE SENSE?
NO. BUY A TRAIN AND DO IT AT HOME.
THAT'S A BIT COSTLY.
BESIDES, OTHER PASSEN-GERS ARE PART OF THE EXPERIENCE.
SORRY. I JUST DON'T GET IT.
...

UM, EARRING BOY...
THE NAME'S TANJIRO KAMADO!
I'M TAMIO ENMU. NICE TO MEET YOU.
WHY CAN'T I DISROBE ON THE TRAIN?
BECAUSE OF BOX LUNCHES!!
BAM
WHAT?
IF YOU SCARE THE PASS-ENGERS...
...THEY'LL FORGET ABOUT THEIR LUNCHES WHEN THEY RUN!
Eek! A butt!
AND THAT'S A PROBLEM!
HMM... I NEVER CONSIDERED THAT.
NOW YOU KNOW!

A TRAIN IS NOW ARRIVING AT...
THANKS FOR THE ADVICE.
HERE. HAVE A YUZU JELLY DRINK!
Shake it first!
OH! THANKS!
FARE-WELL NOW!
RRRING
PANTS
THE END!

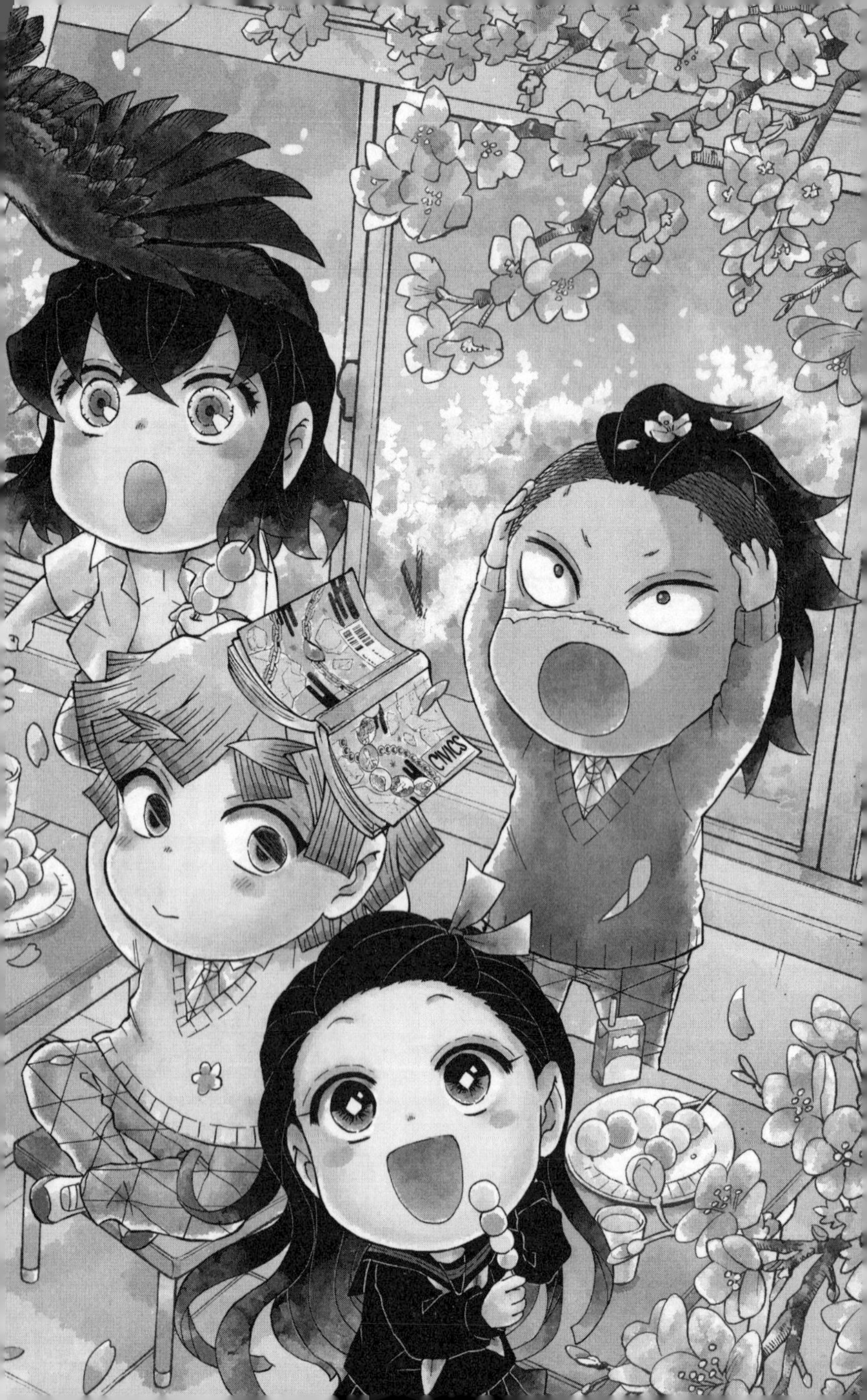
CIVICS

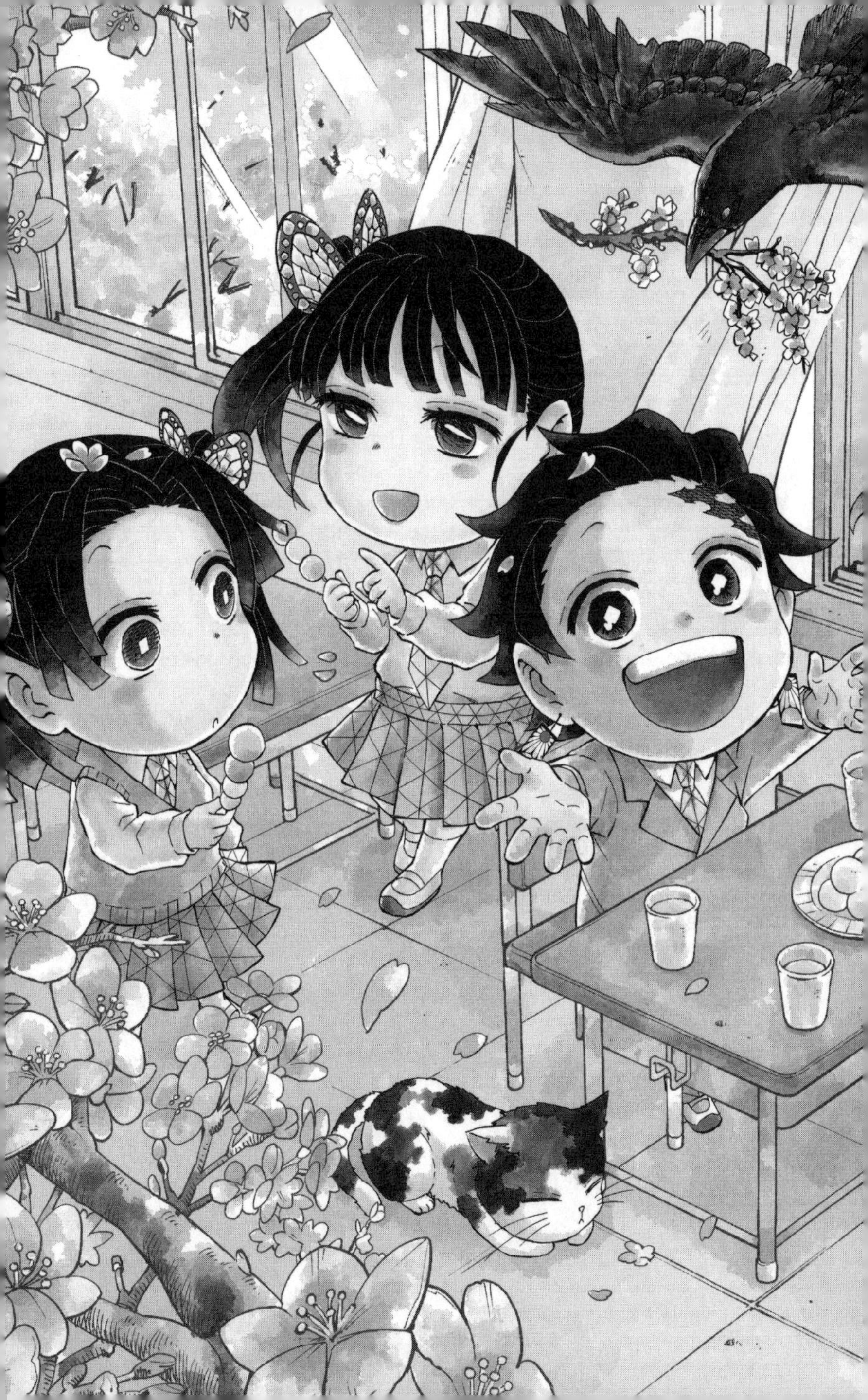

# AFTERWORD

Welcome to volume 2! Thanks for reading! Just like with volume 1, this was only possible through the efforts of a lot of people, so thank you all very much. I'll be counting on you in the future too.

This volume goes on sale in July, and the story takes place from early summer to autumn, so I'm thrilled to see how the seasons have synced up. What a happy coincidence!

The serialized releases never match the actual season, so I drew the preceding two-page spread to match with the real world. Without any connection to the story, the sakura trees are in full bloom! I have to say, I like that illustration, but I was never satisfied with the color illustration of Makomo and the others for chapter 9, so I put them on the back cover of this volume.

I suspect volume 3 will take place from autumn to winter. Nothing is slated yet, though, so here's hoping it gets the green light!

STAFF

REGULARS
Nagashima
Kantaro Kumano
Keisuke Futta

HELPERS
Kojiro
Tachi Biwa

SPECIAL THANKS
Saikyo Jump editor: Toide-san
The *Demon Slayer: Kimetsu no Yaiba* original manga team
Graphic novel editor: Abe-san
Designers: Deguchi-san, Abe-san
Original creator: Koyoharu Gotouge
All the readers!

Natsuki Hokami

帆上夏希.

Good work! This is Gotouge! Volume 2 of *Kimetsu Academy* is on sale! Here's a big thanks to Hokami Sensei, the editors, assistants, and readers! The number of characters playing a role is ramping up, making these pages more boisterous than ever!

As the fun continues to take off, I hope you'll come along for the ride!!

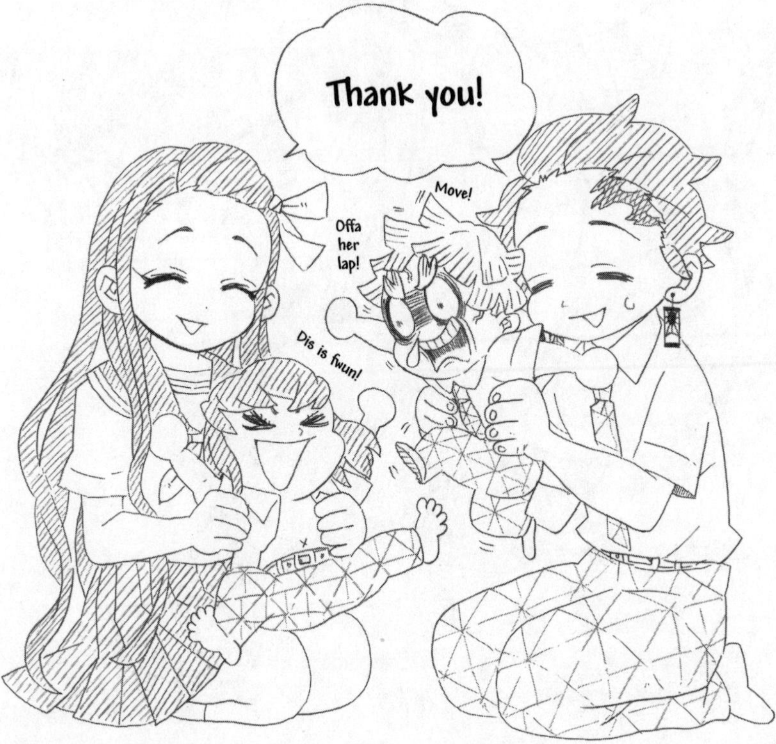
Thank you!
Move!
Offa her lap!
Dis is fwun!

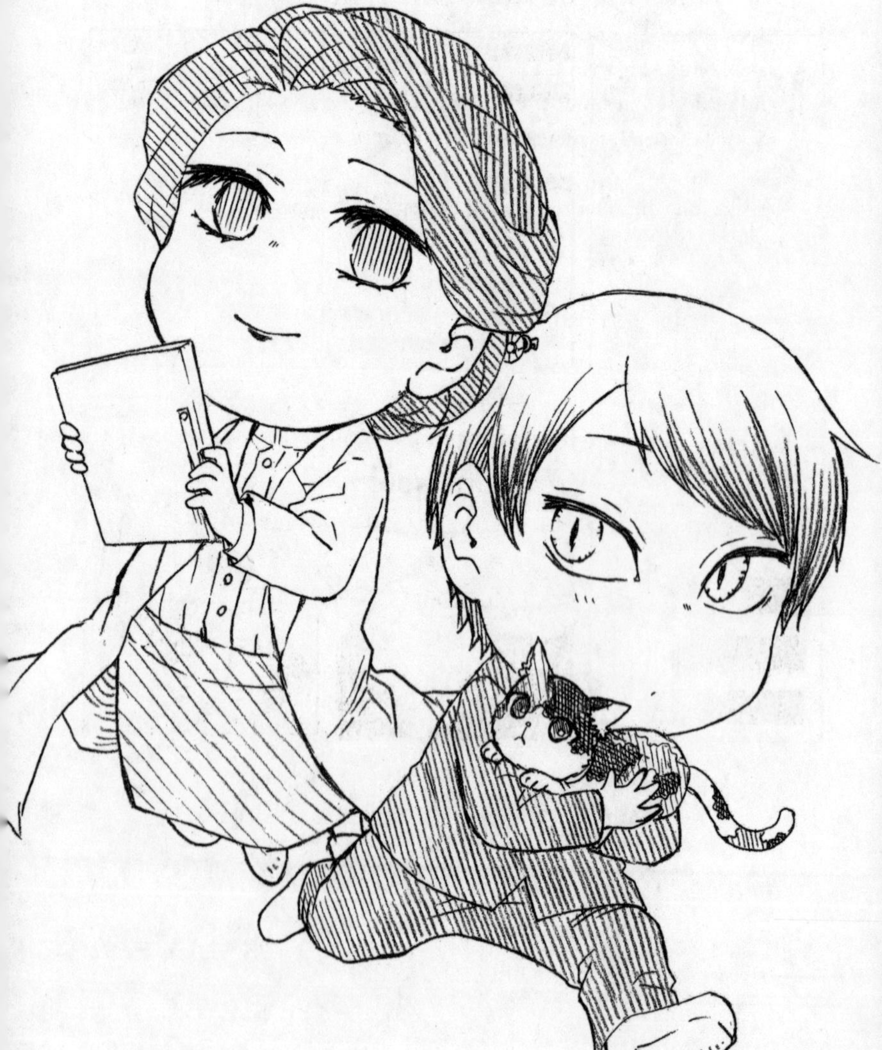

FIRST-YEAR TEXTBOOK DESIGNS FOR KIMETSU ACADEMY HIGH SCHOOL

CIVICS
CHEMISTRY
MATH A
BIOLOGY
HISTORY
ENGLISH
I

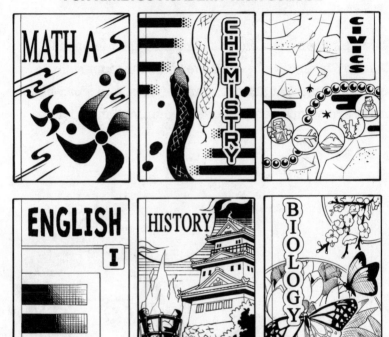

For a while, I only had a rough idea for these, but I asked my staff and they came up with proper designs. The other grades basically look the same.

You're reading the wrong way!

In keeping with the original Japanese comic format, *Demon Slayer: Kimetsu Academy* reads from right to left, meaning that action, sound effects, and word-balloon order are completely reversed from English order.

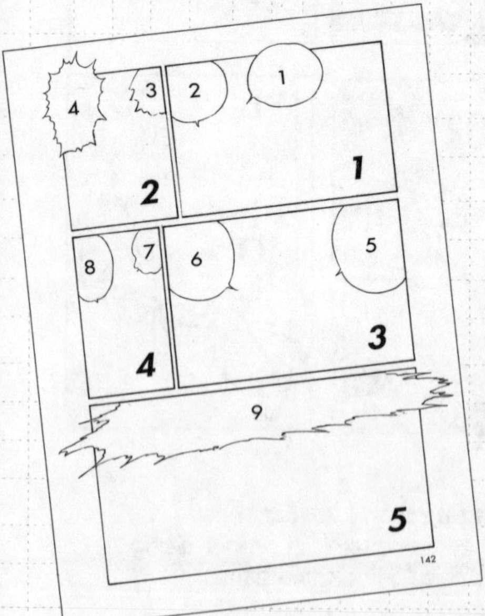
1
2
3
4
1
2
5
6
7
8
3
4
9
5
142

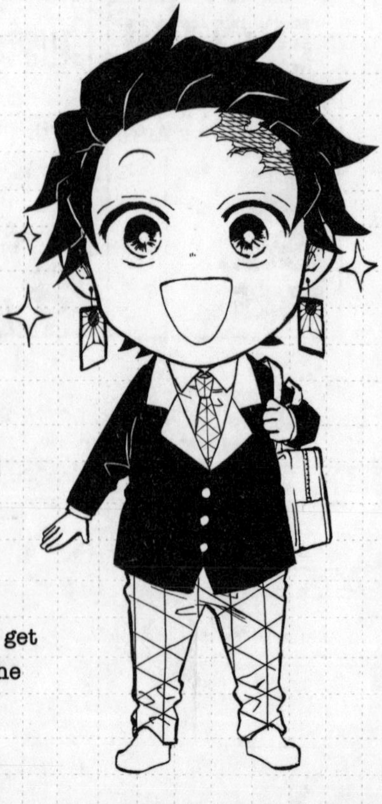

Check out the diagram shown here to get the hang of things, and then turn to the other side of the book to get started!